The City in the Twenty-First Century

Eugenie L. Birch and Susan M. Wachter, Series Editors

A complete list of books in the series
is available from the publisher.

Smarter Growth

Activism and Environmental Policy in Metropolitan Washington

John H. Spiers

PENN

UNIVERSITY OF PENNSYLVANIA PRESS

PHILADELPHIA

Published by
University of Pennsylvania Press
Philadelphia, Pennsylvania 19104-4112
www.upenn.edu/pennpress

Printed in the United States of America on acid-free paper
1 3 5 7 9 10 8 6 4 2

Library of Congress Cataloging-in-Publication Data

Names: Spiers, John H., author.
Title: Smarter growth : activism and environmental policy in metropolitan Washington /
   John H. Spiers.
Other titles: City in the twenty-first century book series.
Description: 1st edition. | Philadelphia : University of Pennsylvania Press, [2018] | Series: The city
   in the twenty-first century
Identifiers: LCCN 2017056085 | ISBN 978-0-8122-5024-4 (hardcover : alk. paper)
Subjects: LCSH: Sustainable development—Washington Metropolitan Area—History—
   20th century. | Economic development—Environmental aspects—Washington Metropolitan
   Area—History—20th century. | Environmental policy—Washington Metropolitan Area—
   History—20th century. | Environmental protection—Washington Metropolitan Area—
   History—20th century. | Environmentalism—Washington Metropolitan Area—History—
   20th century.
Classification: LCC HC108.W3 S65 2018 | DDC 307.1/41609753—dc23
LC record available at https://lccn.loc.gov/2017056085

CONTENTS

ABBREVIATIONS

AAEA	African American Environmentalist Association
AFT	American Farmland Trust
APAB	Agricultural Preservation Advisory Board
BHFA	Beacon Hill Farm Associates
CMA	Catoctin Mountain Alliance
COG	Metropolitan Washington Council of Governments
CPR	Citizens for Property Rights
CSA	community-supported agriculture
CWA	Clean Water Act
DOT	Department of Transportation
EIS	environmental impact statement
EPA	Environmental Protection Agency
FARM	For a Rural Montgomery
FHA	Federal Housing Administration
FHWA	Federal Highway Administration
ICC	Intercounty Connector
ICC–SCAR	Intercounty Connector – Save Communities Against This Route
ICPRB	Interstate Commission on the Potomac River Basin
ISTEA	Intermodal Surface Transportation Efficiency Act of 1991
LBA	Loudoun Business Alliance
MALPF	Maryland Agricultural Land Preservation Foundation
MD SHA	Maryland State Highway Administration
MET	Maryland Environmental Trust
M-NCPPC	Maryland-National Capital Park and Planning Commission
MPOs	metropolitan planning organizations
MTA	Maryland Transportation Authority
NCPC	National Capital Planning Commission
NEPA	National Environmental Policy Act

NIMBY	not in my backyard
PDR	purchase of development rights
PEC	Piedmont Environmental Council
PLUS	Planning and Land Use System
RLP	Rural Legacy Program
RTC	Resolution Trust Corporation
SHA	State Highway Administration
STIR	Stop That Infernal Road!
TDR	transfer of development rights
USDA	U.S. Department of Agriculture
WASA	D.C. Water and Sewer Authority
WSSC	Washington Suburban Sanitary Commission

Introduction

American prosperity was at a historic high during the 1990s. Low unemployment rates and growing incomes gave rise to an explosion of homes, businesses, and new opportunities across the country. The most noticeable boom was in the Southwest, which was home to six of the nation's fifteen fastest-growing metropolises.[1] Scottsdale, a sleepy town outside of Phoenix around 1950, was by the end of the century a sprawling suburb covering three times the land area of San Francisco with barely a quarter of the population. Southern cities featured even more uneven growth than their Southwestern counterparts. The city of Atlanta, for example, grew by an anemic twenty-two thousand residents during the 1990s compared to its suburbs, which ballooned by 2.1 million.

While the rapid expansion of the "Sunbelt"—the large region spanning the South and Southwest—captured national attention, stories of rapid sprawl into rural areas could be found throughout the United States. Loudoun County, Virginia, was the epicenter of this exurban growth in the Washington, D.C., area.[2] In the early 1990s, local voters unseated a preservationist-oriented Democratic majority on the county's board of supervisors in favor of growth-hungry Republicans. For several years, the county rode the high tide of rampant development, even as community activists cautioned more careful planning to curb the environmental and fiscal impact of sprawl. By 2001, hasty suburbanization had doubled Loudoun's population while opening a Pandora's box of traffic congestion, rising taxes, and loss of rural land. The dramatic clashes between growth and the county's rural character were chronicled in newspaper headlines and played out in tense public hearings. At the turn of the century, environmentalists routinely condemned developers as "landscape rapists" for wanting to build on pristine rural land, while advocates of suburban growth cast environmentalists as "frog-kissing Stalinists" who wanted to seize private property and turn it into useless open space for the masses.[3] These struggles over the scale, timing, and type of growth played out in communities across metropolitan America, and the challenge of supporting public interests in the private use of land was made more complicated by the fractured political environment that prevailed in most regions. Dozens of local governments in Atlanta, for example, were inclined to pursue growth to suit their own parochial ends rather than support regional development through a coordinated transportation plan with robust environmental safeguards.[4]

Around the turn of the century, many metropolitan areas that had seemed to thrive on years of rampant development saw a groundswell of support for more careful growth. John Sibley, chair of the Georgia Conservancy, remarked at the time: "Everybody in Atlanta seems to be against sprawl now—developers, bankers, utility companies, all the interests that have profited from it for five decades. . . . You think back two years and the change in the mind-set is stunning."[5] In 1999, the Georgia state legislature gave the governor nearly singular authority, as head of a superagency, to shape land use decisions in Greater Atlanta to control suburban sprawl.[6] In sum, community members, public officials, and even a significant part of the business and development communities, were calling for more gradual, better-planned, and environmentally sensitive—in a word, "smarter"—growth.

When people think of smart growth, Portland, Oregon, likely comes to mind. Public officials in the region used a state law during the late 1970s to draw an urban growth boundary around the metropolitan area in order to concentrate urban uses on the inside and maintain farms and open space on the outside. Since then, Portland's residents, public officials, and organized groups have embraced its metropolitan orientation to a greater degree than most other regions in the United States through a coordinated planning framework, guided by the Metro Council, which promotes clear distinctions between urban, suburban, and rural.[7] This has enabled Greater Portland to regulate growth more extensively than its peers in the West and positioned it as one of the most environmentally conscious metropolitan areas in the country.[8]

While the example of Portland is noteworthy, I would argue that another region—metropolitan Washington, D.C.—is the progenitor of a smart-growth movement that blossomed in the late twentieth century. It followed a familiar pattern of suburbanization as residents, commerce, and industry gravitated quickly to the periphery during the postwar era, producing massive depopulation and disinvestment in the core while generating explosive growth in the suburbs. This decentralization gave rise to more complex patterns of social segregation in the late twentieth century with the formation of mostly white, middle-class communities in Northern Virginia and outside of the Beltway in Maryland, along with poorer and more socially diverse communities inside the Beltway and in outlying areas, where housing was more affordable. By 2014, Greater Washington had over six million people and extended across six thousand square miles of land, both more than double those of 1970.[9]

Metropolitan Washington allows us to explore how a variety of local communities balanced suburban development and environmental protection. The region includes two states and nearly two dozen counties with different political cultures, legal traditions, and attitudes toward growth. This makes it instructive for evaluating different approaches and outcomes for environmental protection in the face of development pressures. Metropolitan Washington is also distinctive for the robust influence of the federal government in all aspects of the region's history and politics.[10] This includes not only the unique federal-local power-sharing arrangement in the nation's capital but also the role of the federal government as a major employer and contract provider, landowner, and investor in the region's development. As a result, federal agencies were often involved in local growth debates where they otherwise would not have been. Metropolitan Washington thus provides a window onto the fullest possible scope of federal government in local environmental affairs while also offering a more diverse mix of state and local policies and grassroots movements compared to more politically bounded regions like Portland or Atlanta.[11]

With Metropolitan Washington as its focus, the broad goal of *Smarter Growth* is to reorient our understanding of the environmental revolution that began in the late 1960s from familiar stories of national politics and policy to grassroots activism and the impact of national policy making on local communities. Many existing narratives recognize how local concerns over industrial pollution and the impact of suburbanization after World War II inspired environmentalism and policy making at a national scale.[12] As a result of this advocacy, federal policies to clean up pollution, along with the aggressive lobbying and litigation of large environmental organizations, became potent forces for change in metropolitan America during the late twentieth century.[13] However, the work of grassroots movements and the impact of federal policies on the ground have received far less scholarly attention. A closer look into metropolitan communities reveal that much of the work of environmental protection occurred at the local level, where public officials, community activists, and interest groups continually debated how to harness the benefits of growth while mitigating its impact—all while protecting private property rights.

As a new national paradigm of environmental protection formed in the late 1960s, its reach and impact on metropolitan growth largely depended on local and regional constituencies. For example, the National Environmental Policy Act (NEPA) and the environmental review process it set up applied to only a small percentage of development projects involving federal lands or monies. Federal agencies also became less stringent over time as national policies, judicial decisions, and administrative practices eroded their regulatory power and devolved political authority to states, localities, and metropolitan planning authorities.[14] In addition, command-and-control policies such as the Clean Water Act (CWA) became fewer as pollution from more diffuse sources, often tied to local development, increased.[15] Last, long-term federal support for highway construction and the consolidation of farming on the urban edge made mass transit and rural land preservation critical for smarter growth.[16]

Compared to other studies of environmental protection, which focus on policy making or regional planning, *Smarter Growth* explores political change through the interests of elected and planning officials as well as grassroots activists.[17] While the development boom of the 1990s fashioned the smart growth movement, the aftermath of postwar suburbanization and the environmental revolution of the late 1960s allowed the movement to take root. Residents of Fairfax County, Virginia, such as local environmentalist Marian Agnew, pushed elected officials to embrace slow growth and protect environmentally sensitive places. In Montgomery County, Maryland, planning board chair Royce Hanson built on a tradition of progressive land use policies to develop a nationally recognized master plan to protect an Agricultural Reserve. Across Greater Washington, environmentalists pressured local and state officials to comply with new federal standards to clean up water pollution by improving sewage treatment. Last but not least, the beginning of construction of the Metro brought Greater Washington a regional mass transit system that would help organize growth for decades to come.

Following this brief window of support for stricter growth management, local communities reembraced rapid development during the 1980s and 1990s. Waves of new residents seeking commodious accommodations in the suburbs and the rural periphery pushed growth outward. Although many benefited from the economics undergirding this expansion, it also created uneven competition for people, jobs, and investment. Poor and socially diverse inner-ring communities were far less insistent on strong environmental safeguards given their competitive disadvantage, lack of existing opportunities, and need to attract commercial revenue to finance an ever-widening array of social services. A good example was Prince George's County, Maryland, where a broad coalition of liberal middle- and upper-class African

American residents and elected officials endorsed the National Harbor commercial development and downplayed concerns about its impact on the Potomac waterfront.

Citizens across Greater Washington galvanized in favor of compact development beginning in the mid-1990s as rampant suburbanization eroded farmland acreage, worsened traffic congestion, increased runoff, and raised taxes to provide outlying areas with infrastructure. When a developer proposed a large religious school in Montgomery's Agricultural Reserve, local environmentalists including Caroline Taylor mobilized in opposition and, in the process, began to offer a broader defense for preserving rural land and farms. Opponents of the Intercounty Connector (ICC) rejoiced when Maryland governor Parris Glendening rejected the highway as being at odds with the state's smart growth policy—his signature legislative accomplishment—adopted in 1997. Voters to Stop Sprawl helped elect officials in Loudoun, led by moderate Republican Scott York, who created a Rural Policy Area to protect the county's western third from large-scale development. Across the Potomac, the thirty-year campaign to assemble Montgomery's Agricultural Reserve concluded in 2009 as officials closed development loopholes, a last group of conservation easements was secured, and civic organizations such as the Montgomery Countryside Alliance touted the values of the reserve. The health of the Potomac improved with new federal regulations, improved regional wastewater treatment, and civic initiatives by the Alice Ferguson Foundation, Potomac Riverkeeper, and the Potomac Watershed Partnership to confront polluters, educate the public, and forge public-private partnerships for cleanup.

While local environmentalists could take pride in many successes in the past two decades, their case-based activism ran up against a broader and more politically influential coalition supportive of large-scale growth. Despite its earlier rejection, the ICC moved forward in Maryland after three decades of intense debate as residents grew more frustrated with traffic congestion. National Harbor was built out adjacent to the Potomac in Prince George's, delivering the upscale shopping, dining, and other leisure opportunities that many African American residents had sought. Rural land preservation suffered setbacks as the Virginia judiciary and a group of local activists known as the Citizens for Property Rights undercut more stringent environmental safeguards in Loudoun's Rural Policy Area. These and other cases have affirmed a half century pattern in which community debates over growth, situated within regional patterns of inequality, yielded variable and incomplete commitments to environmental protection.

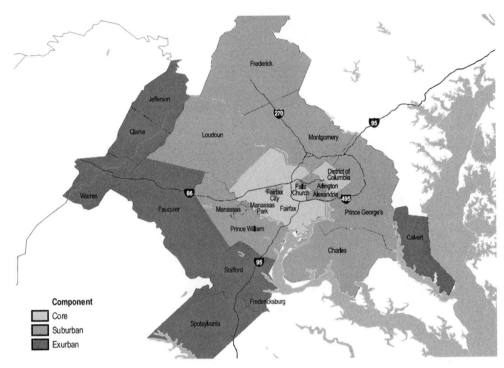

Figure 1. The Washington metropolitan area in the early twenty-first century.
Source: U.S. Bureau of Labor Statistics.

In *Smarter Growth*, I discuss how grassroots activists applied principles of environmental stewardship to advocate for growth that was "smarter" than the models of suburbanization that prevailed after World War II. Their advocacy included a few tenets: promoting compact development that used existing resources rather than new infrastructure and services; preserving rural land and open space; and protecting the air, water, and soil from pollution. Over time, these activists and their allies in government and elsewhere expanded on their concerns about the environment and public health to argue that large-scale suburbanization was also more expensive than carefully planned compact growth. In the early 1970s and around the turn of the century, they were fairly successful at securing more rigorous pollution cleanup, stronger development regulations, and greater strides in rural land preservation as palliatives for the environmental and fiscal impact of growth. Their successes came mostly during high tides of sprawl, when the bucolic quality of life associated with bedroom suburbs was threatened.

Outside of some basic principles, what constituted smart growth was subject to political and public whims. Communities in Maryland had strong support from state officials for promoting compact development, market-based land preservation programs, and funding for land preservation. They were more inclined to organize higher-density growth around Metro stations, for example, than Fairfax or Loudoun Counties in Virginia, which developed largely outside of the Metro service area.[18] Montgomery's Agricultural Reserve was also a testament to local planners and elected leaders who used tools authorized by the state to regulate growth and preserve rural land. Many counties in Northern Virginia, however, favored strong property rights safeguards, permissive land use planning, and aggressive road building. While state support was important for local communities pursuing environmentally sensitive growth, it was not the only factor. Communities that struggled to attract upscale commercial development, like Prince George's, were less willing to insist on robust growth control and environmental safeguards than wealthier peers in Northern Virginia.[19]

Although local environmentalism was full of promise, curbing the impact of development over the long term was a formidable challenge. The construction of homes, businesses, and institutions—key signals of general prosperity—forged enduring coalitions among officials, residents, business leaders, and interest groups.[20] This, combined with the mobile capital of the service-based economy of the late twentieth century, fostered an insatiable appetite for development.[21] Over time, policies and public preferences transformed Greater Washington, like many regions, from a central city hub with dependent suburbs into a diffuse agglomeration of communities with an uneven distribution of people, jobs, and investment.[22] These inequalities left central cities and lower-income suburbs at a disadvantage, pushing their officials and residents to further sacrifice environmental safeguards for marquee projects. The unceasing competition for growth also impaired cooperation on affordable housing, economic development, and regional mobility.[23]

The focus of grassroots activists on community-based struggles also limited the reach of their work. Contrary to the notion of being "laboratories of democracy," local politics frequently did not ensure substantive representation of the public's concerns about suburban development. Endless meetings, complex planning and environmental regulations, and the dominance of growth-oriented officials and business interests often buried civic concerns.[24] Finally, in the adversarial world of community politics, grassroots activists often spent so much time fighting fires that they were rarely able to form broad movements with those of different viewpoints.[25] Indeed, their insistence on the self-evident merits of smart growth at times downplayed the broad value of development, increased housing costs, and elevated their interests in land preservation over the economic concerns of farmers and other rural business operators.[26]

Following a context-setting overview of Greater Washington, *Smarter Growth* includes spatially oriented case studies to explore how movements for smarter growth developed on the ground. The first examines how grass-roots activists improved the water quality of the Potomac River. Aside from construction of the Metro, the river's cleanup was one of the few issues that garnered attention across the region. It is a shining example of how even robust federal policy making established a foundation, rather than a guarantee, for environmental protection. Indeed, as sources of water pollution became more diffuse, civic activism proved more critical than national policy in cleanup efforts. Next, I examine two communities that adopted quite different approaches to waterfront development along the Potomac. The first, in Fairfax, featured a heady group of local environmentalists seeking to protect the ecological resources and natural amenities that they enjoyed from an upscale housing project. The second, in Prince George's, saw an outpouring of political and public support for a landmark economic development project in a county that had been shut out from upscale commerce and whose residents were disinclined to worry about the environmental impact on the Potomac. The next case, a study of a cross-county highway in Maryland, explores how fervent local environmentalism may not be enough to override the widespread view of highways as panaceas for enhancing mobility.

The debate over suburban highways—and about the sprawl of growth more broadly—raised tough questions over how to alleviate the pressures to develop rural land. The final two chapters offer a case of contrasting local approaches to agricultural and rural land preservation. Montgomery County, the site of the cross-county highway, combined progressive land use planning with innovative market-based incentives to help rural landholders earn income by selling development rights in exchange for preserving their land in perpetuity. Meanwhile, rural land preservation in Loudoun County reveals far more political and public opposition, especially at the state level, to robust development regulations and land preservation incentives. The book ends with some general recommendations for promoting environmental stewardship in the fractured political landscape of metropolitan America in the twenty-first century.

An Overview of Greater Washington

Before World War II, the nation's capital was the center of a small region that included the bedroom suburbs of Alexandria and Arlington County in Virginia and the southern third of Montgomery and Prince George's Counties in Maryland. Residents in outlying areas may have had jobs or occasional business in Washington but otherwise lived in rural communities. As the region's major urban center, Washington, D.C., had most of the area's residents, the great majority of its jobs, and its best shopping, dining, and leisure options. During the war, migrants from across the country flooded into the city to work for the federal government. Temporary offices, housing, and a few major federal facilities like the Pentagon were hastily built near the district to accommodate workers and families, commencing the region's suburbanization.[27]

After the war, officials prepared to satisfy the pent-up demand for housing and the desire for a more commodious way of life. The National Capital Planning Commission (NCPC), a federal agency officially responsible for planning the District of Columbia and informally charged with shaping a common vision for the region, favored a compact model of a development-guided mass transit system and a handful of highways. Their desired "wedges and corridors" planning model for the region soon unraveled, however, as rapid and expansive suburbanization took hold and local officials struggled to keep up.[28]

Between 1940 and 1970, the population around Washington quintupled to more than two million, while that of the nation's capital declined from a historic high of 802,178 in 1950 to 756,510 by 1970.[29] There were three major factors that sparked this major demographic and spatial shift. The first was the proliferation of single-use residential zoning and the advent of mortgage incentives from the Federal Housing Administration (FHA) to build homes in outlying white communities rather than socially diverse urban neighborhoods. The second was the emergence of "community builders" that developed large tracts of inexpensive homes on the rural periphery. While the Levitt Corporation in the Northeast is the most remembered, each metropolitan area had some of its own—the Arlington-based Yeonas Corporation was an example in Greater Washington. A young Milton Peterson got his start with the company, becoming one of the most prodigious developers in the region during the late twentieth century.[30]

Like housing, the demand for automobiles skyrocketed after the war. State highway departments rushed to build major highways to enhance mobility and open the countryside for the construction of new homes.[31] In Greater

Washington, the opening of Shirley Highway from the Pentagon to Fairfax during the late 1940s and early 1950s contributed to an eightfold population increase in the Northern Virginia county by 1960, while the construction of the Washington National Pike from Rockville to Frederick County, Maryland, in the early 1950s quadrupled the population of Montgomery.[32]

Even after Virginia and Maryland spent the first decade of the postwar era engaged in an aggressive campaign of road building, political interest in a comprehensive national system of highways persisted. In response, Congress passed the Federal-Aid Highway Act of 1956, which laid the groundwork for transportation and land use planning centered on the automobile for the next several decades. The act offered an unprecedented federal contribution of 90 percent toward building forty-one thousand miles of interstate highways that was paid for by a dedicated Highway Trust Fund that collected taxes on fuel, tires, and heavy vehicles.[33] These highways, along with thousands of miles of primary and secondary roads planned, funded, and built by the states, enabled a type of mobile, suburban lifestyle that many Americans desired. The Capital Beltway, which opened in 1964 to connect the suburbs radiating around Washington, punctuated an era of automobility.[34]

As America's postwar suburbs expanded, they became highly segregated. In Greater Washington, the white middle class moved rapidly out of the nation's capital, settling in Fairfax and Montgomery Counties. This, in concert with an influx of black residents, led Washington, D.C., to become the nation's first majority African American city by 1957. City officials, as in many regions, attempted to curb the exodus of the white middle class through residential urban renewal projects, most notably in the Southwest, but instead displaced thousands of working-class African Americans.[35] Prince George's, on the other hand, became the leading suburb for the region's African American population because of its proximity to eastern Washington and its affordable housing.[36] White middle-class suburbanites tended to overlook how their allegedly "colorblind" desire for socially homogeneous communities actually fostered racial discrimination in housing.[37] Although passage of the federal Fair Housing Act of 1968 broke down the most overt policies of racial discrimination in the real estate industry, housing affordability and public attitudes prevailed as barriers to more inclusive communities.

Employment and commerce decentralized like housing patterns, albeit a little later. Like housing developers, the federal government grew outside of Washington, where land was cheaper and easier to acquire. Cold War–era concerns about the potential impact of a nuclear attack bolstered the idea of dispersing federal installations. In Virginia, Rosslyn and Crystal City in Arlington and Tysons Corner in Fairfax became centers for defense agencies and contractors given their proximity to the Pentagon, while the Washington National Pike (later Interstate 270) corridor became a hub for the biomedical industry near the National Institutes of Health in Bethesda, Maryland. Conversely, Prince George's was often bypassed by the region's major white-collar employers and retailers because of the lack of major highways and the presence of a more socially diverse, working-class population. The result for the nation's capital was that its share of employment and commerce declined despite efforts to revitalize its commercial core.[38]

The postwar suburban boom dramatically increased costs for schools, utilities, and other services. Rather than provoke the ire of residents by continually raising their property taxes, many local officials sought out commercial development to generate tax revenue. Even as outlying areas looked to strengthen their land use planning tools to guide development, the growth imperative—the pressure to add new development to pay for existing and projected commitments of services—discouraged most officials from insisting on robust environmental safeguards. The net result of the growth imperative, based in conservative attitudes about regulating property, was the conversion of agricultural and rural land for suburban construction, rising costs to provision services in more remote locations, and worsening pollution.[39]

Postwar growth especially threatened the Potomac River, which served as both the region's major source of drinking water and the dumping ground of pollution. In 1940, Congress created the Interstate Commission on the Potomac River Basin (ICPRB) to organize the four states and numerous localities in the basin in support of protecting the river's health. The ICPRB, however, lacked any regulatory authority. Instead, states and communities were left to address their individual pollution of the river, which the imperative of growth discouraged.[40] As a result, rapid development tapped the Potomac's water without concerns about supply; produced waves of eroded sediment from site development; and overloaded the region's main wastewater treatment facility at Blue Plains in Washington, which then dumped untreated sewage back in the river.[41] Congress had little pressure to counteract these activities. Instead, it financed individual projects for drinking water, sewage treatment, and hydroelectric power to support postwar expansion.[42]

The widespread material abundance of postwar America, which had given rise to suburbanization, also sowed the seeds of modern environmentalism to counteract its negative impact. It featured two main aims. The first involved a shift of environmental concerns from conservation, which emphasized economical use of the productive capacity of nature, to quality-of-life interests in protecting nature for its scenic, recreational, and open space amenities.[43] A good example of this in Greater Washington was a series of successful civic campaigns to block high-rise apartment construction along the Potomac waterfront during the 1960s.[44] These cases tended to invoke an aesthetic clash between high-rise apartments and the landscape of single-family homes and open space that prevailed in affluent waterfront communities. More critically, the privileging of aesthetic over affordable housing obscured a social bias among the white middle class that viewed the waterfront as an amenity only for those who could afford to live nearby in single-family homes. As local environmentalists continued to advocate for reducing the scale of suburban development and preserving open space, they invited charges of elitism that proved hard to shake during the late twentieth century.[45]

The other major branch of modern environmentalism focused on the consequences of pollution for the environment and public health. Air pollution from industrial facilities and automobiles as well as the unsafe disposal of waste were issues across metropolitan America. Public environmental concern awakened through a combination of high-profile events such as the publication of Rachel Carson's *Silent Spring* in 1962 and the conflagration of the Cuyahoga River in 1969, along with the everyday local concerns about sewage backups, air that was difficult to breathe, and the loss of rural and forested land to development.[46] Near the end of the 1960s, Congress passed several ambitious policies to conserve and protect natural resources.[47]

The most pronounced commitment to environmental advocacy in American history was made during the early 1970s. On January 1, 1970, Richard Nixon signed the National Environmental Policy Act (NEPA) into law. Nixon was not an environmentalist, as his predecessor Lyndon Johnson perhaps was, but an opportunist who acquiesced to political pressure from Democrats and the public for strong environmental regulations. NEPA required federally funded projects or actions undertaken by a federal agency to undergo a comprehensive review process that involved the public. For large projects, an environmental impact statement (EIS) review process would identify the environmental impacts of the project, mitigation measures, and possible alternatives. These policies, an outgrowth of the "rights revolution" of the mid-twentieth century, insisted that ordinary people should have a meaningful voice in political decision-making.[48]

NEPA offered an expansive vision of sustainability at a time before that term came into vogue. It also coincided with a decade of unparalleled national policy making that included passage of the Clean Air Act (1970) and Clean Water Act (1972), the Endangered Species Act (1973), the Occupational Health and Safety Act (1974), and Superfund legislation (1980) to clean up hazardous waste sites.[49] The Environmental Protection Agency (EPA) was created as part of the executive branch in 1970 to consolidate and coordinate enforcement of these policies. Its work soon became highly politicized given the strictness of these new policies and their punitive consequences.

While Congress and the EPA were major policy actors, their work would have been far less impactful without large groups of environmentalists working at all levels of government and society.[50] Ten organizations, ranging from newer and more aggressive groups like the Environmental Defense Fund and Natural Resources Defense Council to older conservation organizations with new agendas such as the Sierra Club and National Wildlife Federation, built an influential lobbing and litigation presence around their expertise.[51] Their members, along with many local civic activists, built grassroots environmental movements across the United States, the coming-out party for which was the first Earth Day on April 22, 1970.[52]

Although this national attention to the environment was quite significant, environmental protection in metropolitan America over time depended less on national policy decrees and more on the results of citizens and officials working on the ground at the state and local levels. This political devolution had its roots in the social reform programs of the Great Society that championed community empowerment during the late 1960s. Under the Nixon administration, devolution continued under the aegis of making federal agencies more responsive to citizens, but it also gave states and localities more flexibility in compliance.[53]

The issue of water pollution is a good example of this shift from policy to advocacy. Passage of the federal Clean Water Act created a permitting system with strict standards governing the discharge of pollutants into rivers and other navigable waterways. It also offered several billion dollars to help states and localities pay for wastewater treatment infrastructure to clean up pollution from sewers, industrial facilities, and other discrete sources. Yet these groups still had to stage the cleanup and determine who would pay the high costs not covered by federal funding. As a result, grassroots activists and national lobbies were critical for creating the political and legal pressure needed to advance environmental progress.[54]

Federal policies played less of a role in curbing suburban sprawl during the late twentieth century. NEPA and the environmental impact statement process, for example, applied to only a subset of development projects involving federal interests and focused more on mitigating impacts based on community concerns rather than ensuring a minimum standard of environmental protection. Federal policies also did little to protect rural land from suburban conversion; indeed, they promoted the consolidation of farming. Secretary of Agriculture Earl Butz highlighted the acceleration of this trend in the 1970s when he famously advised farmers to "get bigger or get out."[55]

As part of the high tide of modern environmentalism, grassroots activities joined with supportive public officials in several Washington-area communities to curb pollution, the loss of open space, and the financial costs of sprawl during the early 1970s.[56] After supporting rapid suburbanization for a quarter century, voters in Fairfax elected local leaders who enhanced land preservation and passed a 1973 ordinance that tied development to the capacity of existing infrastructure. A conservative state judiciary, however, overturned the ordinance as an undue infringement of private property rights. In 1976, voters elected leaders who returned the county to a dogged pursuit of commercial development to offset rising property taxes.[57]

Montgomery County benefited from having a more environmentally conscious population and officials committed to a model of compact planning. Montgomery embraced the wedges and corridors model of planning after World War II.[58] Under planning board chair Royce Hanson, the county took two major steps to bolster growth management during the 1970s. First, officials adopted an adequate public facilities ordinance that was never struck down, unlike in Northern Virginia. Second, they created a master plan to preserve agriculture and rural land by curbing suburban housing and implementing a program that allowed landowners to sell the right to develop parcels of land in exchange for agreeing to permanent conservation easements.[59] Purchasers in this transfer of development rights program could then use their rights to build extra housing in certain areas. Montgomery's planning measures were quite successful in curbing population growth: while Fairfax's population increased 31 percent during the 1970s, Montgomery's rose less than 11 percent.[60]

The contrast between Fairfax and Montgomery Counties highlighted the importance of state support of local growth regulations for achieving environmental goals.[61] In addition, Maryland's land preservation programs offered funding to local communities for permanent conservation, while Virginia's employed temporary protections and did not offer funding for conservation easements until 1997.[62] State support for growth management, however, still required local commitments for environmental protection to be successful. The influx of working-class African Americans into Prince George's County during the 1970s spiked property taxes to pay for infrastructure and services. Rather than seeking to slow growth to rein in the cost of supporting it, residents instead voted to cap their property taxes, joining a tax revolt movement that swept across suburban America.[63] In the short term, this vote accomplished its fiscal objective. Over the longer term, the tax cap intensified the need to attract commercial development, with two results. First, public officials and residents were more likely to discount the environmental impact of development in order to attract the revenue it offered. Second, local officials undermined the value proposition of growth by offering financial subsidies to try and lure businesses to locate.

As its suburbs struggled to manage growth, Washington, D.C., attempted to redefine its image in the face of population loss, commercial disinvestment, poverty, and crime. With passage of the Home Rule Act of 1973, the nation's capital acquired new rights to govern itself. Under Mayor Walter Washington, the city redeveloped commercial areas along Pennsylvania Avenue and the Georgetown waterfront, built a new convention center downtown, and created more public spaces.[64] The city, and its suburbs, also began construction of the Metro mass transit system after overcoming fifteen years of congressional struggles that had delayed financing.[65] Washington was one of the few places where a public transportation system was built in the second half of the twentieth century. It took twenty years to complete, however, leaving the District and inner suburbs hard-pressed to stem the tide of expansion into the outlying counties of Prince William and Loudoun in Virginia and Charles County in Maryland.

Rapid growth returned to Washington in the 1980s and 1990s in step with the rise of political and cultural conservatism. At the national level, the Reagan administration undermined the enforcement authority of the EPA, blocked passage of new regulations, and curbed citizens' use of environmental lawsuits. Although these efforts slowed after 1983, they marked a new legacy in the devolution of American politics inaugurated by the Nixon era. As a result, coalitions of growth supporters regained control in many communities.[66] By 2000, the population of Greater Washington had increased to

Figure 2. Aerial view of Northern Virginia looking northeast toward Washington, D.C.
Source: Carol M. Highsmith Archive.

4.8 million as the region's boundaries doubled to include nearly a dozen new counties in Virginia, Maryland, and even West Virginia.[67] Virginia localities experienced larger population increases and more extensive growth than their Maryland peers due to lower taxes, more permissive land use policies, and vigorous road building campaigns that opened land to development.[68]

The rapid suburbanization of Greater Washington intensified residential segregation as much of the white middle class moved into outlying areas while people of color, immigrants, and the working class settled in the older, close-in suburbs. Four decades after Washington, D.C., became the nation's first major black-majority city, Prince George's became the nation's first black-majority suburban county. Meanwhile, a handful of older suburbs, such as Springfield, Virginia, displaced the traditional role of central cities as gateways for immigrants thanks to their proximity to major highways and recently completed Metro stations. Incomes in the region remained higher than the national average, but this affluence was not shared equitably. High housing prices pushed lower-income workers into communities inside the Beltway or pulled them out to the urban fringe.[69]

Employment and commerce closely followed residential suburbanization. Greater Washington added fifty-five thousand jobs per year between 1980 and 2002 and had lower unemployment rates than the national average. While the region maintained a large federal workforce, there was considerable growth in the technology, business services, education, health care, and leisure sectors. The competition for the highly mobile capital in these industries transformed the business core into a more complex, uneven network of jobs and commerce that tended to favor Northern Virginia because of its strong bias toward unencumbered growth.[70] At the same time, inner-core communities struggled to attract investment, even when they used major financial incentives to lure upscale commercial projects.[71]

The construction of the Metro offered a major opportunity to reorient Greater Washington around a wedges and corridors model of regional development, but the results varied by community. In places where planners and officials had promoted compact development, like Montgomery and Arlington, Metro stations fitted nicely in and helped organize growth. In places where they had not, like Fairfax, much development lay outside of the Metro service area.[72] Just as the last set of original Metro stations opened in the early 1990s, chronic congestion on the Capital Beltway and many of the region's other major highways pulled political attention to the periphery.[73] In Northern Virginia, two toll roads were built in Loudoun to accommodate exurban growth; however, the state of Maryland and its localities focused their planning efforts on improving existing roads and increasing use of Metro.[74]

Compared with the postwar era, the end of the century was a far more cautious time regarding highway building in light of the troubling social legacies of urban freeways and environmental concerns about air pollution. As construction of the interstate system came to a close, Congress passed the Intermodal Surface Transportation Efficiency Act of 1991 (ISTEA). Although ISTEA continued the long-standing tradition of prioritizing highways over transit, it had several features that were helpful for developing highways that were sensitive to the environmental and social context of their surroundings. These included mandating public participation in assessing regional projects, shifting more authority in the decision-making process to states and localities, and requiring regional planning organizations to approve major projects.[75] While environmentalists used ISTEA and related policies to curb regional growth, many citizens and public officials continued to see highways as the only way to enhance mobility, even though these roads would likely perpetuate the congestion that was a by-product of sprawl.

Rampant development between 1980 and 2000 made farming on the urban edge more challenging in Greater Washington. Suburban encroachment, for example, raised land values and therefore property taxes for rural property owners. The agriculture industry also changed as high land costs, nuisance complaints from suburbanites, and low prices reduced the number of animal-based and commodity farming (e.g., wheat) operations. Federal price supports under the Farm Bill as well as the Conservation Reserve Program, created in 1985 to encourage farmers to take environmentally sensitive land out of production, were insufficient to sustain highly capitalized farms on the urban edge. The results of this were not favorable to the region's farmers. The percentage of land in farms in Prince William County dropped from 27 percent in 1978 to 15 percent by 1992, and in Prince George's from 25 percent to 17 percent.[76] As farming costs continued to rise, a growing number of part-time and hobby farmers found success in operating small, specialized farms for produce and boutique items that allowed them to clear higher profit margins and depend on other work for their primary income.[77]

For most of the late twentieth century, public officials and environmentalists on the urban edge had been more concerned with losing the natural amenities of rural land than with farming operations per se.[78] This fostered support for policies that restricted the development potential of land and offered incentives to discourage farmers from selling their land because it was too expensive to work. The tendency to see farms as land to preserve rather than businesses to support frustrated farmers because it was often associated with limiting the infrastructure they needed to support their operations and reducing the developable potential—and thereby the value—of their land as collateral to borrow funds to reinvest in their highly capitalized businesses.[79]

Gradually, environmentalists realized it took more than land preservation to protect farms from suburban encroachment; it also required support for farms as businesses. Montgomery established an Agricultural Services Division in 1996 (renamed the Office of Agriculture in 2016) to help them navigate local planning issues, manage local preservation programs, and provide technical assistance, Loudoun took similar measures.[80] Getting the public to visit farms and buy locally also became more popular. By 2000, there were thirty farmers markets in the Washington area and several farm tours. Some localities, especially in Virginia, had success with marketing local farms as part of a rural tourism strategy including historic sites and outdoor scenic and recreational opportunities.[81]

The feverish growth of Greater Washington during the 1990s sowed seeds of discord for slowing it down. As metropolitan development became more diffuse, sprawl consumed rural land, degraded resources such as water and open space, drove up taxes to pay for public services further out, and failed to resolve mounting traffic congestion. These consequences forged a broad but loose coalition of civic, environmental, antitax, and broader-based groups committed to compact, transit-oriented development—the basis for the smart growth movement.[82]

CHAPTER 1

A River Revived

In a 2012 story for the *Washington Post*, Ed Merrifield reflected on his work over the previous decade as president of the Potomac Riverkeeper Network. The group was one of several civic organizations in Greater Washington devoted to curbing water pollution, enhancing recreational opportunities, and protecting river habitats. In discussing their approach to environmental stewardship, Merrifield avowed, "If it's illegal pollution, we go after it as fast as we can to tell them you have to stop. We use all legal means necessary. We won't back down."[1] Potomac Riverkeeper engaged in political lobbying, like many environmental groups, but was better known for providing environmental education and hands-on activities to cultivate public stewardship of the Potomac. This kind of work proved ever more valuable during the late twentieth century as sprawling development expanded the sources of pollution and encouraged environmentalists to see their work in the context of the smart-growth movement that was taking shape in the region.

Cleaning up the Potomac River was the most unifying environmental issue of Greater Washington over the past half century. In the early 1970s, the river, like many in the United States, was heavily polluted because of inadequate wastewater treatment, storm-water runoff and erosion from land development, and poor regulations on industry. In 1972, Congress passed the Clean Water Act (CWA), which featured strict water quality standards and a permitting system to govern the discharge of pollutants. Over the next decade, state and local officials built and upgraded wastewater treatment facilities to comply with federal policy, but they still had to find the political will and resources to clean up pollution—and that often depended on pressure from grassroots activists. Environmentalists were supportive of cleaning up pollution but worried that increasing treatment capacity would unintentionally spark growth in outlying areas. In the mid-1980s, the limitations of federal policies for addressing indirect or "nonpoint" sources of pollution that were not connected to sewage treatment infrastructure became more visible. Controlling storm-water runoff, for example, was a significant problem in built-up urban and suburban environments with a high percentage of impermeable surfaces such as roads and rooftops.[2] As a result, citizen-led activities that tapped into, and grew, public investment in the health and welfare of the Potomac became even more important.

Through the interplay of policy making and grassroots activism, the "nation's river" is healthier now than at any point in the past fifty years. Citizens pushed officials to clean up the Potomac primarily through community-based debates to address the environmental impact of existing development rather than seeking additional growth. In the mid-1990s, grassroots activists began to take more direct ownership of pollution cleanup. Greater political cooperation across the region supported public-private partnerships between government and environmental organizations. Environmentalists also broadened their approach from a focus on lobbying public officials to more direct activities including trash cleanups, river monitoring, and environmental education. Finally, they adopted a more holistic perspective on river cleanup to address the issues of habitat and species protection, ecological restoration, and open space preservation. The focus of local environmentalists on critiquing both the environmental and financial costs of growth reflected a critique of 1970s metropolitan America that returned with renewed force in the late 1990s under the more formal banner of smart growth. The cleanup of the Potomac, then, was an environmental success story as well as an integral part of metropolitan Washington's smartgrowth movement.

The Potomac in Postwar America

Postwar growth took a heavy toll on the Potomac. The river, which is 383 miles long with a watershed of 14,700 square miles, knits together Greater Washington as it reaches into West Virginia and Pennsylvania. At its southern end, the Potomac has an estuary with the Chesapeake Bay.[3] Beginning in the late nineteenth century, Washington built a combined system to convey sewage and storm-water runoff into the Potomac. By the late 1930s, the most developed sections of the region had their own sewer systems, including the District of Columbia, the City of Alexandria, and Arlington County, and the southern third of Montgomery and Prince George's Counties. In 1938, Washington

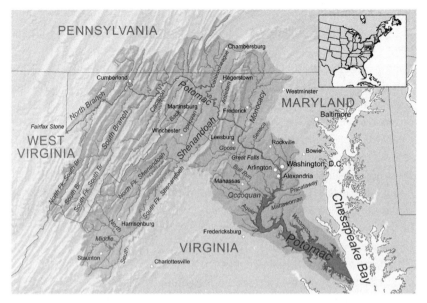

Figure 3. The Potomac River Basin. Source: Kmusser, Wikimedia Commons.

opened a regional wastewater treatment facility known as Blue Plains to screen and remove suspended solids as well as to accelerate the breakdown of organic waste by waterborne organisms. Postwar growth, however, soon outstripped the facility's capacity, resulting in raw sewage being regularly dumped into the Potomac as overflow. Upgrades to expand the plant's capacity and quality of treatment failed to keep pace with population growth, resulting in pollution levels that were higher by 1970 than in the early 1930s.[4]

Insufficient capacity at Blue Plains was not the only problem. Many postwar suburbs relied on septic tanks, which were easier to construct and less expensive than sewers but had shorter life spans and were more likely to leach sewage into local groundwater that made its way to the Potomac. Fairfax, for example, had two thousand such defective tanks by the mid-1950s. A second issue was sediment runoff from site development, where large lots were left bulldozed and without trees for extended periods before construction was completed. By 1960, streams in the Washington area dumped one million tons of sediment into the Potomac each year.[5]

The worsening condition of the Potomac was the result of rapid suburbanization and the unwillingness of jurisdictions in Greater Washington to work together to curb pollution. In 1940, Congress chartered the Interstate

Commission on the Potomac River Basin (ICPRB) to coordinate development of the river's resources. Its members included elected government officials and experts from the federal government, the four states in the Potomac's watershed, and Washington, D.C. The commission regularly warned of the need to build more wastewater treatment facilities, reduce erosion, and undertake regional-level planning for compact, gradual growth.[6] Communities in the basin, however, chose to focus on their local growth and did not feel bound to work together to curb pollution.[7] "Each community now moves independently in a different direction," the producer of a local television series about the Potomac remarked. "The interstate commission sets standards but has no authority, and no one lives up to them."[8] In addition, Congress was unwilling to strengthen regional coordination to require states and localities to clean up pollution. Instead, it encouraged developing water resources to support regional growth.[9] Without strong regulation or coordination, local communities were left to their own devices to address their impact on the Potomac.

Conversations about the river shifted in the 1960s as the impact of suburbanization mounted. The construction of several communities without adequate sewage disposal facilities as well as growth around Dulles International Airport in outlying Loudoun led Congress to authorize construction of the Potomac Interceptor to send wastewater from those areas to Blue Plains.[10] While the project helped convey pollution, it overburdened Blue Plains even more, which then sent raw or partially treated overflow into the river. Even as the Potomac's pollution worsened, few citizens expressed public concern, though the League of Women Voters was a notable exception. Instead, well-off suburbanites with conservationist impulses focused on preserving scenic and open space amenities by seeking to restrict high-rise apartments along the waterfront.

The most prominent case involved the Merrywood tract in the affluent Fairfax community of McLean, the childhood home of first lady Jacqueline Kennedy. When county officials approved three seventeen-story towers for the site in 1962, members of the McLean Citizens Association protested that it would disrupt the low-rise character of the waterfront and overburden the area's schools and roads. The case rapidly gained regional attention from civic organizations, planning agencies, members of Congress, and even Supreme Court Justice William O. Douglas, an ardent conservationist credited with mobilizing support in the 1950s to block a highway proposal and to preserve the 185-mile Chesapeake and Ohio Canal. The most significant actor in the Merrywood case was Secretary of the Interior Stewart Udall, who lived near the property and refused to grant a permit for a sewer line across the federally owned George Washington Parkway. When the developer defied a second ban, Udall obtained a court order to purchase an easement for $744,500 that restricted development to single-family housing. Several years later, after his tenure as secretary of the interior, Udall concluded that the case had established that a "high rise along the edge of the [Potomac] river was intolerable," affirming support for preserving the waterfront for its open space amenities.[11]

Land preservation cases such as Merrywood were rooted in the broad affluence of postwar America and the desire of well-off suburbanites to preserve the local environment from rampant growth. They illustrated how grassroots civic organizing and burgeoning environmental consciousness, paired with political interest, could spark environmental protection. Yet the emphasis on aesthetic concerns and the overloading of existing facilities obscured a social bias among affluent residents. That bias interpreted the waterfront as an amenity to be enjoyed by those who could afford to live in the large single-family homes nearby rather than those who would have lived in the more modestly priced apartments.[12] About a decade after Udall had secured the conservation easement, a developer bought the Merrywood property. By the late 1970s, he had built thirteen single-family homes with five more under construction, which were selling for what was at the time the exorbitant price of $250,000.[13]

As communities struggled to control postwar suburbanization, national officials saw the Potomac waterfront as a prospective test case for a new model of growth management. In a widely touted message to Congress in 1965, President Johnson insisted that the Potomac "serve as a model of scenic and recreation values for the entire county" and directed a task force to develop a program for cleaning up the river and preserving its banks from high-density development.[14] Despite a strong federal commitment, the task force failed because it excluded state and local officials and proposed a model of shoreline preservation that ignored the growth imperative under which many communities operated.[15] As the 1960s ended, much work lay ahead for cleaning up the Potomac.

A Mandate for Cleanup

By 1970, the Potomac was heavily polluted. Wastewater treatment facilities were chronically overburdened, which led to partially treated effluent being dumped into the river. Blue Plains handled 75 percent of Greater Washington's

Figure 4. The Georgetown Gap. Source: EPA.

wastewater treatment, but its 240 million gallons per day (mgd) capacity was regularly exceeded by 30 mgd.[16] Poorly constructed and overloaded sewer lines were also major problems. Sewer lines near the Cabin John Parkway in Maryland spouted raw sewage from manholes—"like 'Old Faithful,'" as one critic noted—into a creek just above the Potomac's water supply intake for Washington, D.C.[17] The worst leak was in one of several incomplete portions of the Potomac Interceptor system, the half-mile-long "Georgetown gap," which dumped 15 million gallons of raw sewage per day from the region's most affluent suburbs.[18] Storm-water runoff from close-in urban communities along with eroded soil from suburban land development added to the river's pollution.

The effects of this pollution were on display as Joseph Penfold of the Izaak Walton League hosted an environmental education boat trip in late 1971. Out on the water, he and his passengers could not see even a couple of inches below the surface because of silt and algae buildup and encountered a stench so bad that in certain sections birds did not fly around it. The smell was worst at Blue Plains, where sewage and sludge left over from treatment was piled four feet deep on forty acres of open land to dry out for a year before being shipped out for disposal or use as fertilizer in suburban communities.[19] Aside from being nuisances, overflowed sewage, storm water, and eroded soil yielded high levels of coliform that threatened drinking water quality and high concentrations of nitrogen and other elements that threatened aquatic life by producing low oxygen levels and large algae growths.[20] Trips made by Penfold and others, including Maryland congressman Gilbert Gude in 1975, dramatized the pollution of the Potomac, the impact on its aesthetic and recreational amenities, and the merits of preserving the shoreline from high-density development.[21] Gude, for his part, was one of a number of Republicans who joined their Democratic counterparts during an era of strong bipartisan political and public support for robust environmental protection in the early 1970s.

Enhancing wastewater treatment was the primary means by which the Potomac and other metropolitan rivers were cleaned up in the 1970s. Passage of the CWA in 1972 confronted political resistance to cleaning up water pollution by setting strict, nationally uniform technical limits on pollution from sources that directly, or as a conduit, dumped pollution into rivers or wetlands. The law employed permitting, monitoring, and reporting systems for facilities' discharges and established deadlines for treatment plants to eliminate 85 percent of conventional pollutants. The CWA reflected a new mentality that pollution should be prohibited unless authorized and that the national government should lead in standard setting. For these reasons, many state officials opposed the command-and-control approach that took away control of an issue long under their purview. On the other hand, the policy recognized the financial impact on states and localities by authorizing a construction grant program of several billion dollars to build and upgrade wastewater treatment facilities.[22]

No single person was as important to this work in Greater Washington as Norman Cole. Born in South Carolina in 1933, Cole grew up in Florida, where he later worked as a nuclear engineer for the navy during the 1950s. He and his wife moved to Fairfax in 1959, buying a house overlooking the Potomac and near a sanctuary for bald eagles that later became the Mason Neck National Wildlife Refuge. Cole was impressed with the undeveloped beauty of the Potomac's shoreline and took a professional interest in water treatment after a "mile-long stinking mat of dead yellow and brown algae . . . came floating down river and blew in on our shore" during a house party in the late 1960s.[23] Cole then joined local citizens to publicize research that found Fairfax had overloaded its sewage treatment plants by supporting rampant growth. They persuaded the Virginia State Water Control Board in

June 1970 to impose a moratorium on new sewer hookups for three plants, thereby halting new development. But Northern Virginia builders persuaded the courts to overturn the ban and force the county to expand the system's capacity and implement new technologies to accelerate the removal of pollutants. The results were dramatic, as Fairfax turned the worst sewer overload in the state into an example of what state-of-the-art technologies and political management could do.[24]

Cole's advocacy soon garnered the attention of Governor Linwood Holton. Holton was a moderate Republican and the first member of his party to occupy Virginia's governorship since Reconstruction. Although he did not start out as an environmentalist, Holton quickly enhanced the state's commitment to cleaning up polluted waterways after taking a helicopter ride to witness the pollution that bubbled out from the Georgetown gap. His single most important decision in this regard was appointing Cole, a fellow Republican, as head of the State Water Control Board. The board had significant powers to shape local development through the approval or veto of sewage treatment plants, but it had rarely exercised its powers to curb growth, which had strong support in law, policy, and culture in Virginia. As an avid outdoorsman and maturing environmentalist, Cole used the agency's powers to dramatic effect to upgrade Blue Plains in order to clean up the municipal and industrial wastes polluting the Potomac.[25]

In the early 1970s, the most egregious issue facing Blue Plains was an overburdening of the facility caused by the Washington Suburban Sanitary Commission (WSSC), which had for years exceeded its allotted capacity by nearly 50 percent while the other users—Fairfax and Loudoun Counties and Washington, D.C.—stayed within their limits.[26] Cole moved swiftly to pressure the WSSC to rectify the situation but encountered a rather blasé attitude from his counterparts. Indeed, one of the agency's officials reportedly approached Cole during negotiations for an interim treatment facility for the Maryland agency and asked, "Why are you trying to clean it up. It's nothing but a sewer. That's the way it is, that's what it always will be. Why kid yourself?"[27] Cole remained undeterred, urging the other users of Blue Plains to sue the WSSC to comply with guidelines set by the Potomac Enforcement Conference, a voluntary group of officials from state and local water agencies.[28] His colleagues were reluctant to be adversarial, preferring a more diplomatic approach. Cole had none of it, writing in a letter, "I believe polluters and people who overload sewage plants should be put in jail."[29] Cole pressed ahead against the WSSC. In October 1971, the agency agreed to restrict its treatment capacity; however, it soon exceeded its new threshold as it granted over five hundred exceptions to a sewer moratorium between March 1972 and January 1973.[30]

The violations of the WSSC, along with rising public frustrations with water pollution cleanup, pushed the other users of Blue Plains to sue the agency under the CWA. Nine months later, the parties reached an out-of-court settlement that allocated capacity at Blue Plains and required each jurisdiction to develop a plan for disposing of leftover sludge. The agreement was signed on June 14, 1974, at a public ceremony with Maryland governor Marvin Mandel, Washington mayor Walter Washington, and EPA administrator Russell Train. The consent decree was a major achievement for the region that made it easier for politicians to sell the expensive work of improving wastewater treatment infrastructure to their constituents.[31]

Between 1974 and 1983, Blue Plains was upgraded. Its capacity was increased from 240 mgd to 309 mgd and the usage apportioned according to the terms of the consent decree.[32] Advanced treatment, the highest level at the time, was incorporated through a process known as biological nutrient removal that fed sewage to large masses of bacteria and other microorganisms. Upgrading Blue Plains was the most prominent action taken in the Washington area to clean up the Potomac during the 1970s and early 1980s, at a cost of $1 billion.[33] Indeed, improving wastewater treatment was the primary means by which states and localities throughout the United States addressed water pollution through the mid-1980s to comply with the CWA.[34]

Norman Cole, the leading power broker behind the upgrades to Blue Plains, continued his environmental work into the 1980s. This included the construction of a major treatment plant in the Occoquan watershed that helped Fairfax reduce its dependence on Blue Plains. The facility, later named after Cole, has won numerous awards over the past twenty years.[35] Cole also went on to serve as an investigator and advisor after nuclear accidents at Three Mile Island and Chernobyl. In retrospect, Cole's commitment to cleaning up the Potomac portrayed a sense of stewardship that transcended his own "backyard." As one commentator noted, "He did what he did out of a deep concern for the safety and pleasure of his own children and out of a love of the outdoor life and a special affection for the Potomac."[36]

While Cole and other public officials upgraded Blue Plains to support development, civic activists sought to curb new growth in the metropolitan area. The most prominent were a group of women known as the "sewer ladies." The sewer ladies were raised in families with a strong sense of civic duty. Most were college-educated housewives with children, who combined their intellect, time, and concern about the future to advocate for strong curbs on development in order to protect the environment. Finally, each used precipitating events in their own proverbial backyards as a springboard to engage with environmental issues at a regional level.[37]

Among the hundreds of sewer ladies, three stood out. The first was Charlotte Gannett, the de facto leader of the group. After living for a while in Germany, Gannett returned with her family to the United States in 1971 and settled in Montgomery County. She soon became worried about rampant development, which had led to overcrowding in the school system and provoked an expensive wave of school building. Now that her children were adults, Gannett could focus on her activism full-time, cofounding the Montgomery Environmental Coalition in 1972 to focus on development issues and water pollution.[38]

The second was Enid Miles. Miles grew up on Long Island, New York, and earned a degree from Cornell University before moving to Montgomery County. There she got involved in civic efforts to limit the development of the Friendship Heights neighborhood and later joined the leadership of the Montgomery County Civic Federation, whose members tended to support compact development and environmental stewardship measures.[39]

The third was Marian Agnew, the wife of an air force pilot who lived in Fairfax. Like many sewer ladies, Agnew started out as a conservationist interested in preserving scenic and recreational amenities. Her first major involvement in a grassroots environmental campaign was in opposition to a luxury housing proposal for the Burling tract adjacent to the Potomac. After the Burling case, Agnew became president of the Northern Virginia Conservation Council. Over time, her interests evolved to focus more on water pollution issues, and she established the Center for Environmental Strategy as an advocacy organization in Northern Virginia.

The sewer ladies combined familiar tools of grassroots organizing with formidable expertise on the technical details of water pollution to become leading environmentalists in Greater Washington. Gannett's ability in particular to master intricate details and sway officials was not only impressive but also disarming to many given her slight appearance. Gannett invited local officials to her home to watch films about wastewater treatment and then gave them thick technical volumes to read on the subject. One Montgomery Council member, Rose Crenca, intimated, "She looked like a simple housewife ... but she was a mental giant on all that technical junk." The sewer ladies attended hundreds of public hearings and private meetings with officials, converting their backyard interests into effective political mobilization. The director of Montgomery's Office of Environmental Planning said of the sewer ladies' expertise: "These women who come in our offices make bureaucrats sit up and listen," and, in many cases, "will tell their staffs to go back and do more work to satisfy the women's questions." The planning director also learned while reviewing case files that the sewer ladies actively lobbied officials at the EPA.[40]

The sewer ladies disagreed with Norman Cole about expanding and upgrading wastewater treatment facilities because they worried that it would open the door for more development that would, in turn, generate more pollution. Gannett and Agnew, among others, were also critical of Cole's technology-driven approach to wastewater treatment that focused on the use of chemicals over preventative efforts to limit pollution.[41] Cole retorted that the sewer ladies' efforts to restrict sewer access as a means to curb new growth instead just made cleaning up pollution more difficult. He also praised more moderate environmental voices that believed that technology could solve pollution problems if there was sufficient political will.[42]

The sewer ladies emerged at a time when government was responsive to greater citizen input in decision making, particularly on environmental issues.[43] On the other hand, many felt ignored in planning processes. The experience of Ruth Allen was a good example. Allen, who earned a Ph.D. in philosophy from Yale and a graduate degree in epidemiology, was hired by the Metropolitan Washington Council of Governments (COG) to oversee the implementation of Section 208 of the CWA to develop regional plans for pollution and water supplies. Allen was supposed to collect public feedback, but her colleagues told her to listen to political officials and technical bureaucrats instead. That bothered Allen, who met Marian Agnew at a committee meeting where environmentalists were advocating for an alternative to incinerating the sludge left over from sewage treatment. Allen's interest in the citizens' views did not resonate well with her superiors at COG, who forced her out. Upon leaving, Allen joined up with the sewer ladies and, in an ironic twist, became a member of the citizen's advisory group for COG, where she challenged her former colleagues to be more responsive to public concerns.[44]

The most prominent case of civic engagement in wastewater treatment issues during the 1970s involved a new facility in Maryland to treat sewage and sludge that Blue Plains could not handle. In early 1973, the WSSC applied for federal funding to build a facility for Montgomery County in

Darnestown. At the time, much of the county was under a sewer moratorium to curb additional growth.[45] The EPA rejected the proposal, arguing that the facility's discharge of treated wastewater near water supply intakes for the Washington area would harm drinking water quality and violate the guidelines of the Safe Drinking Water Act of 1974.[46] As the Montgomery Council tried to determine a new site, the governor intervened at the behest of the state's construction industry to site a new facility in Dickerson.[47] The new location was further away from drinking water intakes, thereby offering a longer distance for dissipating effluent.[48]

While the business community endorsed the Dickerson plant to support current and future growth, environmentalists opposed the high costs and uncertain impact on downstream water intakes. At public meetings, the sewer ladies, in particular Charlotte Gannett, insisted that the agency revisit the facility's costs, which more than doubled in two years, the project's full impact on public health, and alternatives such as composting.[49] Enid Miles and the Montgomery County Civic Federation used data from federal environmental agencies to insist that the plant's discharge points should be below water intakes because existing technologies were insufficient for fully treating municipal sewage.[50] The focus of local environmentalists on critiquing both the environmental and financial costs of the Dickerson project reflected a strain of smart growth in 1970s metropolitan America that returned with renewed force in the late 1990s.

In March 1976, the WSSC applied for $273 million in federal funding to build the Dickerson plant. The next month, a preliminary EPA review raised concerns about the facility's high costs and impact on drinking water. As the agency continued its review, the sewer ladies lobbied against the project. Patty Mohler persuaded the county health department to submit a letter of concern to the county council, while Enid Miles relayed materials through a neighbor to the U.S. Surgeon General, who wrote to EPA administrator Train opposing the health impact of the facility.[51] Shortly thereafter, the agency rejected the project, citing the facility's high costs, slowdowns in projected population growth, and construction of small interim facilities that satisfied demand for the foreseeable future.[52]

While the sewer ladies and other grassroots environmentalists praised the EPA's decision, elected officials as well as the Greater Washington Board of Trade argued the facility was needed to support current and future growth.[53] Montgomery's county executive, James Gleason, rebuked the EPA for wielding heavy-handed regulations to interfere in the local project, "We are being

choked to death by federal bureaucracy," he said.[54] State and local officials
filed suit against the agency to revive the Dickerson proposal, but a federal
judge rejected the appeal.[55]

The defeat of the Dickerson plant left an open question of how to dispose
of waste from Blue Plains. As part of the 1974 consent decree, its users were
given four years to agree to a regional plan for disposing of the leftover sludge.
When they failed to do so, a federal judge ordered each jurisdiction to find
a site to dispose of its share. Montgomery officials decided on a composting
facility as a more environmentally conscious option than incineration, but
their selection of a site near the county's border with Prince George's County
inaugurated a four-year political fight that was only resolved when the county
selected another site.[56]

By the early 1980s, the water quality of the Potomac had improved significantly. Area treatment plants were under the CWA's permitting system
and offered an improved quality of treatment. The Georgetown Gap had been
closed and intermittent raw sewage overflows above the water intake for the
nation's capital eliminated by 1974. The number and variety of aquatic plants
and fish made comebacks, while pollution levels dropped enough in some
places to allow swimming and other activities for the first time in nearly a
quarter century. Boats filled the Potomac in Washington for bicentennial cel-
ebrations, and annual raft races began in 1978.[57]

Despite the gains made in cleaning up the Potomac, political challenges
continued to stymie progress. Upgrading and building new wastewater treatment facilities was expensive and took time. Part of the problem was a complicated federal review process and President Nixon's impounding of half of
the funds for three years before their release in 1975. By 1977, only one-third
of the funds had been spent on less than half of the nation's facilities.[58] Political conflicts over treatment facilities as well as disposing of sludge also slowed
pollution control. Many of the nation's municipal treatment facilities and con-
veyance infrastructure failed to meet federal guidelines for water quality by
the original due date of 1977, leading Congress to push back the deadline five
years. Because of these widespread delays, the Montgomery Environmental
Coalition and the Environmental Defense Fund were unsuccessful in blocking the EPA from renewing a permit that allowed the continued discharge
of untreated or partially treated waste from sixty different overflow points
in the Washington sewer system.[59] Finally, the Section 208 planning process
created under the CWA, which was intended to create a regional approach
to water pollution, was derailed by officials' unwillingness to work together

and openly engage the public.[60] As a result of these shortcomings, states and localities were left to undertake river cleanup on their own schedules.

Perhaps the most vexing environmental concern was that improving wastewater treatment only addressed 40 percent of the Potomac's pollution load in the Washington area. The rest came from nonpoint sources such as storm-water runoff, which the CWA did not address at the time it was originally adopted.[61] Instead, runoff was largely the product of impermeable surfaces in built-up urban and suburban communities. While the expansion of Blue Plains was a major contributor to cleaning up the Potomac, there was a far tougher task ahead of effectively controlling nonpoint pollution through stronger land use and development regulations.

The Potomac in Broader Context

Enhancing wastewater treatment was the primary means by which metropolitan communities cleaned up water pollution during the 1970s and early 1980s. Even after its upgrades, however, Blue Plains was in a state of disrepair. In 1984, the EPA fined the District of Columbia $50,000, mandated repairs to Blue Plains, and required the city to hire nearly three hundred more employees to improve the plant's operations. The EPA's decision reflected a more litigious approach to enforcement after the political and public backlash that followed the Reagan administration's efforts to dismantle the agency.[62] But the users of Blue Plains also recognized the need to improve the facility's operations. In 1985, they agreed to create a regional committee to oversee the facility, allocated capital and operating costs based on use, ensured Washington had priority in using the facility, and required monitoring all sewers with a minimum discharge amount.[63] Unlike the Blue Plains upgrades, which were financed through the CWA, this agreement required states and localities to foot the bill. The agreement reflected a new era of pollution cleanup characterized by more limited federal financing and oversight. With the "command-and-control" era in environmental enforcement now over, community-based strategies led by civic and environmental activists became even more critical, especially given the challenges of controlling runoff and other sources of pollution.

After decades of neglect, the pollution of the Chesapeake Bay, into which the Potomac drains, began to garner attention in Greater Washington and the eastern shore of Maryland. The context for cleaning up the bay, however, was rather different from the Potomac. While environmental concerns were key for the latter, economic concerns centered on the declining stocks of seafood for Maryland's fishing industry drove the former's cleanup. The political landscape had also changed. The bay cleanup began as conservative opposition to environmental protection privileged voluntary agreements over regulations.[64] The governors of Maryland and Virginia and the mayor of Washington, D.C., signed two agreements during the 1980s for cleaning up the bay. While they helped improve water quality for wildlife, expansive regional growth and lax accountability limited their effectiveness. Although the bay's cleanup was less successful than that of the Potomac in the prior decade, it laid the groundwork for treating the river as a regional resource to be protected.[65]

At a more local scale, the cleanup of the Anacostia River shifted the conversation about water pollution in Greater Washington from wastewater treatment to more diffuse and difficult-to-control sources. The Anacostia, a tributary of the Potomac, flowed through primarily urban communities in Southeast Washington and Prince George's. Nearly half of the river's watershed consisted of impermeable surfaces like streets and rooftops that fostered runoff, while the river itself, according to one account, was a "silted wasteland of mud, stench, murk, trash, and sparse aquatic life" that was far more polluted than the Potomac.[66]

Despite environmental conservatism within the federal government, the 1980s and early 1990s became an opportune time for cleaning up urban rivers and waterfronts. In 1987, Congress amended the CWA to better regulate storm water and related pollution, but the standards were more limited than for wastewater treatment and were not fully implemented until the end of the century.[67] Federal investment in cleaning up water pollution had also receded. Cleaning up the Potomac cost about $5 billion between 1970 and 1990, but federal grants subsidized much of the expense. As the EPA's grant program for wastewater treatment facilities wound down, few sources of federal money were available to clean up the Anacostia and other urban rivers.[68]

State and local actors stepped into the void to craft a new model of environmental stewardship. The governments of Maryland and Washington, D.C., signed two agreements in the 1980s to address combined sewer overflows in the District of Columbia as well as heavy erosion and sedimentation in Maryland, which came primarily from quarrying operations.[69] An unusual combination of civic, environmental, and business interests also joined forces to broaden the scope of river cleanup from pollution control to watershed and wildlife restoration.[70]

Compared to the Potomac, the Anacostia garnered little attention for cleanup until the late 1980s because of the geography of the region's population. The Potomac flowed through mostly middle- and upper-income suburbs, where many environmentalists and supportive public officials lived, and featured expanses of open space or low-density development along the waterfront. The Anacostia, however, flowed through industrial sites like the Navy Yard and mostly poor urban communities, whose access to the river was mostly blocked off by highways and whose residents faced far more immediate shortcomings in housing, schools, and police than their suburb peers.[71] District residents, for their part, had been largely absent from discussions about the Potomac. In contrast, they became more involved with the Anacostia as part of a nascent environmental justice movement concerned about the location and disproportionate impact of polluting facilities on poorer communities and those of color.[72]

In 1989, a handful of Washington residents established the Anacostia Watershed Society to encourage citizens to become caretakers of the river.[73] The group's leading figure was Robert Boone, who moved to Washington in the mid-1980s. Boone worked for an environmental agency tasked with monitoring the Anacostia and was outraged about all of the trash, sewage, and toxic chemicals that poured into the river. He turned his frustrations into action, joining lawsuits to contest runoff from the Navy Yard and leaking sewage in D.C. and Maryland. Boone was also an avid outdoorsman, hosting boat trips for schoolchildren, D.C. politicians, and members of Congress to learn more about the river. In a 2008 article reflecting on two decades of service for the society, Boone, now a "grey-haired former hippie with a temper like a wasp," offered a prescient statement on the importance of the public's investment in the river, "We are here to be stewards of this . . . and we have let down our mantle."[74]

The Anacostia's early cleanup featured more hands-on public involvement and educational efforts than with the Potomac. By late 1991, dozens of projects were under way to clean up storm water and trash, reach out to students through environmental education, plant trees along the shoreline, and build hundreds of acres of new wetlands. Between 1987 and 1994, fish populations and underwater grasses increased significantly.[75] One of the most successful projects built a thirty-two-acre marsh to fill in a mudflat near Kenilworth Aquatic Gardens, which restored aquatic life after years of neglect. New recreational opportunities for boating and biking also became more prominent

Potomac vs. Anacostia Class vs. Anacostia

as conditions improved.[76] By the mid-1990s, local concern about the river had reached a high point. A survey by the D.C. Coalition for Environmental Justice found that three-quarters of registered voters wanted more done to clean up sewage and trash in the Anacostia, while 20 percent identified a medical problem caused or worsened by pollution.[77]

The long-delayed cleanup of the Anacostia offered a new approach to improving the health of rivers in Greater Washington. While wastewater treatment had been the focus during the 1970s and 1980s, nonpoint sources such as runoff now received more attention. There were two consequences of this shift. First, the scope of activities to improve river health expanded from pollution cleanup to ecosystem improvement. While passage of the Endangered Species Act in 1973 had conferred federal protection on certain rare species to block harmful actions, restoration activities such as building wetlands offered a more holistic approach to sustaining habitats, not just individual species.[78] Second, members of the public became key partners in cleanup and restoration in concert with lobbying to improve policy making for water pollution.

This new paradigm was evident in the campaign to restore the shad population to the Potomac, which was historically the river's most abundant and commercially important fish. The construction of Little Falls Dam in the late 1950s, overfishing, and pollution had destroyed shad habitats and nearly depleted the fish's ranks.[79] Beginning in 1995, biologist Jim Cummins harvested and fertilized eggs from shad during the spring spawning season in order to replenish the Potomac. Over the next seven years, thousands of volunteers worked day and night and through inhospitable weather to stock 15.8 million shad and create a self-sustaining population.[80] Many participants were local students who participated through educational programs sponsored by the Chesapeake Bay Foundation and the Anacostia Watershed Society, whose mostly white, middle-class members had begun to engage a broader cross-section of the river's community in its stewardship. To support the restocking, a new fishway was created through Little Falls Dam. At a ribbon-cutting ceremony in 1999, Secretary of the Interior Bruce Babbitt remarked on the broader potential of restoring the Potomac: "For seven years, I've watched hundreds of cities restore their communities by restoring their rivers. Now it's our turn."[81]

The shad restoration project was also an example of new efforts to compensate for the impact of large-scale development in Greater Washington.[82] Another example was the expansion of the Woodrow Wilson Bridge between Alexandria and Prince George's, which eliminated two hundred acres of forests, wetlands, and underwater grasses. Government agencies and environmental groups carried out a series of compensatory projects that included transplanting twelve thousand native plants and trees to replace invasive species at a one-acre site in Alexandria; planting twenty-two acres of underwater grasses in the lower Potomac and Chesapeake Bay; protecting an eighty-four-acre bald eagle sanctuary in Prince George's County, and constructing ladders to help spawning fish traverse Rock Creek and tributaries of the Anacostia River.[83] As the sources of pollution became more diffuse, and government willingness (and ability) to regulate them eroded, public investment in the Potomac became more critical to the river's health. The challenge would be to scale up from individual projects to an ecosystem-based approach that transcended political boundaries.[84]

Direct Action and Collaboration on the Potomac

Metropolitan growth was a major contributor to the pollution of the Potomac, with runoff from built-up areas being the fastest growing source of pollution.[85] Compared to forested land, developed land offers far lower levels of water infiltration and soil conservation; and this exacerbated the overloading of wastewater treatment plants.[86] Close-in communities experienced "urban stream syndrome" characterized by "increased flash floods; elevated concentrations of nutrients and contaminants; altered stream morphology, including incised channels that cut off vegetation from its water source and increased sedimentation from eroded stream banks; and reduced diversity, with an influx of more tolerant species to counter the loss of more sensitive species."[87]

Large-scale industrial farming outside of the metropolitan area also contributed ever-higher pollution loads as their operations expanded and came to rely on pesticide-intensive agriculture.[88] As exurban growth made its way into West Virginia during the 1990s, the state's poultry industry more than doubled and dumped 4.6 million pounds of bird carcasses a year into the Potomac, which overburdened rural municipal treatment facilities that then dumped pollution back into the river.[89] This was a major reason why American Rivers, a national nonprofit conservation organization, ranked the Potomac one of the ten most polluted rivers in the late 1990s.[90] Many environmentalists, however, tended to discount the environmental impact of farms because they valued their open space, bucolic aesthetic, and wildlife protection. In a more critical light, one could argue that environmentalists held a sentimental view of farming that elided the industrial nature of its operations, particularly with chemical usage and waste.

Federal policy making proved far less effective in dealing with nonpoint pollution than it had been with using command-and-control regulations to upgrade and build wastewater treatment facilities. The primary reason was that nonpoint pollution was generally a consequence of land use planning, which was traditionally the domain of local communities. The federal government had no mandate to intervene into zoning and land use planning except where federal monies, lands, or other interests were at stake. In addition, many federal agencies supported development through housing, highways, and business creation as well as overseeing an industrial model of agriculture that lacked strong pollution controls. Finally, controlling pollution from farms was largely the province of states and localities, whose imperative for growth often led to weak standards for compliance.[91]

Even as more environmental actors turned their attention to nonpoint pollution, wastewater treatment remained a challenge as development continued apace in Greater Washington. During its inspections of Blue Plains in 1995, the EPA found deteriorating conditions, maintenance issues, and other violations of the facility's federal operating permit despite a mandate nearly a decade earlier for the plant to add personnel and invest in operations. After filing a lawsuit against the District of Columbia, the EPA reached a settlement requiring the city to use its existing revenues to make upgrades and repairs over the next two years. By 2000, the D.C. Water and Sewer Authority (WASA), which operated Blue Plains, had invested $100 million and were able to cut the facility's pollution by half.[92]

At the turn of the century, however, Blue Plains dumped three billion gallons of raw sewage per year into the Anacostia and Potomac as overflow during periods of heavy rains. Environmentalists sued WASA, and in a 2003 settlement the agency agreed to undertake a $143 million project "to upgrade pumping stations, reroute some sewage pipes and install dams in others." A year later, it had reduced overflows by 24 percent. In 2004, WASA settled another lawsuit with the EPA when it agreed to build three underground water storage tunnels to eliminate more than fifty sewage overflow discharge outlets into the Potomac and Anacostia Rivers and Rock Creek.[93]

After years of planning, WASA deployed a special machine nicknamed "Lady Bird"—in homage to the former first lady's commitment to conservation—that began digging thirteen miles of underground tunnels in July 2013.[94] Two years later, the machine had completed the first four-mile section of the tunnel, which measured twenty-three feet in diameter. Unlike the upgrades at Blue Plains, which were largely financed with federal money, the $2.6 billion tunneling project received less than 10 percent of its funding from federal sources.[95] This discrepancy was a by-product of the declining influence of environmental issues in national politics in relation to the rise of homeland security, reviving a struggling economy amid the financial crisis of 2007–2008 and a more conservative fiscal and political climate. Federal environmental agencies had also chosen to spend more of their money, time, and resources on legal action and implementing court orders than congressional mandates or capital financing.[96]

In a highly pluralistic and competitive interest group environment, it was difficult to find common ground for improving water quality on a large scale.[97] Environmental lobbying and litigation were often restricted to well-funded national organizations or affluent local environmentalists who had the skills to act on the political stage. In addition, these activities had a limited ability to inculcate a keen sense of public investment in environmental issues beyond updating constituents about the latest issues or asking for money to finance political activities. The rise of environmental education and local direct action in the early twenty-first century was a way to break through the political deadlock to continue improving the Potomac's health.

One of the earliest and most successful organizations doing this kind of work was the Alice Ferguson Foundation. Its namesake was an artist who in the 1920s bought the 130-acre Hard Bargain Farm in Accokeek about twelve miles south of Washington in Prince George's. Ferguson managed the farm and later purchased hundreds of acres of nearby land, which she resold to conservation-minded individuals who built homes scattered throughout to block against intensive development. Alice's husband, Henry, established a nonprofit foundation in her name in 1954 to protect the site's environmental and cultural resources. In the 1960s, the bottom half of the now 330-acre site was deeded to the National Park Service as part of Piscataway National Park. In the early 1970s, the foundation established an educational center that offered classes for thousands of elementary and middle school students each year, encouraging them to develop a sense of environmental stewardship by visiting the Potomac waterfront and learning about its natural resources and farming history through hands-on activities. Programming was later added to support K–12 school curriculum and to bring high school students to the site. At present, the foundation serves four thousand elementary school students per year in one- and two-day environmental and agricultural programs at Hard Bargain Farm, reaches out to six thousand middle and high school students visiting national and state parks in the Washington area through its Bridging the Watershed program, and trains hundreds of teachers in outdoor environmental education.[98]

The Alice Ferguson Foundation is best known for its an annual spring-time Potomac Watershed Cleanup. The first cleanup began in 1989 at Hard Bargain Farm with fifty volunteers. In 2000, the event had grown to three thousand people at 110 sites. By 2006, it had brought together over thirty-five thousand volunteers, many of them young people, to remove 2.5 million pounds of trash since its inception. The organization's website proudly documents the number of volunteers, cleanup sites, total trash, and items found to showcase the tangible benefits of the cleanups.[99]

Over the past decade, the foundation has expanded its outreach about the harm of litter. In 2006, it hosted the First Potomac Watershed Trash Summit to better understand why trash volume increased year after year. Two years later, it published a survey of residents' attitudes that found nearly two-thirds were bothered "a lot" by litter in the Potomac watershed and wanted to see government do more about it. Yet the survey also revealed that most people littered out of laziness and a mistaken belief that others will clean it up or that it would wash down a storm drain and be filtered.[100]

Admittedly, the amount of trash collected through public cleanup campaigns was a small part of the Potomac's overall pollution. However, cleanups and environmental education could inspire a sense of environmental stewardship that reached beyond the typical white, middle-class, college-educated residents who traditionally engaged in environmental advocacy. This possibility was on display when a group of fifth graders from nearby Bowie, Maryland, took a two-day field trip to Hard Bargain Farm. While there, the group viewed the open space of the Potomac riverscape, observed plant and animal life, and learned about pollution through an exercise where they were given a gallon of water and fourteen different containers of pollutants commonly found in the Potomac to add to the bucket to understand the impact of pollution. They also enjoyed team-building exercises, socializing, and cooking out at night. The lessons learned about the pollution of the Potomac were clear. When asked, "Who polluted the Potomac?" one student aptly responded, "All of us did."[101]

A growing sense of stewardship also manifested itself in more aggressive public surveillance of conditions along the Potomac and the threat of legal action to rectify concerns. The most notable organization undertaking this work was the Potomac Riverkeeper Network, founded in 2000. The group was part of a national and international network of water-keeper organizations dating to the 1960s, when commercial and recreational fishermen in New York organized to protect their way of life and save the Hudson River from industrial pollution. Like many groups, it sought enforcement of existing pollution laws governing the Potomac watershed through media campaigns, lobbying, and litigation. It also had a broad range of environmental concerns, including erosion and runoff, illegal dumping of trash and toxics, the loss of wetlands, air pollution, and changes in fish populations.[102]

In 2003, Ed Merrifield became the first Potomac Riverkeeper. A former chiropractor and longtime sailor of the Potomac and Chesapeake Bay, Merrifield joined the organization after reading a history of the river-keeper movement and being inspired by its argument that people had enjoyed the legal right to fish and enjoy waterways for centuries in America. As president of the Potomac Riverkeeper Network from 2003 to 2012, Merrifield focused on fund-raising, building a leadership team, and cultivating alliances with Washington-area law schools and private law firms to secure discounted or pro bono legal aid to reinforce civic action. By the second decade of the twenty-first century, the Potomac Riverkeeper Network had nearly three thousand members across the watershed, including at least a couple hundred trained "riverwatchers" who regularly surveyed the Potomac's water quality and investigated illegal pollution.[103] Other groups also undertook this work, including the Potomac Conservancy and Arlington's local government.[104] As one environmentalist explained, "I think the stream monitoring program is a really good way for volunteers to take ownership for helping the environment."[105] In addition, the work of nonprofits like the Potomac Riverkeeper in some ways compensated for the decline of government monitoring over the past fifteen years that was a product of neoliberalism.

What distinguished Potomac Riverkeeper from other groups was its tenacity. Speaking to a *Washington Post* reporter about the group's philosophy, Merrifield noted, "If it's illegal pollution, we go after it as fast as we can to tell them you have to stop. We use all legal means necessary. We won't back down."[106] Mike Bolinder, the current Anacostia Riverkeeper, affirmed Merrifield's commitment to swift action and holding polluters accountable as an inspiring model of activism: "The thing I learned from Ed that will make me a better riverkeeper is never accept weasel words like 'showing improvement' or 'making progress.'"[107]

In its first few years, the group's biggest success was compelling the Maryland Department of Natural Resources to clean up lead pollution from an old shooting range. In 2003, it sued the agency for allowing members of the National Capital Skeet and Trap Club to operate a shooting range for half a century on state land that discharged lead bullets in and around the Great Seneca Creek, a tributary of the Potomac. The case generated a media investigation that publicized the CWA violations the group had identified. Four years later, the lawsuit was settled in an agreement that required the Maryland agency to clean up the lead pollution and to conduct testing for the next fifteen years to ensure its success.[108]

The Potomac Riverkeeper Network also publicized the impact of endocrine disruptors on fish and public health. Appearing in dozens of news stories and testifying before a congressional committee in 2006, Merrifield and the organization discussed how products like soaps and medications, cleaning agents, lawn fertilizers, and plastics contained toxic chemicals that sparked massive fish kills in the Potomac near West Virginia and produced intersex bass, rendering male bass as female. These chemicals in the Potomac also posed a public health concern for Washington-area residents, who received nearly 90 percent of their drinking water from the river, because they could not be filtered out using existing technologies and because the EPA does not yet regulate them. The public health impact of endocrine disruptors is not yet clear; however, there is research suggesting that these chemicals, for which there is no known safe level of exposure, can produce developmental, reproductive, and neurological conditions, with the greatest impact on fetuses and newborns.[109]

The Potomac Riverkeeper Network's greatest success to date has been its litigation against a familiar foe: the Washington Suburban Sanitary Commission. In February 2014, it joined the Environmental Integrity Project and the Chesapeake Bay Foundation to sue the WSSC for dumping millions of pounds of sediment, aluminum, and other pollutants into the Potomac in the process of purifying and supplying drinking water for homes and businesses in suburban Maryland. Their claim argued that excessive amounts of pollution harmed fish, underwater grasses, and other aquatic species, although the public health impact was not clear. These activities, along with failure to properly monitor pollutants, had been ongoing for nearly twenty years and were in violation of the commission's federal water control permit. To add insult to injury, the commission's permit had expired in 2002 but was continued without being updated. The Maryland Department of the Environment joined grassroots activists in their lawsuit to get the WSSC to clean up its act.[110]

Twenty months after the lawsuit was filed, the parties negotiated a consent decree. The WSSC agreed to make long-term improvements to comply with the conditions of its permit and relevant federal and state clean water policies. The terms required WSSC to overhaul or replace its water filtration plant, to immediately undertake $8.5 million in pollution control projects at the existing plant, including $1 million to reduce sediment pollution, better monitor pollution, and find ways to minimize the need to discharge pollution. The improvements will reduce pollution by over two million pounds in the first year and greater amounts in later years. The agreement also included $100,000 in civil penalties to be paid to the state. According to the agreement, which has to be ratified by the U.S. attorney general and the U.S. District Court, the WSSC would have up to ten years to comply or face an additional $1 million in fines.[111]

The legal director of Potomac Riverkeeper noted, "the work of restoring the Potomac River and Chesapeake Bay will take a big step forward with this agreement," as the settlement "ensures that years of unmitigated pollution discharges into the Potomac are at an end."[112] In thinking about how to use the money, an attorney for the Chesapeake Bay Foundation recommended farm conservation projects in western Maryland to prevent runoff at its source rather than trying to clean it up later.[113] The WSSC's general manager, however, worried about the high costs of long-term improvements to the existing plant, built in the 1960s, which he estimated could exceed $100 million.[114] This was in addition to the commission's struggle to pay for $1.5 billion of work to reduce sewer spills required under a 2005 agreement as well as undertaking an independent program to replace aging water pipes. Forty years after agreeing to rein in its pollution, the WSSC continued to face sharp criticism for polluting the Potomac, suggesting that perhaps the more things change, the more they stay the same.

Today, the Potomac is healthier than it has been in decades. In part, this is due to the CWA and federal lawsuits to force compliance with cleanup and water quality standards. The bulk of the river's cleanup, however, has been the result of state and local action on the ground. Upgrading wastewater treatment facilities was the primary way in which public officials at these levels have acted to clean up the Potomac. Environmentalists during the 1970s contested these efforts out of concern that they would catalyze growth, which they did, although the scale of the Potomac's pollution certainly warranted cleanup. The emergence of nonpoint pollution as a more significant issue in the late 1980s accentuated the importance of efforts to curb runoff through land use regulations that reduced erosion, preserved open space, or limited the scale of development. Unlike the command-and-control regulations of

Figure 5. The Great Falls of the Potomac, just upriver from Washington, D.C.
Source: Carol M. Highsmith Archive.

CWA, improving land use planning and restoring local habitats has varied in scope and success across communities.

The case of the Potomac confirms that grassroots activism to harness the tools of smart growth in support of environmental protection was central to the cleanup of the river. In focusing on policy over politics, scholars have obscured the crucial role of citizens in lobbying and litigating for compliance with environmental policies, blocking undesirable treatment facilities and development projects, educating the public about the importance of environmental stewardship, and undertaking hands-on activities to put environmental ethics into practice. Moreover, citizens have been primarily responsible for broadening the view of the Potomac from more traditional conservation-based values of open space to modern ideas of pollution cleanup to newer practices of ecological restoration. In short, more citizens became more involved in a variety of ways to act as stewards of a river that not only knits together Greater Washington but also serves a symbolic role as "the nation's river" in the capital area.

Other cases of citizen involvement produced markedly different outcomes for development and illustrate the fractured nature of local politics in the context of metropolitan growth and preservation. The next chapter examines how a high tide of environmental consciousness in the early 1970s inspired a dramatic grassroots movement in an affluent community in Fairfax County to preserve one of the last forested landscapes in the county. The following chapter moves us into the turn of the century, where Prince George's County saw a groundswell of support for upscale commercial development in a county long passed over for it. These two cases underscored how an unequal distribution of people and development could favor environmental protection in certain communities while undermining it in others.

key historiographic argument

CHAPTER 2

Where Have All the Forests Gone?

In the spring of 1970, a national television crew traveled to Fairfax County to record the public's involvement in a dramatic environmental movement. Just a month earlier, millions of Americans had participated in the first Earth Day, raising awareness and learning about environmental issues locally and globally.[1] Earth Day was a headline event in a banner year for modern environmentalism, but so too was the news story the television crew covered.

The event in question was a public hearing on a proposal to preserve a forested landscape along the Potomac from being converted into a luxury housing project. More than two hundred people attended and more than fifty testified, including a number of teenagers.[2] The highlight of the meeting was a stirring rendition of a folk song written by high school student Susan Daniel. Modeled after Woody Guthrie's iconic "This Land Is Your Land," Daniel's song offered a reflective, youth-centered perspective on the environmental impact of postwar suburbanization as she called for preserving the hills, plans, wildlife, and Potomac waterfront that the Burling tract offered.[3]

The year 1970 is often remembered for national events like Earth Day and the creation of the EPA. Indeed, the decade more broadly represented a golden era of environmental policy making reinforced by the rise of national environmental organizations as a potent force in American politics. Even as environmental politics was scaling up, the Burling case testified to the enduring importance of grassroots activism. Indeed, local environmentalists in Fairfax defined the contours of "smart growth" two decades before the term came into official use.

After a quarter century of rampant suburbanization, residents, officials, and organized interests in Fairfax spent 1970 debating whether the Burling tract should be developed for upscale housing or protected as a park and nature preserve. A year earlier, a local development firm acquired the

336-acre parcel in the mostly white and affluent community of McLean. The firm proposed unusually significant measures to control runoff into the nearby Potomac associated with developing the site's steep slopes and to preserve half the land as open space. A small group of nearby homeowners, however, had strong misgivings about the potential loss of one of the few wild, forested landscapes left in the county. As they organized for a battle in their backyard, they were joined by hundreds of high school and college students who wanted a nature preserve in the midst of suburbia. A new generation of local elected officials committed to reining in runaway growth joined an intense community struggle to convince the Burling tract's developer to preserve the landscape for future generations.

The Burling controversy showed how environmental consciousness among the white middle and upper classes grew as suburbanization intensified. The leisure time that came with the material abundance of postwar America fostered public interest in protecting nearby nature not for its productive capacity, as was the case with traditional conservation, but for its scenic, recreational, and open space amenities.[4] But suburbanization did not just encroach on open space; it also degraded ecologically sensitive areas such as wetlands and hilly terrain and polluted the water, air, and soil.[5] As residents in more affluent communities became frustrated with the environmental impact of rapid growth and higher property taxes to support development further out, they embraced land preservation as a way to improve their own quality of life.[6] The idea that growth could be too expensive—environmentally and financially—was a cornerstone of the smart growth movement in the mid-1990s. This concept was manifest in the Burling case, in which a county that supported rampant postwar suburbanization saw an unprecedented constituency mobilize in favor of environmental protection instead.

While the Burling case represented a certain triumph of an early smart growth movement, it also highlighted the biases among the mostly white, middle-class environmentalists in suburbia. Postwar housing policies and practices had not only created exclusive communities but also differentiated access to opportunities that improved people's lives, including good schools, public services, well-paying jobs, transportation, and low incidence of crime.[7] Even as historically marginalized peoples gained political influence during the 1960s, social segregation reinforced the voices of affluent whites over other groups.[8] At the time of the Burling case, conversations about inclusive housing had shifted from racial discrimination, which had been outlawed with passage of the Fair Housing Act of 1968, to affordability.[9] In affluent,

white-dominated communities, however, many residents downplayed the
need for affordable housing to focus on protecting environmental resources
for their own enjoyment, even in cases where land preservation could be
expensive.[10] Thus, environmental activists did not challenge the systems
underlying community formation, which benefited them, but instead sought
to block specific projects that impaired their access to natural amenities.[11]

Postwar Suburbanization and Open Space

Fairfax County was the epicenter of postwar suburbanization in Greater
Washington. The county developed its first zoning code and subdivision
regulations in the 1940s, but these proved inadequate to manage the growth
ignited by the postwar baby boom and the pent-up demand for housing. By
the mid-1950s, its transformation from a quiet rural county to a bustling suburb was well under way.

Late in the decade, officials reduced the density of development in the
western two-thirds of the county in order to maintain its rural character. The
Virginia Supreme Court, however, rejected the move, concluding in a case
brought by a developer that the policy unfairly restricted housing to those
who could afford large lots.[12] The court went even further in doubling the
allowable density of the area from one house per two acres to one house per
acre. The case reflected the unusual control that the state legislature and judiciary exerted over Virginia localities in land use planning, and the tendency
of the state to elevate interests in revenue-generating development over local
efforts to manage growth.[13]

Residential suburbanization and the decentralization of employment and
commerce continued to flood Fairfax with development during the 1960s. By
1970, the county had 455,000 residents, a tenfold increase from 1940. Local
elected officials and planners, however, had little interest and fewer tools for
managing growth than Maryland counties like Montgomery, which developed its own wedges and corridors plan to promote compact development
that was based on the regional plans of the National Capital Planning Commission. Indeed, most residents had little concern about suburbanization
except when their communities were threatened with the loss of open space
or with high-density development projects.[14]

Fairfax made some progress in preserving open space despite conservative political leadership and limited planning tools. In 1950, local officials

established a county park authority that administered six regional parks totaling 3,198 acres by 1960. This paled in comparison to the nearly 9,000 acres of parkland in Montgomery, where there was earlier and broader support for pairing open space preservation with compact growth.[15]

As suburbanization accelerated, residents and county officials contemplated how to protect the natural amenities that made living in the county appealing.[16] Local planners offered several proposals: reducing the density of development, lowering property taxes on rural land and open space, and increasing public financing for conservation easements or purchasing land outright for parks.[17] But there were numerous barriers at the state level to moving forward with these strategies. Historically, the state courts had narrowly defined how zoning and other tools could be used to regulate private property rights. In addition, the state constitution precluded the use of financial incentives to encourage landowners to preserve land rather than develop it. Although communities in Virginia could use public funds to pay for conservation easements or acquire scenic and historic areas, they had to seek state authorization for each case.[18] In sum, the state constrained localities in their ability to manage growth and preserve rural land.

As suburbia consumed more land, residents and officials in mostly white middle- and upper-class communities stepped up their support of open space preservation. By 1969, parkland in Fairfax expanded to 5,000 acres from 3,200 at the beginning of the decade, although Montgomery's increased to nearly 15,000 from 9,000.[19] While local officials, as well as regional park authorities, played an important role in parkland acquisition during the 1960s, federal financing through the Land and Water Conservation Fund was crucial to many local projects. Created by Congress in 1965, the fund included a state assistance program that provided matching grants to help states and local communities protect land for parks, recreation, and nature preserves. Among the three large suburban counties in Greater Washington, Fairfax was the biggest beneficiary of the federal program, receiving $2.85 million between 1966 and 1969, while Montgomery received $463,000 and Prince George's $260,000.[20]

The motivations behind land preservation in postwar metropolitan America highlighted a shift from the conservation-oriented values of a production-based economy to the environmental and quality-of-life values of a consumer-based economy. Indeed, the commitment to open space preservation that blossomed in the 1960s was made possible by postwar material abundance and the willingness of officials and their constituents, albeit mostly in white middle- and upper-class communities, to invest in land preservation. The protection of specific sites from suburbanization had deep roots in a search for health and well-being that defined the suburbs as better off than central cities. As suburbanization consumed ecologically sensitive resources like hillsides and wetlands, concerns about pollution and the loss of wildlife grew. With the Burling tract, the stage was set for a dramatic grass-roots campaign that argued that certain places were too ecologically sensitive, too rich in natural splendor, and too special to develop.[21]

A Controversy Forms

The Burling tract was one of the few properties in Greater Washington adjacent to the Potomac River that had not been significantly developed or permanently preserved by 1970. It was named for Edward J. Burling Sr., a midwesterner who moved to Washington, D.C., during World War I and bought 336 acres of hilly and mostly forested land in McLean in the early 1920s. The property, located twelve miles from the White House, was positioned atop 150-foot cliffs looking down on the Potomac rapids to the north and the waterfall of Scott's Run to the west. It was situated at the northernmost portion of the Scott's Run watershed, which drains directly into the Potomac, and offered scenic water views, a remarkable collection of wildflowers, forests of ancient hemlocks, and abundant wildlife.[22] Burling, who became a prominent Washington lawyer, had a log cabin built overlooking the rapids. But he refused to have electricity installed, preferring to use kerosene lamps and a wood stove rather than allow a utility company to run wiring underground. Despite not having modern utilities, the estate became a gathering spot for political and social elites, artists, and intellectuals.[23]

In 1967, Burling died, leaving his waterfront property in trust to his family. Shortly thereafter, a fire destroyed the house, leaving only a flagpole, swimming pool, and a fireplace on the site. Less than two years later, his heirs sought to sell the estate because they could not afford the taxes, which amounted to over $30,000. Burling's son went to Stewart Udall to see if the Department of the Interior would purchase the land and turn it into a park or wildlife preserve. Although Udall was interested and had intervened a few years earlier in the Merrywood case, five miles away, the agency did not have the necessary funds. With the existing tax burden and no offers forthcoming to acquire and preserve the property, the Burling family contracted to sell the property to a local development firm in mid-1969.[24]

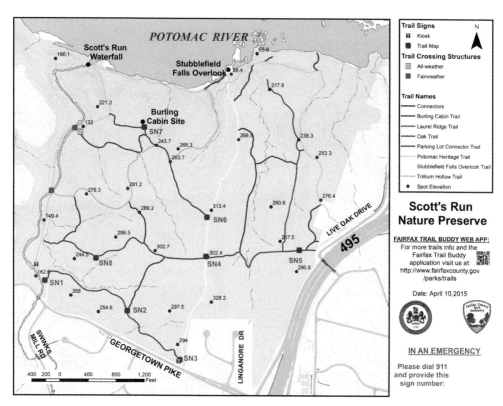

Figure 6. Scott's Run Nature Preserve, formerly the Burling Tract. Source: Fairfax County Park Authority.

The firm of Miller & Smith proposed building a luxury residential community on the Burling estate, whose southeast corner was conveniently situated at the intersection of two major thoroughfares, the Capital Beltway and Georgetown Pike. The plans included three hundred homes clustered on half-acre lots rather than distributed across the entire tract as was common in many suburbs at the time. This left half of the land undeveloped, including strips along the Potomac waterfront to the north and Scott's Run to the west. In July 1969, officials in the county land development office offered the first approval for preliminary site plans without a public hearing, which was possible because the plans did not conflict with existing single-family zoning. Nearby residents, however, soon became aware of the developer's plans.[25]

In the fall of 1969, Betty Cooke, a local artist who lived across from the Burling tract in a 150-year-old pink house, noticed a small green sign on the property announcing a hearing on the development plan before the county planning commission. On September 18, twenty of her friends and neighbors met at the home of Graydon Upton to review the plans and organize a "citizens committee" to advocate for reducing the proposed density and thereby the impact of the project. The membership drew from that of the Old Georgetown Pike and Potomac River Association and included Sharon Francis, a former aide to beautification advocate Lady Bird Johnson; David Dominick, head of the Federal Water Pollution Control Administration; John Adams, a Washington lawyer for a Richmond firm who was a conservationist and admirer of the Burling tract; and Townsend Hoopes, a former official with the Air Force.[26]

As middle- and upper-middle-class homeowners living in an affluent community experiencing rampant development, the members of the citizens committee sought to buffer themselves from sprawl while preserving access to the natural amenities that made their communities desirable. Many also had conservation or environmental interests that were piqued by the ecological sensitivity and natural amenities of the Burling tract. Finally, they could draw on their professional knowledge and connections to the community and government to adeptly navigate the political decision-making process that would shape the site's destiny. Thus this group of citizens was well positioned to influence decision making in the Burling case.[27]

The citizens' committee from the Old Georgetown Pike and Potomac River Association moved quickly to raise objections to the environmental impact of Miller & Smith's development proposal. First it commissioned a siltation and erosion study, which discussed how a large-scale project would degrade the site's slopes and pollute the Potomac. The county government was attuned to these concerns and had instituted a policy requiring developers to control erosion and sedimentation during the land preparation and construction phases of projects. At the first public hearing for the Burling tract project in late October 1969, members of the citizens committee used their study to criticize the developer's inadequate conservation safeguards and the lack of much usable parkland. They recommended reducing the number of homes to be built on the site from 309 to 100 to lessen the project's impact, but also asked for another hearing to give them time to possibly secure funding to buy the property for use as a public park.[28]

By the next public meeting on December 15, the Old Georgetown Pike and Potomac River Association was in talks with Walter J. Hickel, Udall's newly appointed successor at the Interior Department, to seek funds through the Land and Water Conservation Fund to preserve the Burling tract for the public. Hickel, continuing a long tradition of federal officials commenting on development matters in Greater Washington, urged county leaders to reject Miller & Smith's proposal. In his words, a large-scale residential development near the Potomac "'would entail destruction of the natural area and, by eroding the steep slopes, add dramatically to the pollution of our national river.'" Hickel recommended preserving the site for the community and hinted that his agency might help buy the property.[29] The interests of the citizens committee and Hickel at this point were strongly influenced by the recent national attention to ecological concerns such as erosion and pollution. Over time, however, their discourse shifted to highlight the Burling tract as a landscape whose wilderness and open space amenities should be preserved to counterbalance the loss of nature to suburbanization.

Before moving forward with its plans, Miller & Smith was required as a condition of Burling's will to consent to a conservation agreement with the property's heirs. In January 1970, the developer submitted a proposal to the Fairfax and Northern Virginia park authorities for preserving several dozen acres of land. The local park authority declined to sign on, presumably because it could not afford the maintenance costs given its shoestring budget. The regional park authority, however, approved the conservation agreement in late February. It stipulated that twenty-five acres would be reserved for the westward extension of the George Washington Memorial Parkway, which was intended to preserve a low profile landscape along the shoreline. In addition, it transferred to the park authority a twenty-six-acre strip of land along Scott's Run and the Potomac for a park. Last, it placed permanent conservation easements on the entire tract including limiting it to single-family housing, restricting development of the crests of the slopes, and preserving most of the land ceded to the park authority as open space. In exchange, the park authority agreed not to take or support the taking of the property by any government agency through eminent domain.[30]

The regional park authority accepted the conservation agreement for several reasons. It wanted the land to be preserved and had taken the lead over the past few years to create larger parks throughout Northern Virginia and in Fairfax in particular, using matching funds from the Land and Water Conservation Fund to acquire land in a county where development pressures inflated its value.[31] The agency's five-year capital improvement program also did not include enough money to buy a significant part of the tract outright.

In addition, the agency felt that the agreement was the best deal it could get without going into condemnation proceedings to take the property through eminent domain, which would be quite expensive.[32] Once the park authority accepted the agreement, the developer had to submit it, along with its plans for the entire Burling tract, to the county planning commission and the board of supervisors, the county's top elected leadership. This subjected the plans to multiple stages of public review, giving residents the opportunity to influence the decision-making process.

The Burling case generated considerable attention in Fairfax and Greater Washington as an opportunity to redress the environmental impact of subur-banization. A writer for the *Washington Post* captured the heady mix of envi-ronmental concerns and political interests in a February 1970 article. "There are questions of siltation and erosion of land, removal of fully-grown trees to make way for new homes, placement of homes on steep slopes, establishment of parks in a burgeoning metropolitan area and the Federal government's role in preserving what remains of undeveloped America."[33]

Right before the planning commission met to consider the developer's site plans and the conservation agreement, Interior Secretary Hickel offered to con-tribute up to 50 percent of the costs for purchasing the Burling tract and con-serving it as a park. His offer, valued at up to $1.2 million, was nearly 40 percent of the Land and Water Conservation Fund's contingency reserves.[34] While the ecological impact of development had previously motivated Hickel, his interests now were more rooted in open space preservation. A spokesman later noted: "The Burling tract is not just a piece of land; it is also an opportunity. It's so close to a dense population area that in future years—even now—we'll want open space."[35] Hickel's deepening interest in the case was a major federal commit-ment to land conservation at a time of rising environmental consciousness that blended environmental objectives.[36] Also, the fact that the property was nearby made it easier for him to be involved and to potentially use the Burling case as a primer for publicizing the value of the Land and Water Conservation Fund.

On February 9, the county planning commission approved the conser-vation agreement and development proposal, which sent the project to the board of supervisors for final approval. However, the commission urged concerned parties to continue seeking funding to buy the property for use as a park.[37] By the time the supervisors held their first public hearing in mid-March, civic concern about the Burling tract had expanded beyond the neighborhood level.

Marian Agnew, who became one of the most prominent "sewer ladies" working to clean up the Potomac during the 1970s, got her start in environmental activism with the Burling case. Agnew, the wife of an air force pilot, was looking for a place to walk her two dogs one day when she realized how little park space, not to mention wooded areas, was left in Fairfax. While working as a substitute teacher at Langley High School, she advised a group of students, including her son, on a school project to plan a system of bike trails for McLean. Agnew and the students soon learned about the Burling case and decided to get involved based on their interests in outdoor recreation. Over the next several months, she and the students were at the center of a grassroots movement that called not simply for reducing the density of development at the Burling tract but for protecting the entire site as a park and nature preserve. In an interview after the case was over, Agnew explained the approach she came to adopt in her environmental activism: "I realized that confrontation is often the only way to get action."[38]

The board of supervisors hearing on March 11 was the first of several high-profile events in a burgeoning campaign to protect the Burling tract from suburban development. The hearing began with testimony from Miller & Smith representative John "Til" Hazel, a staunch growth advocate who was fast becoming the most prominent land use and zoning lawyer for developers in Northern Virginia. Hazel acknowledged civic interest in mitigating the impact of building on the hilly terrain and harming its flora and fauna. To that end he stressed the developer's unusually robust conservation measures: clustering housing to keep half the land as open space; creating a hiking trail; building ponds to collect soil runoff during construction; and grading small sections of land at a time to control erosion.[39]

Nearly everyone else at the hearing had strong reservations about the project. A representative from the Interior Department reiterated its commitment to help buy the Burling tract for conversion into a park.[40] Of the two-dozen residents in attendance, only three supported the developer's proposal. The rest, which included several high school students associated with Agnew, argued that developing the site would erode its steep slopes and asked the board of supervisors to find a way to preserve the property.[41] The appearance of the students marked the beginning of the sustained involvement of young people in debates about the Burling tract. Their concern came from the loss of recreational open space associated with suburbanization and was enhanced by the rise of environmental education in the United States.[42]

Despite growing civic opposition, the board of supervisors unanimously accepted the developer's plans. Harriet S. Bradley, who represented the district where the Burling tract was located, believed that the project aligned with long-term plans for single-family housing in the area. While having a reputation for being critical of developers, she suggested that in this case, local officials had "'a unique opportunity to work with a developer who is sufficiently concerned with the [environmental] problems of development.'" Finally, she noted that McLean already had a large park—the Turkey Run Recreational Area—that was adjacent to the Potomac.[43]

An equally important rationale was the high cost of buying the property from Miller & Smith. While the Department of the Interior had offered up to $1.2 million, that money was contingent on the county and the state matching the offer. Fairfax's share was 20 percent, which translated to nearly half a million dollars, while the state would have to contribute over $700,000. Although Fairfax was a rather wealthy county, it was struggling to pay the bills for an ever-widening array of services as residents settled farther out and sought to lower their tax rates. Dedicating such a considerable amount of money to preserve land that would not generate tax revenue seemed a losing proposition, even though the prospective development of the Burling tract threatened the amenities that many residents saw as contributing to a high quality of life.[44]

The differing viewpoints of public officials and environmentalists highlighted the challenges of translating the value of the environmental goods and services that land offered into the economic calculus of the real estate market. Public officials continually searched for revenue-generating development to pay for public services.[45] In doing so, they were disinclined to support robust environmental policies that might ward off developers because of their costs for compliance and because of the high costs of paying for land preservation in "hot" real estate markets.[46] Given that the developer was looking to align its project with the single-family residential character of the community and was willing to offer relatively strong environmental safeguards, it made sense that local officials were open to the site's development.

In contrast, members of the Old Georgetown Pike and Potomac River Association were critical of the decision for setting a bad precedent. As group member John Adams asked, "If you develop this piece of land now, what is to keep other pieces from being developed later?"[47] Adams' question echoed of "the tragedy of the commons," a phrase popularized by Garrett Hardin in a 1968 article about global population pressures that also spoke to the issues surrounding growth and environmental protection in modern America.[48] It questioned how the law and the mechanisms of the market privileged individual actors and their private property rights, particularly in the short-term pursuit of profit, over a robust commitment to ensuring the public's investment in long-term access to environmental goods and resources.[49] Thus, the development of a single property would be interpreted as a rational, individual act rather than part of a broader pattern of growth with a cumulative environmental impact. The concept of the tragedy of the commons cut to the heart of modern environmentalism, which insisted that law, policy, and cultural values needed to evolve to promote a more ecologically sound and equitable use of nature to counterbalance the selfish tendencies underlying private property.[50]

Although citizens who supported preservation of the Burling tract felt that this served the public good more than building yet another housing development, their claims were not immune to scrutiny. Most were predominately middle- and upper-class professionals, or their children, who could afford to live in communities where large amounts of open space increased housing values.[51] This charge was quite valid for groups such as the Old Georgetown Pike and Potomac River Association and reflected the tendency for higher income areas experiencing rapid growth to see popular support for open space preservation.[52] Moreover, many residents who supported preservation failed to acknowledge how postwar housing and land use policies had privileged white middle-class interests over others.[53] This led a columnist for the *Washington Post* to recommend that the local money to help buy the Burling tract could be better spent on expanding housing and social services for lower-income residents.[54] For supporters of preserving the Burling tract to be successful, they would have to position their environmental interests as more important than the imperative for growth.[55]

The Possibility of a Park

Over several months, a small but growing coalition of residents had opposed plans to develop the Burling tract. Initially, they sought to mitigate the ecological impact of building homes on the site but soon concluded that the property's natural features should be preserved for public enjoyment. As local interest in preservation expanded, the board of supervisors held another hearing on April 8 to allow the public to air its views. In the preceding month, more than one hundred high school students had organized a petition drive to solicit support among residents in the Dranesville District for paying a special property tax assessment to help the county purchase the Burling tract for use as a nature park.

At the hearing, a group of thirty students representing Fairfax Students for Preservation of the Burling Tract delivered petitions signed by 2,300 district residents. This was an unusual statement of financial support for land preservation in a fiscally conservative county that had long been devoted to attracting suburban development.[56] The move, however, made sense given that Fairfax was experiencing rapid suburbanization, which degraded environmental resources that many residents felt were critical to their quality of life.[57] While offering to pay to preserve the Burling tract, the signatories did not expressly question the political economy underlying suburbanization or the legal and cultural endorsement of private property rights that made public acquisition the only sure way to protect the property.[58]

The presence of the students at the April 8 hearing confirmed the central role of young people in the case. They testified about their interests in hiking to the waterfall on the property at Scott's Run, confirming the influence of recreational interests on open space preservation.[59] Many of the students went to the same high school and were in the gym class of Marian Agnew, an early supporter of preservation. Some people contended that Agnew had duped her students into participating in the hearing to advance her own interests. In response, one parent wrote to a local newspaper that her son and the other students had not been "indoctrinated" but believed in their cause.[60] The prominent role that students would play in the Burling case confirmed their bona fide environmental interests.

Even with vocal civic support, the board of supervisors voted five to two to reject a civic appeal to consider its approval of the site plan. Residents in attendance loudly voiced their disapproval, forcing the board to take a fifteen-minute recess before resuming its agenda. During the break, John Adams cornered two of the supervisors who had voted against the appeal, asking them to change their votes. When the hearing resumed, one of the supervisors asked the board to reconsider its decision. In a highly unusual turn of events, the precise reasons for which are not clear, the two supervisors that Adams had lobbied changed their votes, helping to pass a 4-3 motion that retracted the board's support for development of the Burling tract.[61]

Following the decision, the board asked the county's park authority to consider the feasibility of buying the Burling tract to serve as the district park for the Dranesville District.[62] If it reached a positive conclusion, the board would put the property on the county's public facility map, giving it the ability to issue $600,000 in bonds that had been approved by voters in 1966 for a district park.[63] Three weeks later, and just a few days after the first Earth Day was celebrated in communities across the United States, the Fairfax Board of Supervisors held a hearing on the results of the district park study. The park authority concluded that the Burling tract had the qualities needed for a district park, emphasizing its natural features, its location adjacent to the Potomac, and its accessibility to over seven thousand residents within a two-mile radius.[64] Even with the county park authority's endorsement, which allowed the county to issue $600,000 in bonds, and the offer of $1.2 million from the Interior Department, the existing financing was still not enough to buy the land.

Elected officials remained unconvinced of preservation. Harriet Bradley reaffirmed her support for the developer's project for its compliance with the local master plan and for offering several measures to mitigate the impact of development, including fifty-six acres of parkland. She was also skeptical about of the petition drive undertaken by Fairfax Students for Preservation of the Burling Tract, insisting that residents did not know they were expressing support for paying part of the costs for acquiring the Burling tract.[65] The students responded by conducting another petition drive, obtaining 2,350 signatures over the next month.[66]

The growing movement to preserve the Burling tract suggested that people were more responsive to environmental issues when they felt an intimate connection with nature. Initially, residents affiliated with the Old Georgetown Pike and Potomac River Association had gotten involved in a "backyard" case to scale down prospective development at the site to curb the erosion of its hilly terrain and runoff into the Potomac. Over time, however, the tract's wildness became a source of admiration as more citizens desired to preserve its amenities. This included "the dramatic bluffs of the palisades, the breathtaking waterfall of Scott's Run, the Potomac River frontage, the abundant wildlife, the unique array of wildflowers, and scientifically acclaimed forest of high quality tulip, oak, hickory, and hemlock."[67] As local residents came to interpret expansive development as destructive, preservation advocates gained ground in their fight to protect the Burling tract.[68] Developing an appreciation for nature and the various roles it fulfilled thus went a long way to cultivating a sense of responsibility for its protection.[69]

With local environmentalism on the rise, the board of supervisors agreed in early May to allow residents of the Dranesville District to vote on whether they would pay a special tax to help the county purchase the Burling tract for a public park. Although officials intended the ballot measure to be advisory, the county attorney concluded that if voters approved the tax, the outcome would be legally binding and enforceable by the local circuit court.[70] A week later, Gordon Smith announced that his development firm, after ten months, had finally purchased the Burling tract for $3.36 million and was planning to proceed with their approved development project.[71] Because the purchase price exceeded the funds available from the Interior Department and a local park acquisition bond, the special tax assessment—estimated at $1.5 million—was a prerequisite for acquiring the Burling tract.

On May 28, the Fairfax planning commission held the tenth public hearing on the Burling tract, at the request of the board of supervisors, to outline the costs to homeowners of the referendum measure. While familiar points of view were aired in what had become an intense debate, the atmosphere was incredibly lively. Cameras from a national television station recorded a public hearing that drew over two hundred attendees. Fifty-one people signed up to speak, most favoring preservation. Many in attendance were local teenagers, several of whom broke with the traditional approach of offering written and oral testimony to be more creative. Some of the youth showed a film explaining the merits of preserving open spaces. The high point of the meeting, and a watershed moment in the case, came when high school student Susan Daniel performed a folk song she had written in support of preserving the Burling tract.[72]

Daniel's song offered a youth-centered meditation on the environmental consequences of postwar suburbanization. The song began by noting that many children of the suburbs did not have recreational access to nature but instead played on the "concrete and the tar" of the streets and driveways in single-family residential communities or, at best, in neatly bordered yards or small neighborhood parks. The song lauded the Burling tract for its hilly and forested landscape full of diverse plants, wildlife, and waterways, and intimated that its preservation was a critical opportunity for the community to offer current and future generations of children a gateway into a preserve of nature before sprawl engulfed what was left of such places. One particularly intriguing aspect of the song was its lyrical parallel to Woody Guthrie's iconic "This Land Is Your Land." Both songs included a narrative of wandering and a sense of wondering, in Guthrie's case across America and in Daniel's, in a "living forest" in the midst of man-made suburbia. A chorus line from the Burling song—"This land is your land, but it should be our land"—was a modification of Guthrie's line that reinterpreted the Burling site from private property to a landscape whose natural richness in the midst of suburbia should serve the public not as the site of another housing project but as a park and nature preserve.[73] Daniel's song was not only a creative reflection on the impact of postwar suburbanization but also a call to arms for hundreds of high school students concerned about the environment and their futures.

At the end of the hearing, the planning commission put the Burling tract on the county's public facilities map, making it possible for the park authority to issue $600,000 in bonds to help pay for the land.[74] Between the public hearing on May 28 and the ballot referendum on July 14, debate over the Burling tract heated up. By this point, protecting the site's amenities had mobilized thousands of supporters. Members of the Old Georgetown Pike and Potomac River Association, who had organized early in the fight, saw their membership grow and increased their lobbying efforts. Prior to the vote, Marian Agnew, the teacher whose students had helped undertake the petition drive to initiate the referendum, wrote to McLean's local newspaper urging residents to vote for the special tax assessment. Recognizing the investment young people had in the campaign, Agnew stressed "the opportunity to preserve this tract for open space and recreation now and for the future; the right to believe that outdoor living and study is both possible and necessary here and now."[75]

Although many were not old enough to vote, members of Fairfax Students for Preservation of the Burling Tract went door-to-door handing out promotional materials and explaining the importance of preserving the Burling tract as a recreational park and nature preserve.[76] Among the materials that members of the group, including Susan Daniel, distributed was a brochure featuring a smiling tree on the front.[77] The tree symbolized the greenery of undeveloped forests and open spaces that were threatened by suburban encroachment. The contents of the brochure underscored how losing the Burling tract to suburban development would leave children without places to enjoy nature. It concluded that generations of residents have natural spaces that people were willing to proactively save from the bulldozer of growth.

As public interest in preserving the Burling tract reached a fever pitch, the voices of those supporting development of the property, which had been relatively quiet, grew more vocal. Those voices included Harriet Bradley, who represented constituents in the district where the Burling tract was located; the county's planning commissioner; the county executive; and most of the business community in the county. More surprising was the inclusion of the Northern Virginia Regional Park Authority, which had signed a conservation agreement with the developer, and the McLean Citizens Association, which had mobilized several years earlier to restrict development on the Merry-wood property.[78]

Business leaders took out an ad in a local newspaper raising several questions about the preservation of the Burling tract even as they articulated general support for local parks.[79] The thrust of the ad focused on the costs to local taxpayers of acquiring the Burling tract either through outright purchase from the developer or through eminent domain. Although Fairfax was a wealthy community and thereby able to offer the kinds of fiscal resources needed to support land preservation, a $1.5 million tax assessment on only a portion of the entire county for a few hundred acres of land was a tough proposition, even during a high tide of environmental consciousness.[80] Many stakeholders were not interested in spending public funds to acquire developable land for a park that could generate tax revenue and pay for public services. Conversely, the idea of growth management to curb the mounting environmental and fiscal costs of sprawl was not yet well formed, despite some efforts by preservation advocates to contrast the pressures that more housing would put on public facilities and natural resources with the environmental benefits that would accrue from open space preservation.[81]

The Referendum and Its Aftermath

As Virginia residents went to the polls on July 14 for the primaries, those in the Dranesville District of Fairfax encountered a ballot measure asking if they would pay a special tax assessment of $1.5 million to help buy and preserve the Burling tract. Leading up to Election Day, three hundred students campaigned tirelessly to generate support for preserving the Burling property, passing out bumper stickers and flyers, calling voters, and going door-to-door to talk with most of the seventeen thousand registered voters in the district. On the day of the elections, local students were out in force at local polling stations and helped get voters to the polls even though they could not vote themselves. The *Washington Post* called the students' involvement "virtually without precedent in a Northern Virginia election."[82] The referendum saw nearly six thousand residents turn out to vote on it. After a vigorous debate, the final vote was 3,208 residents in favor of paying the tax to buy the tract and 2,758 opposed. The results were a vindication for the hundreds who had organized to protect one of the most environmentally sensitive landscapes in Fairfax from suburbanization.[83]

At a time when inflation and taxes were high, suburban residents had agreed to tax themselves to preserve the Burling tract in support of the common good, a decision that many local officials had opposed. The vote was also a testament to the power of grassroots environmental organizing to shape local decision making on suburban development. Even after the vote, however, county officials still had to negotiate with the developer to acquire the Burling tract. The next night, the developer remarked that the property "is still not for sale."[84] After working within the political system and through the democratic medium of a referendum, the question now was whether public officials would follow through with voters' wishes by forcing the developer's hand in taking the Burling tract through eminent domain.[85] This action, which allows a government to take private property under its "police powers" if it serves the public welfare, required the county to file a condemnation suit and a jury to establish a purchase price. The legalistic nature and potentially high price of acquisition in a market where demand kept land prices high, made widespread land conservation difficult.[86]

Following the referendum, the controversy over the Burling tract escalated. Two days later, a large yellow bulldozer appeared on the property just long enough to build dirt mounds to block demonstrators' access to the site.[87] While a representative for the developer insisted that the action was to prevent trespassing, the timing was hardly coincidental. Although local residents had agreed to tax themselves to help buy and preserve the Burling tract, the developer wished to proceed with construction. Continued delays meant money lost while the property remained undeveloped. According to a spokesperson, the company spent $1,000 a day in taxes and interest on its loan for the project and had to keep forty to fifty laborers on the payroll. A week after the vote, Virginia governor Linwood Holton entered the fray. Holton, whose concerns about the pollution of the Potomac River led him to appoint Norman Cole as chair of the State Water Control Board that summer, wrote a letter to the developer expressing a "hope that it might be possible to preserve it [the Burling tract] as an open space," although he did not promise state money to help finance the purchase.[88] A day later, the developer rejected a bid from the Fairfax County Board of Supervisors to buy the property for $2.5 million. The county responded by directing local officials to not issue construction permits. "Til" Hazel, the developer's outspoken lawyer, called the county's offer and tactics "absurd."[89]

In late July, the board of supervisors began the process of acquiring the Burling tract.[90] On July 27, the supervisors voted unanimously to condemn the Burling tract as the first step of acquisition through eminent domain, which required a jury to establish a purchase price. The county had three sources of funds totaling $3.6 million: $1.5 million from the voter-approved tax assessment; $1.5 million from the Land and Water Conservation Fund (a slight increase from an initial offer of $1.2 million); and $600,000 in unused county park bonds. Fairfax did not put up money at the outset of the proceedings since that would have obliged county officials to buy the property regardless of the jury's price tag. The consequence was that the developer was able to develop the site until the jury had reached a decision.[91]

The decision to condemn was extraordinary in a county known for its strong deference toward private property rights. Since 1966, Fairfax officials had filed eight suits for park acquisitions, and only in one case—when they paid $68,000 for twenty-four acres of land near Burke Lake—did they see a lawsuit through to its conclusion.[92] The $2.1 million in local funds that the county was prepared to spend on the Burling tract was an unprecedented move in favor of open space preservation. The use of eminent domain, albeit a recognized police power of localities, also presaged the growing importance of litigation to support environmental activism during the late twentieth century. Indeed, the court system became an integral venue for challenging the exercise of private property rights when prospective development inflicted injuries other than economic or physical (e.g., environmental) on the public.[93] While the developers of the Burling tract stressed their rights as owners of the property to develop it, those who supported its preservation claimed the best interest of the public, as confirmed in the referendum, would be served by making it a park and nature preserve.[94]

On July 27, the day that the Fairfax County Board of Supervisors condemned the Burling tract, a group of seventy protestors, mostly young children and their mothers, formed a picket line across the street to greet bulldozers sent by the developer to prepare the site for construction. The group sang protest songs and carried hand-made picket signs. Some of the signs included a bulldozed tree with the phrase "Please Don't"; others asked, referring to the onslaught of suburban sprawl in surrounding communities, "Where Have All the Forests Gone?" while still other signs proclaimed "Green Is for Trees" in criticizing the developer's pursuit of profit over environmental protection.[95] The assemblage of women and children was a fitting symbol for the sense of civic responsibility, middle-class family values, and maternal care for the environment that had guided organizing efforts.[96] The demonstration confirmed the ability of an emotive appeal for preserving the land for its natural amenities to generate more interest than a more rational, science-driven argument about the ecological impact of home building on the site's steep slopes, which had animated early organizing efforts.

The day after the county attorney filed the condemnation suit, the developer sent two bulldozers to knock down trees on the site, creating a swath twenty-five feet wide and nearly two thousand feet long. Approximately seventy-five picketers occupied the site and sang songs, although they did not interfere with the work.[97] While stopping work in the early afternoon to talk with county officials about possible acquisition of the property, the developer resumed bulldozing after a circuit court judge denied the county's request for a temporary injunction to halt activities on the site.[98] The judge's ruling, which acknowledged the authority granted to the developer to undertake construction while the condemnation suit was in court, reflected the strong protections afforded private property rights in Virginia localities.

By the time officials condemned the Burling tract, what started as a local matter had gained regional attention. Like many issues in Greater Washington, the Burling controversy attracted the interest of environmentally conscious members of Congress looking to gain public support for their stances without potentially upsetting their constituents. Two Democratic senators, Fred R. Harris (OK) and William B. Spong Jr. (VA), along with one Republican senator, Edward W. Brooke (MA), spoke out against development and in favor of its preservation based on environmental concerns and the decision of residents with the ballot referendum. Senator Harris, for example, sent letters to the Department of the Interior, the Fairfax Board of Supervisors, and the developer that called for halting work on the site during the condemnation case because it was "doing irreparable damage" to the tract.[99] While eliciting congressional interest, the Burling controversy, like most development cases, was settled at the local level. Even with the expanded scope of federal involvement in environmental matters, the move to preserve the Burling tract was exempted from federal oversight under the National Environmental Policy Act because that law dealt with mitigating the impact of development projects involving federal interests rather than preserving land.

On August 5, the Fairfax Board of Supervisors reached an agreement with Miller & Smith to purchase the Burling tract for $3.6 million, the maximum amount the county had available. The bulk of the financing included $1.5 million from the Department of the Interior's Land and Water Conservation Fund that was matched by $1.5 million from the special tax assessment.[100] Near the end of the negotiations, Governor Holton gave Fairfax $300,000

toward purchasing the land from monies allocated to the state through the
Land and Water Conservation Fund, freeing up half of the county's park bond
money.[101] On September 4, Fairfax officials submitted a check for the property and filed a deed with the county clerk claiming title and full ownership
of the land.[102] Shortly after the agreement was reached, a group of thirty-one
residents filed a lawsuit to overturn the referendum that had led officials to
pursue acquisition. But the judge upheld the purchase in early January 1971,
bringing to a close more than a year of intense debate that dominated the
political agenda of Fairfax County.[103]

At a time when political and public concern about the environment
peaked in the United States, residents in McLean mobilized when a developer sought to convert an environmentally sensitive parcel of land into an
upscale residential project. Their grassroots organizing drew on recent social
movement tactics and an expanded scope of public participation in political
decision making to address the environmental impact of suburban sprawl
on their community. The time, energy, and money invested in the Burling
controversy were unprecedented for Fairfax County and drew the attention
of people across Greater Washington. One of those who followed the story
was Stewart Udall, who wrote an article about the case entitled "Youths Save
a Public Park." In it, he recounted the critical role of high school and college
students in the civic campaign to preserve the Burling tract as a public park
and nature preserve. The viewpoint of Udall's article was confirmed by Sharon Francis, who was a leading activist in the case. Working for the Conservation Foundation in Washington, Francis concluded that local teenagers "were
dedicated and remarkably clever" in their activism and had "won big."[104]

Despite an intense year of public debate, plans for converting the Burling tract into a public park and nature preserve lagged. Two decades after
the county purchased it, the local park authority finally established a master
plan for the site, which had been expanded to 385 acres and renamed Scott's
Run Nature Preserve. A few improvements were made including a system of
guided trails, parking lots on the west and southeast corners, stepping-stones
at main crossings, and the installation of trash cans. Otherwise the hilly and
forested landscape that appealed to preservationists in 1970 has remained
largely intact. The main activities at the site today include hiking and walk-
ing, with opportunities to observe geological formations and a rich variety of
trees and wildflowers. Local park officials and volunteers also offer occasional
interpretive programs. By the early twenty-first century, Scott's Run Nature
Preserve was part of nearly 2,600 acres of parkland in McLean, almost 16

Figure 7. Potomac River waterfall at Scott's Run Nature Preserve. Source:
NortyNort, Wikimedia Commons.

percent of the community.[105] In light of the suburban sprawl that Northern Virginia experienced during the late twentieth century, Scott's Run became a welcome retreat from traffic gridlock and shopping malls. A 2009 article in the *Post* celebrated the nature preserve as "a scenic touch of wilderness in the heart of suburbia."[106]

The Burling controversy was a wake-up call that suburbanization would likely continue to unduly harm the environment unless public officials and citizens intervened. Even though the outcome of the Burling case was a victory for preservation, environmental advocates began to realize that a case-by-case approach to environmental protection would not change the prevailing political, legal, and cultural motivations underlying rapid and uncoordinated growth. The Burling case sparked the push for smarter growth in Fairfax and Greater Washington more broadly for a brief time in the early 1970s. Although the term "smart growth" was not yet in use, the basic features of the Burling campaign had laid the groundwork: promoting compact development to use existing resources rather than employ expensive new infrastructure and services; proactively preserving rural land and open space from suburban encroachment; and better protecting the air, water, and soil from pollution.

On the heels of the Burling campaign, the Fairfax Board of Supervisors adopted one of the most progressive approaches in the United States to curbing growth. During the fall of 1971, with the seats of the entire nine-person board up for election, the issue of growth management took center stage in the campaign. Voters elected a mostly new slate of supervisors committed to curbing growth through land use policy changes. The board's partisan makeup shifted radically, from five Democrats and four Republicans to eight Democrats and one lone Republican. Jean Packard, a resident who had frequently commented on environmental matters before the supervisors, was among those who were elected to the new board.[107] After her election, Packard spearheaded a nationally significant campaign to control growth in Fairfax.[108]

The hallmark of the board of supervisors' efforts was an eighteen-month study that resulted in the Planning and Land Use System (PLUS), approved in 1973. The foundation of PLUS was an adequate public facilities ordinance to time development with the availability of infrastructure that was modeled on one created in Ramapo, New York. The program was supported by bans on rezoning and processing development applications for up to eighteen months, drawing on earlier policies that blocked and delayed plans for infrastructure and new development, bringing growth almost to a standstill. With a slate of land use policies and a cooled national economy and regional housing market in the early 1970s, growth management appeared promising.[109]

By 1975, however, two circumstances changed the conversation about growth in the county. The first was the eagerness with which the Virginia state and local courts intervened into local land use decision making to rule against growth control measures in cases brought by those looking to develop land. The second was the erosion of support among residents as tax burdens increased with the absence of significant new commercial and industrial development. By 1976, Fairfax voters elected a new board of supervisors headed by Jack Herrity, who returned the county to a path of aggressively pursuing suburban development and limiting robust environmental protection through the end of the century.[110]

The Burling case was a critical moment for grassroots environmentalists in Fairfax and Greater Washington. Many came together to form the Dranesville Environmental Force, which spent the 1970s addressing local pollution issues before fading from the spotlight.[111] The Old Georgetown Pike and Potomac River Association spent three years after the Burling controversy engaging in a successful campaign to have the Georgetown Pike designated, in 1974, as Virginia's first Scenic and Historic Byway. The group later partnered with local homeowners' associations and historical societies to limit modifications to the highway as residential development splintered off of it and commuter traffic increased congestion during the 1980s and early 1990s. The association was finally able to secure an agreement from the state department of transportation in 1994. It has also remained committed to park development along the Georgetown Pike, which has eleven parks along its corridor.[112] Finally, Marian Agnew, who became one of the most visible figures in the Burling controversy, made a career of environmental activism that included cleaning up the Potomac River as one of Greater Washington's sewer ladies during the 1970 as well as a regional battle to (unsuccessfully) block the construction of Interstate 66 in Northern Virginia.

The development firm of Miller & Smith initially struggled after the Burling case but found its footing and continued to develop properties in the Washington area through the end of the century. Ironically, the firm could have saved itself a lot of political trouble by building conventional-style detached homes on one-acre lots, because such a project would not have been subject to multiple layers of public review. Instead, its choice to cluster housing on the Burling tract to increase open space subjected its proposal to more stringent review. After the Burling case, Miller & Smith turned to building more modest housing in Maryland as the luxury market dried up in the mid-1970s, allowing it to secure financing from the Federal Housing Administration. Gordon Smith quipped, "It is really very much like selling to veterans right after World War II."[113] Smith's comment, while harkening back to the postwar era of Levittown, hinted at the growing push for affordable housing in the 1970s, although the success of fair housing policies in fostering racially integrated communities still remained limited.[114] Toward the end of the century, however, Miller & Smith sought to capitalize on rising incomes by turning toward high-end development, but in a more pedestrian, urban-oriented setting that also included tree preserves and a protected wetland, nods to the environmental protection measures that came to differentiate "smarter growth" from postwar suburbia.[115]

The Burling controversy was a milestone for the Washington area to inaugurate the late twentieth century. Over the prior quarter century, postwar suburbanization had degraded environmental resources and hastened the loss of open space and other natural amenities that attracted people to the suburbs in the first place. While localities had created parks, and residents had protested intensive development in their communities before 1970, citizens had a limited ability to influence local decision making that heavily favored growth and lacked robust environmental protection. The Burling case occurred at the time when public concern about the environmental impact of suburbanization was at a historic high. When a developer looked to build a residential subdivision on the Burling site, environmentalist residents initially lobbied to mitigate its impact. Soon, however, they mobilized to block development entirely and to instead preserve the natural landscape of the land as a park for public enjoyment.

The Burling case revealed that managing metropolitan development and protecting environmental resources during the late twentieth century depended primarily on local responses to regional forces. While Congress initiated several major environmental policies during the 1970s, and the EPA emerged as a major administrative agency, the national government was most effective in regulating pollution, habitat destruction, and public health. State and local action proved more important in shaping environmental protection related to metropolitan growth and development during the late twentieth century. Land use and community planning was crucial not only to mitigating the impact of development projects but also protecting agricultural land and open space from suburban encroachment.

The Burling case also underscored a larger trend of environmental protection in the American metropolis during the late twentieth century: that the protection of ecological and open space resources often depended on effective local responses to larger regional growth pressures. In the Burling case, successful land preservation depended on using public funds to acquire private land. For this reason, land preservation required a deep resolve, not just from local officials but also from residents, who would have to foot the bill. Over the longer term, such financial and political commitments proved difficult to sustain for two reasons. First, public commitments to paying for land conservation declined.[116] Second, the uneven growth of Greater Washington during the late twentieth century produced a tremendous competition to attract the tax revenue and commercial opportunities of economic development, which proved far more difficult to refuse than a housing project.

CHAPTER 3

Desperate for Growth

During the 1990s, Prince George's became the first suburban county in the United States to have an African American majority and the only county in the country where the median income rose in the process. As waves of middle- and upper-class residents moved in, however, they were frustrated to find a lack of upscale retail and leisure opportunities that other, primarily white communities in Greater Washington enjoyed. At the turn of the century, residents and public officials hoped that a landmark project along the Potomac at Smoot Bay would bring the growth for which they clamored. Testifying at a 1999 hearing in support of a recent proposal, Amy Alexander highlighted why most residents downplayed the project's environmental impact in favor of what it offered. "I love the birds and I love the deer and I love to garden," she said. "But when we go out to find a restaurant, when we go to find a clothing store, when we go to the library, it is a small town. . . . Prince George's, I feel, is ready to grow."[1]

Alexander's comments underscored the pervasive inequality that emerged in metropolitan America not only between a central city and its suburbs but among the suburbs themselves during the late twentieth century. Although the Fair Housing Act of 1968 helped eliminate racial discrimination in real estate, housing affordability and private choices remained barriers to integrating majority-white communities.[2] This led African Americans to settle in particular suburban housing markets—in Greater Washington, that tended to be Prince George's. As white flight escalated in response to the influx of African Americans and legal mandates for school desegregation during the 1970s, suburbanites pressured officials to reduce residential property tax burdens, just as the demand for public services was on the rise.[3] Racial segregation also limited access to other opportunities like jobs, commerce, and leisure.[4] During the 1970s and 1980s, Prince George's fell behind in attracting economic development because the workforce, infrastructure, and consumer base of other, more affluent and predominately white communities were more appealing to the region's developers and investors. Beginning in the 1990s, local officials increased their use of financial incentives and streamlined the planning process to attract upscale development that would provide tax revenue to improve county schools and services and would provide the kinds of opportunities needed to recruit and retain more affluent residents.

Three different projects were proposed for the Smoot Bay property after 1980. After the first two failed to materialize, a third—National Harbor—garnered widespread support. Unlike the first two, which offered employment or housing that directly benefited local residents, National Harbor capitalized on the tourist appeal of the national capital area to secure tax revenue while offering retail and recreational opportunities that middle- and upper-class residents could also enjoy. Public and private support was unusually strong for the project. In addition, the demand for development muted public discussions about the adverse impact of developing the Smoot Bay property. Environmentalists did not reject National Harbor outright, as one might have expected with the smart growth movement of the late 1990s. Instead, they insisted that the developer of National Harbor better address its impact on the environment and local businesses, but their ranks were small and they were often branded as elitists for seeking to advance their own desires for environmental amenities while disregarding widespread support for the project's economic and social benefits.[5]

The politics of Smoot Bay thus illustrated how regional inequalities impaired local commitments to environmental protection for large-scale economic development. It also confirmed the primacy of local and state decision making over federal environmental review. Part of the site included a piece of land owned by the federal government, which agreed to transfer it to the property's owner(s) in exchange for federal oversight of an environmental review process under the National Environmental Policy Act (NEPA) to guide the entire site's development. Although the review process required public participation and considered a range of environmental and social impacts, state and local interests largely shaped the substance of the environmental impact statement (EIS). The resulting document offered a cursory assessment of National Harbor's impact while reinforcing its need and benefits.[6] Once federal environmental concerns were dispatched, local and state decision making took over. While a group of residents secured concessions to further mitigate the project's impact on local businesses, public officials soon approved National Harbor, which was built starting in 2008.

The Struggle for Commerce in Prince George's County

The policies and personal preferences underlying postwar suburbanization stratified metropolitan America. Several factors contributed to segregating housing markets in favor of white middle-class residents including zoning and land use policies, real estate practices, home loan programs, and personal preferences for homogenous communities.[7] Because of white flight from Washington, D.C., the postwar baby boom, and the broadened material prosperity of the region, Fairfax and Montgomery became mostly white middle-class communities. Prince George's, in contrast, became the leading suburban county for African American migrants given its proximity to black neighborhoods in Washington, D.C., and its affordable housing stock.[8]

Although the Fair Housing Act of 1968 broke down de jure racial segregation, real estate practices such as blockbusting and steering, white resistance to black residence—especially after a federal order to integrate the county's public schools—and housing affordability remained barriers to socially inclusive communities.[9] In 1970, Prince George's had a population of 660,567, of which 91,843 were black. By 1980, the number of African Americans jumped to 247,860, while the number of white residents dropped by 170,000.[10] In the process, the Capital Beltway became a line of demarcation between black working-class and poor urban communities on the inside and mostly white middle-class suburban communities on the outside.

Deepening segregation undermined Prince George's ability to build a strong employment base of middle-class jobs. Although federal legislation broke down legal barriers, the availability of jobs and investment depended heavily on a locality's workforce, ability to offer public facilities and services, and the socioeconomic status of its consumers.[11] Compared to Northern Virginia, which became a center for the defense industry, and Montgomery, which specialized in medicine and biotechnology, Prince George's share of federal jobs included only military bases and a few research agencies. In the Washington area, having federal employers was a major source of economic development on its own as well as attracting private employers.

As the locus of commerce in Greater Washington shifted from downtown to a more diffuse array of suburban centers, Prince George's residents also enjoyed less access to retail outlets. Approximately sixty-five retail facilities were built in the county during the 1960s and 1970s, but nearly all establishments were neighborhood-oriented facilities rather than destination stores. Indeed, the only major retail center built in Prince George's before 2000 was Laurel Mall, which opened in 1979. By contrast, two of Greater Washington's largest malls were built in Fairfax during the 1970s, while Montgomery had four large retail centers by 1980. Because retail commerce is heavily shaped by the distribution of nearby consumers, residential segregation excluded Prince George's residents from middle-class retail and leisure opportunities.[12]

The exodus of the white middle-class and the influx of working-class residents destabilized the county's tax base while increasing calls for public expenditures for schools, housing and social services, and other activities. Mostly white property owners, who had resisted school desegregation and equal spending across the county, soon protested property tax increases intended to compensate for the lack of commercial tax revenue.[13] In 1978, residents voted to cap local property taxes, part of a "tax revolt" movement that swept across the United States.[14]

The tax cap had unintended consequences. As county officials struggled to provide services without raising taxes, they also avoided taxing new development at rates sufficient to support infrastructure because they feared that it might ward off investment. Even though voters eliminated the cap in 1984, they kept restrictions on the rate, which continued to undermine the financing of public services. The tax revolt, combined with the county's existing marginalization in the regional economy, pressured local officials to lure commercial development, which generally paid more in taxes than it cost in services, more vigorously than ever before. In the process, however, they discounted concerns about the environmental impact of development. The most prominent case involved a large site in Oxon Hill known as Smoot Bay.[15]

In the 1920s, Lewis Egerton Smoot acquired a five-hundred-acre parcel of land in Oxon Hill, about seven miles south of downtown Washington, to extract minerals for a building materials company. As part of its operations, the Smoot Sand & Gravel Company flooded two hundred acres of land along the Potomac River to create a bay for dredging. During World War II, the rural, sparsely populated community began its suburban development as workers and families flooded into the national capital area to serve in the war effort. Oxon Hill's postwar residents largely worked for nearby federal employers in the county including U.S. Naval Research Laboratory and Bolling Air Force Base. During the mid-twentieth century, Smoot Sand &

Gravel became the premier building materials company in the Washington area, literally building the region's suburbs. Bonnie Bick, whose father was a scientist at the U.S. Naval Research Lab, grew up in Oxon Hill and watched the mining operations near her home.[16] In the early 1960s, Lewis Smoot died, putting the future of the Smoot Bay property in question. Shortly after his death, the Anacostia Freeway and the Capital Beltway were opened less than one mile to the north, making the site eminently attractive for development. Although Bick later moved out of Prince George's to go to college and start a family, she would return to her family's home later in life, as plans to bring upscale commerce to Oxon Hill and the county unfolded.

Nearly two decades after Lewis Smoot's death, James H. Burch reached an agreement with Smoot's widow in 1980 to acquire the defunct industrial site. Born in Washington, D.C., Burch spent his early life in Northern Virginia and devoted nearly a decade to becoming a priest before giving up the vocation. After running unsuccessful campaigns in the 1970s for seats in the Virginia House of Delegates and the U.S. Congress, he went to work for his father's land development company in Fairfax. At the time he purchased the Smoot Bay site, Burch had never built a project on his own. Despite his limited experience, he had an ambitious goal to create a large, mixed-use commercial project geared to middle-class residents. The Smoot Bay site was one of the most promising pieces of property in the county for such a project.[17]

By the early 1980s, Prince George's officials were eager to attract large-scale projects for housing, employment, shopping, and other opportunities. This included Parris Glendening, who was finishing up eight years of service as a county councilman. About a year before he won election as county executive in 1982, a position he held for twelve years before becoming governor of Maryland, Glendening was inspired by Burch's plans to shepherd passage of legislation to allow large-scale, mixed-use development in the county.[18] The prospect of developing at Smoot Bay—a place that was often overlooked for federal employment, lacked major retail facilities, and had a less affluent population than its neighbors—was quite appealing.

In early 1983, Burch issued plans for Bay of the Americas, a massive $500 million project whose scale was unprecedented for the county. Its centerpieces were a waterfront hotel and conference center and a one-thousand-boat marina and yacht club. It also included one thousand townhouses and two million square feet of office, retail, and restaurant space. Over half of the site was reserved for public open space.[19] Local residents were mostly enthusiastic about the project. "'Prince George's needs an uplift badly," one

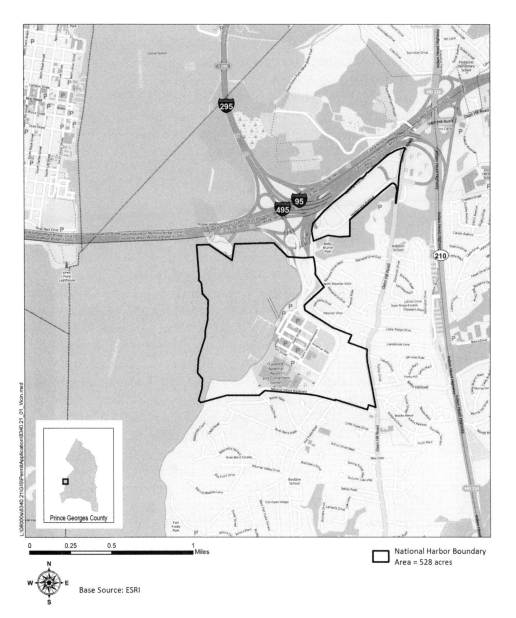

Figure 8. Smoot Bay site (with National Harbor project designated). Source:
Wetland Studies and Solutions, Inc.

couple wrote to county officials. "A project such as Smoot Bay would spur a higher income clientele here. We don't need a low-cost bedroom society."[20] Some residents were concerned that it would pollute the Potomac via runoff, harm wildlife, and increase traffic congestion, but they were in the minority.[21] Local officials were eager to support Bay of the Americas, hoping to translate the success of Baltimore's Inner Harbor waterfront revitalization project to a rural residential area.[22] Even with this support, Burch did not move forward with the project. Although the reasons were not clear, the size of the project and the difficulties of securing financing, particularly given his lack of development experience, were the most likely causes.

By the mid-1980s, the property tax limitations of the previous few years had made funding public services quite difficult. Officials stepped up their efforts to attract commercial investment to increase revenue. During his first term as county executive, Glendening won approval for a record $117 million in capital bonds for infrastructure to attract large-scale development, including $80 million for highways. His later record as governor and reputation as a leading figure of the smart growth movement, however, has obscured his earlier commitment to large-scale growth as a local official in a county starved for it. Two years into his tenure as county executive, Glendening gave a searing speech endorsing a pro-business posture and criticizing "a small group of misguided citizens" as "false prophets of no-growth" in a county where a legacy of low-income and scattered development plagued residents' quality of life.[23] "Whether we like it or not, growth will come to Prince George's County," he said. "Our challenge is to decide what type of growth we went and, then, how to manage it."[24]

Glendening's views positioned him as more committed to careful land use planning and compact development than his elected counterparts in Fairfax, but less progressive than his peers in Montgomery, where the existing state of development and more affluent population supported robust implementation of the wedges and corridors plan. His stance made sense for Prince George's, which had a limited tradition of land use planning, a desperate need for the jobs and tax revenue that commercial development offered, and a growing cadre of residents frustrated about the lack of employment and leisure opportunities. After winning reelection, Glendening reflected on his record of securing development as county executive: "our message was very clear and very pointed: We need these projects to keep ahead."[25]

Burch's failure to develop Bay of the Americas left a major void in Prince George's that many hoped would be filled when James T. Lewis bought the

Smoot Bay property in 1984. Lewis had extensive experience with large commercial projects, with a career dating to the late 1960s.[26] In 1985, he announced preliminary plans for PortAmerica, a project similar to Burch's but with a far more distinctive centerpiece: a 750-foot, fifty-two-story office tower that was taller than any other structure in the region, including the Washington Monument.[27] Such a bold waterfront project was comparable to Georgetown, Old Town Alexandria, or the Inner Harbor in Baltimore.[28] Initial estimates suggested that the project would bring with it nine thousand jobs and $2.5 million in annual tax revenue, not to mention the prospect of being, in the words of one county councilman, "the shot in the arm we need" to attract more development.[29]

PortAmerica would have made its way quickly through the local approval process were it not necessary to extend the Anacostia Freeway through federal parkland to bring traffic to the site. In December 1985, Maryland Democratic congressman Steny Hoyer shepherded a bill through Congress that directed the Department of the Interior to transfer the parkland to the bi-county planning commission for Prince George's and Montgomery in exchange for giving the National Capital Planning Commission (NCPC) authority to review development plans.[30] In essence, this gave the NCPC veto power over development as well as oversight of an environmental review process under NEPA that required the input of numerous agencies and the public before construction. As a result, environmental concerns would have more of a bearing with regard to the site's development than without federal oversight, particularly given the widespread support for large-scale growth in the county.[31]

PortAmerica encountered two major obstacles. The first was the height of the office tower in relation to the capital skyline, which generated sufficient political concern to garner a congressional subcommittee hearing.[32] At the hearing, the chairman of the D.C. Fine Arts Commission called it "the single greatest threat to the visual and symbolic integrity of our Nation's Capital that I have seen proposed in my decade and a half on the Commission." A representative of the Conservation Foundation agreed that the federal government should get involved to protect the capital skyline, whose embodiment of the democratic values of American society transcended base, material interests.[33] Growing environmental concerns about the Potomac and Chesapeake Bay also stoked worries among the Chesapeake Bay Foundation and the Maryland chapter of Bassmaster—a recreational fishing organization—about the impact of a large-scale project on water quality, shoreline erosion, and aquatic life.[34]

Even with these pointed criticisms, PortAmerica had widespread political and public support for bringing jobs, tax, revenue, and a sense of pres-
tige to Prince George's County.[35] To satisfy his critics, Lewis scaled down
the skyscraper to an octagonal twenty-two-story tower with six ten-story
buildings, reducing the estimated number of jobs for the project from
10,000 to 6,500.[36] Other modifications tweaked the mix of commercial, residential, and open space.[37]

Like its predecessor, however, PortAmerica was not built. After nearly a
decade-long boom, the commercial real estate market in the Washington area
cooled. In 1992, Lewis defaulted on a loan and had to relinquish 80 percent
of the site. He later lost most of the rest to foreclosure. By 1995, PortAmerica had consumed $125 million in loans and cash without any construction.
At mid-decade, Smoot Bay remained empty, an unnerving symbol of Prince
George's difficulty in attracting upscale commercial development.[38]

National Harbor

Milton V. Peterson became the third developer to try his hand at Smoot Bay
when he purchased the site in late 1995 for $5.6 million.[39] Peterson was one
of the most prodigious developers in Greater Washington during the second
half of the twentieth century. Born in Massachusetts, he earned an undergraduate degree from Middlebury College in Vermont before moving to
Fairfax in 1958. He began his career working for several years for Stephen
Yeonas in Arlington before starting his own residential development company in 1965. Peterson partnered with politically savvy land use lawyer John
"Til" Hazel in the 1970s to lead the Hazel/Peterson Companies, which built
several large housing projects in Fairfax and other counties. Peterson went on
to establish his own firm and moved into mixed-use development, building
millions of square feet of real estate in Virginia and Maryland by 1995. Peterson had a long track record of success executing large-scale commercial projects, drawing on a comprehensive in-house staff, adeptness at navigating the
development process, and his own tireless energy. "Milt," as many knew him,
prided himself on running a family company and serving the community.
Peterson would need all of his skills and energy to find success at Smoot Bay.[40]

At the time that Peterson acquired Smoot Bay, Prince George's was in
the midst of a historic transition to becoming the only suburban county in
the United States to have an African American majority where the median

income also rose in the process. Middle- and upper-class subdivisions sprung up across the southern and eastern sections of the county outside the Belt-way. Inhabiting those new homes were families who often preferred to live in majority-black communities rather than face the potential tensions and hostilities of integrating into mostly white suburbs.[41] By 2000, Prince George's was three-quarters African American and on the leading edge of a wave of migration into Maryland in which African Americans accounted for nearly two-thirds of new residents while the state's white population dropped slightly.[42]

Even as the county's class profile shifted, enduring patterns of racial segregation impeded access to upscale commercial and leisure opportunities that could be found in the region's white suburbs. While Fairfax, for example, had a sound tax base thanks to its large affluent population and property taxes, professional job base, and upscale commerce, Prince George's had higher taxes and less adequate services.[43] In addition, a number of new shopping centers were built in Prince George's during the 1980s and 1990s, but most provided only basic products and services rather than more expensive and eclectic consumer items.[44] As a result, 80 percent of county residents surveyed in 1994 found the lack of retail stores a major problem and often had to go elsewhere to purchase more specialized consumer goods.[45] On the other hand, many working-class and poor residents in the county suffered because of commercial disinvestment, including the loss of several tenants in the county's one major mall in Laurel.[46]

The rise of the black middle class and their frustrations over the quality of public services and the state of development inaugurated a new chapter in Prince George's history with the election of Wayne K. Curry as county executive in 1994. Curry's election reflected a belief that African American leaders could best serve the interests of a primarily black constituency.[47] A lifelong county resident, Curry was born in 1951 into a family that helped integrate their neighborhood and public schools. During the 1970s, he earned an undergraduate degree and worked as a staffer for the county executive. Curry earned a law degree from the University of Maryland in 1980 and worked as a real estate and development lawyer before establishing his own practice, which he operated from 1984 to 1992. With his election as county executive, Curry became the first African American to hold a county's top elected leadership position in suburban Washington.[48]

Curry's commitment to attracting jobs and commerce resonated with voters. Of those surveyed in one poll, only a quarter reported a big problem with growth and development, an indication that most residents wanted more of it.[49] Curry avidly catered to developers and investors, explaining in a 1997 interview: "You give me all the things that we need—the tax base, jobs and pride—and I'll back you all the way."[50] His views contrasted with those of his predecessor, Parris Glendening, who gradually lost the support of the business community as he became more committed to a more compact and environmentally conscious model of growth while governor of Maryland.[51] Given the deficits that Prince George's faced, public officials like Curry, as well as many residents, were supportive of doing everything possible to attract investment and far less concerned about the environmental or fiscal impact of development.[52]

In 1997, Milt Peterson issued his initial plan for a project called National Harbor. It featured a resort-style convention center and hotel complex with upscale retail, entertainment venues, and recreational amenities. National Harbor's selling point was not in bringing jobs and housing but in attracting tourists and providing, albeit indirectly, higher-end retail and entertainment options for middle- and upper-class African Americans frustrated with having to go to white suburbs for their shopping and leisure.[53] The project also promised tax revenue without requiring expensive new services associated with residential development, such as schools. One resident who lived near the site quickly embraced Peterson's National Harbor: "We've been waiting for, asking for, pleading for upscale businesses to come to us," she remarked.[54]

The county council was eager to see National Harbor built and made several concessions to keep the project from failing as two prior ones had. First, the council allowed more intensive development than originally permitted. Second, it required only a general site plan before construction could begin, rather than a detailed site plan as was customary. This decision suggested a reduced scrutiny of the project's details and overall approval. Finally, the council agreed to fast-track the entire review process, a step they had taken two years earlier to lure the Washington Redskins to relocate from Washington, D.C., to a stadium in Landover.[55]

Peterson issued more detailed information about National Harbor in February 1998. Plans for the 534-acre site presented an urban destination resort with "a combination of resort, marketplace and street fair with fanciful architecture and high-tech attractions that offers something of interest to every demographic segment."[56] They included a convention center with 3,750 hotel rooms; nearly four million square feet of entertainment, retail, and restaurant space; and over one million square feet of office space and parking. The waterfront parcel—the focal point of the project—had five zones each with its own design, uses, and personality to provide distinct visitor experiences.[57] Peterson's vision was for an upscale, family-oriented resort that capitalized on the tourist potential of Greater Washington and served residents' consumer interests and the county's desire to secure additional revenue to improve public services.

Although Peterson had strong backing from local officials, his project still had a major hurdle to clear. It involved a decision made back in 1985 to transfer a parcel of federal parkland, needed for extending highway access to the Smoot Bay site, to the local planning authority in exchange for giving the NCPC oversight of a federal environmental review process.[58] In the late 1990s, however, the NCPC exchanged its long-standing interest in a park-oriented waterfront for support of greater development of close-in communities—a vision of smart growth. The agency endorsed large-scale economic development like National Harbor that could capitalize on the region's tourist potential to bring in needed tax revenue without having to provide expensive public services like schools and social services.[59]

As the NCPC began public hearings on National Harbor, the voices of the project's supporters proved far louder than those of its critics. The most prominent were the Indian Head Highway Area Action Council, a federation of three dozen civic and neighborhood associations in the southern half of Prince George's; the Chesapeake Bay Foundation, whose members worried about prospective pollution from site development; and the Coalition for Smarter Growth, a recent Washington-area confederation devoted to reducing the environmental, fiscal, and social impact of suburban sprawl and large-scale development. The groups did not reject National Harbor outright, as one might have expected with the smart growth movement of the late 1990s. Instead, they urged officials to transfer most of its facilities away from the waterfront further inland to reduce their impact.[60] This recommendation did not gain traction, however, as a significant part of the site's appeal was its waterfront location.

One issue that threatened the project's construction was the identification of a nest of bald eagles on the Smoot Bay property. Because the eagles were a federally protected endangered species, the developer had to undertake a study to confirm that National Harbor would not seriously impact them before proceeding with the project. After reviewing a study commissioned by Peterson, the U.S. Fish and Wildlife Service gave approval to move forward.[61]

Most residents and public officials lauded National Harbor at the NCPC's hearing in May 1998. "Prince George's County needs this project for a host of reasons," one resident insisted, "including additional tax revenue, jobs, access to quality entertainment, food and retail opportunities within our county borders and in Southern Prince George's County."[62] Despite catering to tourists, National Harbor's size and focus on middle-class consumers was a big selling point. "'Tourists are a benefit, if that is what will bring in the upscale businesses,' one resident explained. 'If it brings more tax dollars and jobs into Prince George's County, it's welcome.'"[63] The county council, with Curry's support, approved the site plan a month later.

After several hearings, the NCPC created a draft EIS for public discussion at a meeting held on January 20, 1999. The document found that National Harbor would have unavoidable impacts to nearby residential areas and the natural environment, including damage to wetlands and aquatic habitats as well as air quality from automobile traffic and loud noises. But it concluded there was not a serious enough impact to warrant blocking the project. Five hundred people packed into the Oxon Hill High School auditorium for this hearing compared to one hundred at the first hearing eight months earlier. Clearly, the stakes of the project were high.[64]

The main goal of environmentalists and their allies was to mitigate the impact of National Harbor. Andrew MacDonald, an environmental scientist with the Coastal Plains Environmental Council, reiterated a widely shared view among environmental advocates that the bulk of development should be relocated to protect the river and trees on the property.[65] One Oxon Hill resident added, "We built our home because of the trees and the woods. . . . We know there's going to be progress. We're not against that. But it doesn't have to be so massive."[66] Robert Boone, president of the Anacostia Watershed Society, as well as members of the Maryland Bassmaster Federation, were among those who revisited concerns about the impact on the bald eagles' nest at the site.[67] While environmentalists were critical of National Harbor, the substance and tenor was far less strident and pervasive than for other projects in Greater Washington at the time.

Most local stakeholders supported National Harbor and did not want the environmental review process to sidetrack its approval. Wayne Curry was among those who maintained that the environmental concerns were marginal compared to the tax revenue and commercial and leisure opportunities the project offered the county.[68] An African American small business owner added that National Harbor offered an opportunity for Prince George's to emulate the economic success of waterfront development that Alexandria and Arlington enjoyed across the Potomac.[69] While public officials tended to focus rather narrowly on the tax revenue and jobs National Harbor offered, many residents felt that the project would have a marginal environmental impact compared to the increased access to upscale consumer goods that it offered.[70]

Some residents were also critical of the motives of environmental critics, most of whom lived in Northern Virginia, where there was already a sufficient level of upscale development. Alexander, for example, faulted the insistence on protecting bald eagles, explaining "there's all this land and all this space, and I think the birds should move aside. There's plenty of space for them down the river."[71] Another resident was more pointed about the outsider status of many critics of National Harbor: "I would like to say that that's a very lofty position that you can afford to take if you live in affluent Alexandria, with its many jobs, shopping centers, and restaurants."[72] These kinds of comments—that environmentalists were elitists for focusing on eagles over people's quality of life—generated wide applause at the public hearing.[73]

The differing views about National Harbor reflected a familiar story about the tensions between development and environmental protection. However, the views of the African American Environmentalist Association (AAEA) challenged the conventional wisdom of environmentalists as obstructionists to large-scale growth. The founder of the AAEA was Norris McDonald, who began his environmental career in the late 1970s with Friends of the Earth, an assertive grassroots organization based in the United States that also had a worldwide network of activists. McDonald left the organization to establish the AAEA in 1985.[74]

Initially, the AAEA's profile was little different from that of mainstream environmental organizations, but McDonald reoriented the group's work to focus on environmental matters pertaining more directly to African American communities. Part of his motivation was to better position the group within the environmental justice movement, which insisted that the costs of development disproportionately fell on communities of color and that these communities deserved robust protections like their white counterparts. McDonald's experiences with mainstream, white-dominated national environmental groups had also been particularly frustrating. He believed that organizations like the Sierra Club were more interested in preserving nature for the enjoyment of the white middle class than addressing pollution and other issues that had a disproportionate impact on black communities.[75] He also contended that such organizations had done a poor job of bringing African Americans into membership and leadership positions. In a 2005 interview, McDonald contrasted his philosophy of environmental justice with what he saw as the elitism and nature-first bias of white-dominated environmental organizations, saying: "It is arrogant. It is racist. It is an indicator of how they feel about the black community and individual blacks."[76]

Unlike other environmentalists, McDonald and the AAEA supported National Harbor. McDonald himself was already critical of what he called an "opposition" orientation among mainstream environmental groups that was hostile to most development projects without considering their social context.[77] For McDonald, growth had to be considered in the context not only of its environmental impact but also on criteria such as the impact of projects on African American communities, the extent to which the costs and benefits were equitably distributed, and the nature of political and public support.[78] Taking a mix of factors into consideration, McDonald concluded in testimony before the NCPC: "The benefits to county residents and visitors alike to such a site far outweigh the disruption of wetlands and aquatic habitats that would be generated by shoreline alterations and waterfront activity."[79]

McDonald's analysis raised intriguing points about how social geography shaped commitments to environmental protection. Mainstream environmental organizations, however, considered his views highly suspect not only because he downplayed the need for additional environmental safeguards for the project, but also because he supported the use of nuclear power and even DDT—both of which were widely scorned in environmental circles.[80] McDonald's views, and the fact that he seemed to be the only representative from the AAEA involved in advocacy issues, pushed a leader of the Prince George's chapter of the Sierra Club to argue that McDonald was "trying to portray a wedge [in the environmental community] where it doesn't exist."[81] Conversely, some county residents agreed with McDonald that the elitism of mainstream environmentalists threatened to keep the county from enjoying the much-needed material benefits of a large-scale commercial project.[82] One small business owner, for example, wondered, "whether or not racism when it comes to this project is not still alive and well."[83] Although the AAEA was a small organization at best, and a mouthpiece for McDonald at worst, it challenged the tendency of mainstream environmentalists to oppose large projects and to present their interests in protecting nature as beyond scrutiny.

After voluminous public discussion on the draft EIS for three months, the NCPC released a final version in April 1999. It reiterated that National Harbor's economic benefits outweighed its environmental impact, which could be effectively mitigated.[84] While several groups contested this assessment, political and public support of the project remained strong. In late

1999, Congressman Hoyer intervened to secure approval of a rider to a congressional bill that removed the NCPC's veto power over development at Smoot Bay prior to approval of its final EIS.[85] Local officials forged ahead to approve the project, unencumbered by prospective federal lawsuits by citizens under NEPA or related federal legislation. Over the next several years, environmental concerns faded from the spotlight as a broader array of questions arose about the project's benefits to residents, impact on traffic, and threats to local businesses.

Moving Forward

By 2000, the prospects for development at Smoot Bay appeared promising after years of setbacks. In January, Milt Peterson scored a major victory when the Gaylord Entertainment Company agreed to build a hotel and conference center complex to anchor National Harbor. Gaylord was a Nashville-based media, entertainment, and hospitality firm that, in addition to owning the Grand Ole Opry, had built the Opryland hotel and convention center and was constructing a resort and convention center in Florida. Its $560 million proposal, which included four hundred thousand square feet of exhibition and meeting space and two thousand hotel rooms, would be the largest private project ever in Maryland. While larger than the existing Washington Convention Center in downtown Washington, it was smaller than the facility under construction to replace it.[86]

The Gaylord complex fed the already large public appetite for National Harbor. As one resident explained, it was "just what the doctor ordered for the wealthiest majority African American community in the world, a community that for some strange reason (race) has been overlooked by upscale commercial developers."[87] Wayne Curry gave a speech to the county Chamber of Commerce, of which he used to be president, to reiterate his pro-growth philosophy and support of the project.[88] Elected state officials representing Prince George's also jumped on the bandwagon. State delegate Rushern L. Baker III, the chair of Prince George's House delegation and later its county executive, insisted that the Gaylord project was critical to attracting other investors to National Harbor to make it a landmark for the county.[89]

Local officials, with growing support from their colleagues at the state level, renewed their push to make National Harbor a reality. In 2000, county officials offered to issue $122 million in bonds to widen existing roadways, build parking garages, and help market National Harbor as a way to close the deal. State elected officials, captivated by estimates that National Harbor would bring in nearly $70 million per year in tax revenue once completed, promised a $137 million package of incentives for improving local roads and interchanges, parking, and preparing the Potomac shoreline for a boardwalk.[90]

The combined offer of nearly a quarter of a billion dollars was the largest commitment of public funds ever for a private development project in the state. The justification was based on two basic premises. The first was that businesses made location decisions based on the cost of business. The second was that large-scale economic development provided revenue above and beyond the cost of the incentives. Such a large financing package reflected the growing use of incentives by states and localities during the late twentieth century to outcompete their peers for the jobs and revenue offered by commercial development that helped to offset the expensiveness of public services for residents.[91] For many county residents, the single most important reason for supporting National Harbor was the tax revenue it would generate to improve the schools.[92]

Other residents were skeptical about such a large financial lure. Some questioned whether the property, hotel room, sales and other taxes from the project would cover the investment costs, much less offer additional revenue to fund public services.[93] One of the more strident critics was Stan Fetter of the Indian Head Highway Area Action Council. Fetter lived more than a dozen miles away in a leafy neighborhood in Fort Washington, near the Alice Ferguson Foundation, which offered environmental education activities and hosted Greater Washington's most prominent annual trash cleanup campaign. Fetter generally supported the revenue and opportunities that National Harbor promised, although he worried about the project's environmental impact on the Potomac. In a May 2000 letter to the editor, he argued that the public financing offer would be better spent on improving communities along the Indian Head Highway corridor rather than devoted to a single project that was not going to substantially enhance the county's employment profile. "Let's remember what we're getting here," Fetter wrote. "Oxon Hill is not going to become the next Interstate 270 corridor because of this project, and it isn't worth giving away the store (again and again) and misleading the public (again and again) in its behalf."[94] Fetter raised an important question about what kinds of projects were best suited for public investment. His point about reinvesting in existing communities rather than supporting lavish new projects also bespoke a smart-growth ethos that had gained cachet across metropolitan America by this point.

The location of National Harbor near the urban core seemed to align well with Maryland's Smart Growth and Neighborhood Conservation Act. Passed in 1997, the act sought to curb sprawl by concentrating development, building on existing resources, and supporting targeted improvements in underserved communities. Its leading advocate was Governor Glendening, who had built his political career in Prince George's by trying to attract projects big and small to close-in communities as development moved farther out. Glendening supported National Harbor. Although he, like many, found National Harbor's tax revenue, opportunities, and job-creation potential desirable, he also interpreted the project as consistent with smart growth and supported large-scale state financing to make it happen: "The state needs to invest in good, solid economic development projects," a spokesperson explained, "to create jobs, to raise tax revenue and to build solid communities."[95]

Looking more closely, however, National Harbor seemed a poor fit for smart growth. At a basic level, it seemed incongruous with the surrounding community. The president of the Indian Head Highway Area Action Council, Helen O'Leary, railed: "We don't want an amusement park in a residential neighborhood."[96] Moreover, the lack of planned Metro service increased the odds that the project would worsen traffic congestion and promote sprawl. In addition, the tourist-driven profile of National Harbor ensured that most jobs would be low-paying service-sector positions rather than the kinds of middle-class positions envisioned under the state legislation.[97] Finally, the upscale businesses would likely compete with local shops, which invested more in local communities, thereby undermining neighborhood conservation.[98]

As National Harbor came closer to fruition, Oxon Hill community members mobilized to limit the project's impact on themselves and local businesses. Their leader was Bonnie Bick. Bick grew up in Oxon Hill and watched the operations of the Smoot Sand & Gravel Company as a child. She went to college at the nearby University of Maryland in the early 1960s, becoming politically active after attending a lecture by political philosopher Hannah Arendt on the subject of individual responsibility. Bick moved to New York City after college and went on to demonstrate against the Vietnam War and U.S. involvement in Central America during the 1970s. She moved back to Maryland, to Calvert County, in 1985 and invested her energies in local environmental issues.[99] Bick was the leading activist behind preserving the Mount

Aventine estate and Chapman Forest from a major project in the 1990s and
had worked with Glendening and Steny Hoyer to secure state funding for the
project. Unlike both politicians, however, Bick was highly critical of National
Harbor's impact.[100]

In 1999, Bick, now middle-aged, moved back to her family's Oxon Hill
home after the deaths of her parents and husband. A longtime member of the
Sierra Club, Bick shared the concerns of other environmentalists about building National Harbor. But she was one of the first to recognize the potential
impact of National Harbor on local businesses.[101] Bick led a group of residents
who brought a series of lawsuits against the Peterson Company to make compensatory investments to revitalize local businesses. In 2001, she joined with
Donna Edwards to cofound the Campaign to Reinvest in the Heart of Oxon
Hill. Edwards was an attorney with a distinguished record of commitment
to liberal causes. Getting her start as a volunteer in Democratic presidential
campaigns in the 1980s, she went on to serve as a lobbyist for Public Citizen,
founded by consumer advocate Ralph Nader, and started the National Network to End Domestic Violence, where she was a leading figure in the passage
of the Violence against Women Act in 1994.[102] Bick and Edwards were formidable opponents of Peterson and used their understanding of the development process and influence with local officials to pressure him to compensate
for the impact of National Harbor on Oxon Hill.[103]

Between 1998 and 2004, the Campaign to Reinvest in the Heart of Oxon
Hill waged a fairly successful campaign to secure the community's interests
against National Harbor. Reflecting on its motivations, Bick insisted, "We
said it is not OK to have glitz at National Harbor but squalor in downtown
Oxon Hill."[104] Employing a mix of tactics including negotiations, grassroots
activism, and legal action, Bick and Edwards were able to reach a 2004 settlement that offered several tangible outcomes. These included preservation and
investment in the Potomac Heritage National Scenic Trail along the waterfront; the hiring of a consultant to develop a business plan for improving
the downtown; a commitment to connect downtown Oxon Hill to National
Harbor and the waterfront; and help in bringing a Metro station.[105] As the
legal battle with Peterson wound down, county officials voted to condemn
Bick's home and demolish it to make way for a drainage ditch to support
the widening Oxon Hill Road to accommodate National Harbor. The irony
was certainly not lost on Bick, but in an unusual display, Edwards and Peterson jointly opposed taking Bick's house and were successful in the process.[106]
Once the Campaign to Reinvest in the Heart of Oxon Hill had rested its case,

no major barriers remained for National Harbor. There was also a reasonable amount of goodwill. Speaking in 2008 about her relationship with Peterson, Bick maintained, "We are friends now."[107]

With a commitment to build a convention center complex, and with public concern about the project assuaged, officials moved quickly to tie up the loose ends for National Harbor. After serving as county executive for eight years, Wayne Curry completed his final term in 2002. Curry had been the biggest cheerleader for National Harbor and the value it offered to the county's growing African American middle class. His successor, Jack Johnson, also supported National Harbor but focused more of his energies on improving schools and enhancing public safety.[108] In 2004, the Prince George's County Council, with a long-standing Democratic majority that was also strongly pro-development, took two major steps to bring the Gaylord project to fruition and kick-start National Harbor. The first was to include the Gaylord complex in a special tax district to reduce the facility's tax burden. The second was to issue $160 million in bonds to pay for road and sewer infrastructure, which was nearly $40 million higher than Curry's initial offer.[109] Both measures paid off.

In early December 2004, the Gaylord organization broke ground for the National Resort and Convention Center at National Harbor. The ceremony featured a who's who of Maryland politics including Governor Robert Ehrlich, two U.S. senators and a representative, the current county executive Jack Johnson, and Wayne Curry. This assemblage of supporters affirmed National Harbor as a critical step for enhancing the tax base of Prince George's, improving the image of the county, and increasing shopping and entertainment opportunities for residents.[110]

Successes and Challenges

As the Gaylord complex was built, it began to fulfill its economic promise. Less than a year after its ground breaking, the county council approved a request from Peterson to add 2,500 condominiums and townhouses to National Harbor, where no residential component had existed previously. Peterson made the request to provide regular traffic for his project's retail outlets and to capitalize on local demand for upscale housing.[111] This suggested that while tourism could be a prominent engine for economic development, local demand remained essential for ironing out the seasonal unevenness associated with tourism.[112]

The Gaylord center also began to establish a niche for all-inclusive conference and resort facilities, which no single property in Washington could offer.
Seventeen months after its ground breaking and before it even opened, it took
three conventions from Washington's largest hotel. In April 2008, the facility opened. With two thousand guest rooms, an eighteen-story atrium, and
nearly five hundred thousand square feet of function space, Prince George's
had the largest convention center complex on the eastern seaboard.[113] Prior
commitments from five hotel chains added another one thousand rooms and
time-shares to those in the Gaylord complex.[114]

Despite widespread fanfare, National Harbor has experienced significant
limitations because of its lack of mass transit. Although a Metrobus line, private water taxis, and a shuttle bus provided access to some visitors, the great
majority arrived by automobile. Even after the widening of the Woodrow Wilson Bridge, the construction of interstate highway ramps to National Harbor,
and improvements to local roads, traffic congestion could be considerable. A
2011 charity race became a public relations nightmare when traffic jams and
poor planning for parking delayed an event for twenty thousand participants.
National Harbor was also less competitive in attracting federal agencies to
lease office space because it did not have reliable public transportation, which
federal agencies had to grant preference to in making location decisions.[115]

The most significant environmental issue to date has been a sewage overflow. In early 2008, more than seven million gallons of sewage overflowed
into Broad Creek, located fifteen miles south of Washington, D.C. Wastewater treatment engineers with the Washington Suburban Sanitary Commission attributed the overflow to a series of bad storms and a power outage
at a substation at National Harbor. The EPA, however, had already found
inadequate the agency's plans for preventing sewage spills. While residents
of nearby Fort Washington were obviously bothered about the overflow, they
did not see the incident as an indictment of National Harbor but instead a
temporary setback. No other significant environmental issues have yet mate-
rialized, although the long-term impact of intensive development on the
Potomac may take years or even decades to emerge.[116]

The first few years were lean times for National Harbor as a national,
indeed global, recession hit the construction industry hard, creating a conservative investment climate. Getting financing for condominiums and
townhouses was particularly difficult, while plans for retail chains, upscale
restaurants, and a mini-Disney resort dissolved. Peterson reported losing
more than $10 million on the project between 2008 and 2012.[117] While the

Gaylord complex became a major employer, the recession curbed convention tourism throughout the United States, which required businesses at National Harbor to rely more on local traffic. The decision to invest a quarter of a billion dollars in public funds to attract the Gaylord complex now seemed shortsighted. In the rush to support large-scale development, officials and residents had not only shortchanged the environmental impact of National Harbor but also chosen a project geared to tourists rather than local communities. Wayne Curry, perhaps the biggest enthusiast for National Harbor, had a more tempered assessment by 2012: "It could still be an extraordinary commercial location with its entertainment and hotels. . . . I think it still has that promise but it's changed quite a bit."[118]

As the national recession wore on, many states and communities pursued licensed gambling, a highly controversial political subject, as a source of tax revenue and jobs. Three states neighboring Maryland—Pennsylvania, West Virginia, and Delaware—were among those that bet on gambling, earning over $2.1 billion in combined tax revenue in 2012.[119] Maryland joined its mid-Atlantic peers as voters approved three casinos, the first of which opened in 2010. Two years later, voters approved six new casino licenses, which were distributed quickly. At the beginning of 2014, state officials awarded Prince George's the final casino license. Now, it was up to local officials and the public to decide whether they wanted a casino.

Discussions about the prospect of having a casino at National Harbor had come up early on but now assumed renewed interest. Early in the century, Milt Peterson disavowed gambling at National Harbor after Glendening had come out in opposition. His successor, Republican Robert Ehrlich Jr., supported a large casino at National Harbor, as did a number of Republican state officials and Congressman Albert R. Wynn, a Democrat, all of whom cited the much needed tax revenue for the county's public school system. Donna Edwards, who co-led the Campaign to Reinvest in the Heart of Oxon Hill, opposed gambling: "It jeopardizes the kind of community and county that we want to be."[120] As the views of the political establishment in Maryland changed, so too did Peterson's view. Peterson had donated thousands of dollars to state and local lawmakers for their campaigns, including nearly $26,000 to Wynn by 2003.[121]

As the recession wore on, county officials escalated their pursuit of gambling. County executive Rushern L. Baker III and Milt Peterson agreed that a facility that combined slots with table games would be a good fit for National Harbor's tourist-driven profile and a boon for tax coffers. Peterson then signed with MGM Resorts International to launch a public campaign to generate support for a casino.[122] Elected county officials, who had opposed gambling earlier in the century, were now supportive. The proposal encountered some opposition, primarily from the Indian Head Highway Area Action Council, which promised to "fight it tooth and nail," and Donna Edwards, whose defeat of eight-term congressman Wynn in the 2008 Democratic primary paved the way for victory in a special election after Wynn vacated his seat.[123]

In 2014, the Prince George's County Council rushed headlong into evaluating a proposal from MGM for a casino on the northern parcel of National Harbor. Baker expedited the planning process, citing the four thousand jobs and $40-45 million in projected annual tax revenue the county would receive as major imperatives for approving the casino. Residents and environmentalists aired familiar concerns about the moral dilemmas of gambling and traffic congestion.[124]

On July 21, however, the county council voted eight to one to approve the MGM casino. Council members were enthusiastic about the prospects. "We are ... on the precipice of a substantial step forward in economic development," council chair Mel Franklin remarked. His colleague Obie Patterson, who represented Oxon Hill, had his reservations assuaged. The approval of a casino doubled down on support for using tourism as a way to bring tax revenue, upscale shopping, and leisure opportunities to Prince George's growing middle-class population. It also underscored the ongoing challenges the county faced in attracting commercial development outside of tourism that provided not only tax revenue but also opportunities for a wide swath of its residents.[125]

Today, much of National Harbor's waterfront parcel has been developed. Over forty retail shops and galleries, thirty dining and entertainment options, and a Tanger Outlets location with over eighty-five stores are open for business. Four sightseeing cruise operators and seven boat charters were available to take visitors for tours and entertainment along the waterfront. The venues at National Harbor hosted dozens of regular and special events each year. More recently, commissioned art has been added as well as a 180-foot Ferris wheel that offers riders panoramic views of the Washington skyline. The casino opened in December 2016 with 3,300 slot machines, 140 gambling tables, and a 308-room hotel, along with restaurants, shopping, and a 3,000-seat concert venue.[126]

With the construction of National Harbor, Prince George's finally had a landmark upscale commercial development along its Potomac waterfront after more than a quarter century. For many, the project culminated a

Figure 9. Panorama of National Harbor. Source: MamaGeek, Wikimedia Commons.

long-term effort to improve commercial opportunities for county residents, generate tax revenue to enhance public services, and change the image of Prince George's in the eyes of outsiders. While activists from the Indian Head Highway Area Action Council and the Campaign to Reinvest in the Heart of Oxon Hill—particularly Bonnie Bick and Donna Edwards—could mitigate the impact of National Harbor on the environment, local businesses, and residents' broader quality of life, their voices were muted. Instead, local officials such as Wayne Curry, a broad swath of county residents, and environmental justice advocates including Norris McDonald positioned environmental concerns as less important to the common good than satisfying the material interests of residents.

The case of Smoot Bay revealed how local decision making was entangled within regional patterns of inequality that created a fundamental divide between suburban development and environmental protection in metropolitan America. As Greater Washington expanded, residents, jobs, and investment moved farther out, leaving inner suburbs struggling to attract commercial development that could offset the growing demand for ever more expensive public services. In response, suburban localities offered greater incentives to influence the location of commerce, which reinforced the social inequality of residential settlement. The zealous commitment of local officials and residents to upscale commercial development in a county starved for it quashed environmental concerns about the development of Smoot Bay. Even activists like Bonnie Bick did not oppose National Harbor entirely so much as seek to mitigate its impact. The case of Smoot Bay drew into sharp relief how environmental attitudes and political decision making were dependent first and foremost on contextual factors such as the existing state of development and, only later, the availability of policies and tools to support environmental protection.

The lack of economic development geared to the middle and upper classes in Prince George's—significantly influenced by the racial diversity of the county—hampered local commitments to robust environmental protection. The story was quite different in neighboring Montgomery County, which was a bastion of the white middle class in Metropolitan Washington and benefited from the presence of many white-collar employers as well as upscale retail opportunities. Because the county did not face the trouble of attracting economic development that Prince George's did, public officials were willing and able to use progressive land use planning and extensive regulations in order to promote compact development. Even so, a single county could not fully deflect the growth pressures that operated in a large metropolitan region.

At the same time, sprawling development patterns in metropolitan Washington sparked an ongoing demand for major highways that proponents of smarter growth argued could only be stopped through a commitment to compact growth organized around mass transit. The Intercounty Connector, proposed to connect Montgomery and Prince George's Counties, sparked a long-standing debate about the need for a new highway to alleviate existing traffic congestion and stimulate development, versus the likelihood that it would exacerbate sprawl. Compared to the postwar era, the late twentieth century offered grassroots activists far more opportunities to mitigate the environmental impact of a highway, particularly in a county where residents had a comparatively high level of environmental interest and public officials were committed to coordinating transportation and land use planning. As the debate wore on, however, political and public support persisted for highways as panaceas for the existing woes of growth and conduits for future prosperity.

CHAPTER 4

The Road to Sprawl

The growth of modern metropolitan America has been inextricably tied to highway construction. Even with the Metro mass transit system, highways still structured much of Greater Washington's growth.[1] Indeed, just as the last Metro station from the initial plan was opened in the early 1990s, the Washington area began to experience exurban sprawl. As traffic congestion, environmental degradation, and the loss of open space worsened, local environmentalists organized in support of compact growth in order "to permanently reduce our traffic problems, and save what's left of our shrinking farmland and ecological treasures.[2] Expanding mass transit and concentrating development around it was the linchpin of the smart growth movement that began in the 1990s, but this vision had far deeper roots in earlier anti-highway efforts.

One such effort was in opposition to the Intercounty Connector (ICC). Toward the end of the 1970s, the Maryland State Highway Administration proposed the ICC to accommodate existing and future growth in Montgomery and Prince George's Counties. Over the next quarter century, the region's stakeholders intensely debated whether it would alleviate traffic congestion and promote economic growth, or whether it would catalyze sprawl into the region's wedges of open space and worsen mobility. As rampant growth reached a fever pitch during the 1990s, the governor stopped the project because of its environmental and fiscal costs. Shortly thereafter, however, a political shift at the state and local levels, worsening traffic congestion, and federal assistance to streamline the environmental review process brought the project back to life.

The case of the ICC reveals the nascent smart growth movement in action as environmentalists lambasted the faulty logic of building one's way out of congestion without modifying land use policies to concentrate development.

The project established the foundation for a more context-sensitive approach to transportation planning in Greater Washington through environmental policy making, support for multimodal urban transportation, and legal and political mandates for greater public participation and decision making at the local level.[3] Civic and environmental activists used these innovations to challenge sprawl and pollution as well as to support neighborhood conservation and protection of ecologically sensitive land.[4] The case of the ICC demonstrated more broadly how the struggle over transportation planning was the foundation for managing the environmental and fiscal impact of metropolitan growth during the late twentieth century.

Environmentalists struggled to gain the upper hand against a large and diverse coalition of residents, officials, and organized interests who saw building more roads as the only solution to the traffic woes and growth imperative of metropolitan America. As federal policies devolved responsibility for regional transportation planning, local and state support for highways thwarted concerns about environmental protection. Officials were effective at managing public participation in a way that allowed numerous, piecemeal modifications to limit a project's impact without undermining it as a whole. This was possible because the federal environmental review process that governed large regional projects like highways was driven by procedural concerns rather than substantive outcomes or defined thresholds of unacceptable harm.[5] As a result, the decision-making process undermined the efficacy of public opposition to highway construction.[6] Instead, the default approach to regional mobility was based around the automobile, which reinforced scattered land use by thwarting the use of transportation to promote compact growth.

Origins of a Highway

Greater Washington experienced a flurry of highway building in the postwar era that fostered rapid suburbanization. Passage of the Interstate Highway Act of 1956 culminated a decade during which federally subsidized suburban homeownership, auto-based mobility, and the formation of socially homogenous communities became inextricably tied to the American dream. Urban planners with the NCPC recognized this when they issued a *Comprehensive Plan for the National Capital and Its Environs* in 1950. Their plan included several radial highways to connect Washington with its suburbs, which would be tied together by beltways to circulate traffic around the region. The largest of those, known as the Capital Beltway, opened in 1964. State highway officials thought that construction could keep pace with mounting traffic loads and had little political incentive to develop highways that were sensitive to community or environmental concerns.[7] Indeed, the disconnect between land use planning, which operated at the local level, and transportation planning and funding, which operated at the state and federal levels, was a major culprit in discouraging compact growth. Instead, suburban communities depended on more and wider highways as a panacea for enhancing mobility.

By the early 1960s, the liabilities of highway-induced sprawl had become more apparent to public officials and their constituents. Reflecting their tendency to get involved in backyard issues, Congress passed the National Capital Transportation Act of 1960. The policy offered support for a "balanced solution" of highways and mass transit to address the region's transportation needs, which the region's planning organizations, including the NCPC, adopted.[8] Planners in Montgomery and Prince George's bolstered support for mass transit with passage of the wedges and corridors plan of 1964 that called for directing growth to existing areas, including through mass transit, while leaving wedges of open space free from development.[9]

As the suburbs rapidly built highways, grassroots activists in Washington, D.C., waged one of the most intense campaigns against freeway construction in postwar America.[10] Numerous civic groups, organized under the umbrella of the Emergency Committee on the Transportation Crisis, argued that freeways would destroy poor and working-class communities of color to cater to the interests of mostly white, middle-class suburban commuters.[11] The push for mass transit was complicated by the fact that the nation's capital lacked home rule. Instead, Congress drove local politics, and perhaps no one was as influential in doing so as William Natcher. A conservative Democrat from Kentucky and chair of the District of Columbia House Appropriations subcommittee, Natcher blocked congressional funding for the Metro system for years as he insisted that the region start building a series of major highways. Activists in the Washington area, however, harnessed grassroots demonstrations, testified at public hearings, and filed lawsuits to prevent construction of several freeways.[12]

As the environmental, fiscal, and social impact of highways became more apparent, public policy evolved to offer support for mass transit. Revisions to the national Highway Act in 1973, for example, allowed urban areas to reallocate funding for highways to subways, but the legislation excluded Washington at the behest of Congressman Natcher and his colleagues on the D.C. Appropriations Subcommittee.[13] That same year, the nation's capital secured home rule, which gave the city more control over its finances and governance. The city's activists and public officials used this new authority to keep up the pressure for Congress to hear their calls for greater autonomy. In 1976, congressional Democrats persuaded Natcher to release funds for the Metro system, but only after the secretary of the national Department of Transportation offered to fund the entire system.[14] As Metro was built over the next two decades, it offered new opportunities to rein in sprawl and promote more compact development, but communities varied in their willingness to take advantage.

Growth was the dominant political issue in Greater Washington during the 1970s, thanks to rising taxes to fund services, unmet growth predictions, environmental concerns, and the construction of the Metro. These issues, along with an energy crisis that dramatically cut highway tax revenue, undermined suburban interests in highway construction. As a result, Maryland and Virginia officials nixed plans dating back to the 1950s for an "outer beltway" to connect suburban highway five to ten miles outside of the Capital Beltway.[15] While Maryland agencies also eliminated plans for most of other proposed highways, nearly all of Virginia's highway mileage had already been built or would be completed.[16]

The demise of the outer beltway and the region's focus on compact growth was short-lived. Development regulations in Montgomery had environmental and fiscal benefits, but they also inadvertently increased residential property taxes to compensate for the lack of additional commercial development. Traffic congestion also worsened as Metro stations had yet to be built in the suburbs.[17] In 1979, state highway officials revived a twenty-two-mile portion of the outer beltway and rebranded it as the ICC while adding a ten-mile spur road called the Rockville Facility. State officials sought federal funds for the highway, which obliged them to assess the highway's environmental impact and, if necessary, develop an environmental impact statement for approval by federal agencies and other stakeholders. Over the next three years, the State Highway Administration held public hearings on the project.[18]

The highway administration released its first report on the ICC and Rockville Facility in early 1980 after holding six days of workshops. The report laid out the basic contours of an intense debate for the next three decades. While most participants supported some version of the highway, there was a vocal minority of opposition. Many participants were concerned that a large highway would increase traffic congestion and promote sprawl. "'I don't think we should

Figure 10. The Intercounty Connector planning corridor. Source: Federal Highway Administration (FHWA), Maryland Division.

spend any more money on building big highways here," one resident explained. "It will just flood the communities with cars and trucks."[19] The legacy of postwar freeways was clearly visible in such comments, as was the realization that a major east-west highway like the ICC and Rockville Facility would disrupt the wedges and corridors that concentrated development along a north-south axis. The ongoing construction of the Metro also bolstered support for mass transit as an alternative or complement to the highway, although the system did not serve the same area. Finally, workshop attendees expressed concerns, bolstered by the Clean Air Act of 1970, about air pollution associated with building a highway in an area far removed from existing development.[20]

In a March 1981 report, the State Highway Administration revised the highway proposal in light of additional public feedback. First, the maximum width of the ICC was reduced from eight to six lanes and that of the Rockville Facility from six to four. Second, state officials endorsed light rail along parts of the highways. Third, they supported including recreational trails and other parklike elements along the highways.[21] While these revisions suggested state officials were responsive to public concerns, none of the measures undermined the highway's intent or legitimacy.

Public skepticism of the project grew as state officials continued to hold meetings and issue studies supporting the project. Sammie Young, a former military man and administrator with the Federal Drug Administration who lived in Silver Spring, reportedly attended hundreds of public hearings and civic meetings about the outer beltway and later ICC. Even as someone accustomed to accepting authority, Young "got angry" at the "highway system" that supported ever-more highways when there were existing roads that could be widened instead.[22] His frustration over what he felt was a rigged plan to build the ICC persisted for years.

Young served on a citizens advisory committee to the Montgomery County Council that concluded that the ICC was unnecessary. "A legitimate case has not been made for (these disruptive) highway plans," Young insisted."[23] Frank Vrataric, another opponent of ICC on the committee, was an inaugural founder of the Coalition on Sensible Transportation, created the same year. The local ad hoc group was formed to oppose the imperative for building the highway to alleviate traffic congestion and to advocate instead for road improvements and mass transit instead. Vrataric, an electrical engineer who lived in the working-class community of Wheaton, was active in the ICC debate into the late 1990s. He regularly criticized the highway administration's justifications for the highway, arguing that officials "made a mockery of the environmental impact process, of public hearings and sound traffic planning'" by pushing ahead with an unwanted and unnecessary project.[24] Montgomery county council members, however, disregarded the findings of the advisory committee. Their counterparts in Prince George's, on the other hand, dropped the ICC from local plans, likely out of concern that the highway would siphon off development to Montgomery, which helped explain why the latter continued to support it.

The state highway department maintained the ICC and Rockville Facility were necessary for easing traffic congestion, keeping pace with projected growth, and not losing out on revenue-generating development to communities in Northern Virginia.[25] In October 1983 it released its draft EIS, and in early December the Montgomery Council approved a twenty-mile version of the ICC between Gaithersburg (in the county) and Laurel (in Prince George's). The Maryland General Assembly, however, later defunded the Rockville Facility after reassessing its need. In the spring of 1984, Maryland's transportation secretary authorized the ICC pending approval of a final EIS. Securing this approval was a far greater challenge than anyone could have imagined, as the ICC became the single most contentious development issue in Greater Washington during the next two decades.[26]

The Debate Heats Up

As the debate over the ICC escalated, its supporters argued that the highway was necessary to alleviate congestion on the Beltway by providing another route for east-west traffic in suburban Maryland. A 1986 study by the Metropolitan Washington Council of Governments—composed of the region's elected leaders—suggested that by 2005, travel on the Beltway would be a minute per mile slower if no new highways were built.[27] Supporters also argued that the ICC would attract revenue from commercial development. "The Intercounty Connector provides vital traffic access between the I-270 employment corridor and the larger Baltimore-Washington development corridor along I-95," the Montgomery planning board insisted. "Without such access, the I-270 Corridor will not attract the necessary jobs to balance the planned residential growth."[28] State highway officials, representatives of the business and development community, and elected state officials such as state representative Carol Petzold argued that future growth would fill in east-west wedges of open space anyhow and that a highway, rather than mass transit, would be the most feasible option to accommodate it.[29]

One of the few politicians who opposed the ICC at the time was state senator Idamae Garrott, who was winding up a storied career as a civic activist and politician. Garrott started out her career as a government and history teacher in the Baltimore public school system. She then moved to Montgomery, where she helped establish a local chapter of the League of Women Voters in 1952 and was active in the organization over the next fifteen years. Garrott used her civic background as a springboard into politics. From 1966 to 1974, she served on the Montgomery County Council, including a term as council president, during which she led the implementation of the county's adequate public facilities ordinance. After failed races for county executive and the U.S. Congress, she turned to state politics, winning election to the

Maryland House of Delegates from 1979 to 1987 and later serving two terms as state senator.[30]

Garrott was an energetic liberal who was effective in building coalitions and employing careful analysis to slow the growth-driven machine of politics. She was firmly committed to comprehensive land use planning, environmental protection, and limited development. In a 1983 op-ed, she argued that the highway's east-west routing "with its big promotion of additional sprawl, will cause the General Plan to fly out the window!"[31] Garrott and civic opponents of the ICC understood the value of planning transportation and land use together to protect the environment and local communities from sprawl. She was also the leading state legislator responsible for eliminating state funding for the Rockville Facility. Before "smart growth" became a buzzword, Montgomery activists were endorsing one of its key principles.

On May 31, 1988, the Maryland state highway department and the county councils of Montgomery and Prince George's held a joint public hearing on the design of the ICC before a packed house. State highway officials began the proceedings. Neil Pedersen, a career employee who became the resident expert on the ICC, insisted that a highway was needed to address traffic congestion in the two counties. But he placed greater attention on the potential of the ICC to stimulate economic development. "The proposed ICC is a critical component of the Baltimore Washington regional economy," he explained. "As the area emerges as one of the most rapidly growing investment markets in the country, the ICC will provide the necessary link between the two major north south corridors, I-270 and I-95." Maryland highway officials, more so than their counterparts in Virginia, however, were attuned to public concerns about highways. As an example, Pedersen stressed that the new route would have no significant environmental impacts on prime farmland or federally protected endangered species and that the ICC's impact on water quality due to erosion and other pollution could be effectively mitigated.[32]

Representatives from several civic organizations disagreed with Pedersen. They insisted that the highway would worsen traffic congestion by promoting sprawl and would harm parks, wetlands, and recreational areas. This familiar criticism assumed a more strident tone as more residents believed state highway officials had already made up their minds to build the highway. Vrataric argued that the state had withheld information about design proposals and failed to make a draft EIS available for public review in a timely manner.[33] Allen Bender, another member of the 1983 citizens advisory committee, criticized officials for holding a design hearing on the ICC when the final routing had not even been approved.[34] These and other procedural lapses engendered a sentiment that officials were more interested in supporting new development than addressing the impact of the ICC on the environment and local communities.[35] "It is cheered on by the politicians, real estate developers, wealthy land owners, and asphalt tycoons," one resident argued, "who claim it as progress despite the havoc it will wreak on existing residential areas of the County."[36] The hearing was a formative moment for opposition to the ICC as local environmental organizing picked up during the 1990s.

Competing Perspectives on Highways

Throughout Greater Washington, local environmental organizing proliferated in the early 1990s, particularly in response to electoral politics. While grassroots activists had worked locally for years, many environmentalists had focused their attention on national lobbying over the past two decades.[37] As national policy making became more gridlocked and environmental protection devolved to the state and local level, local electoral and environmental politics took on more importance. This was confirmed by the formation of new groups such as the Montgomery County League of Environmental Voters and the Montgomery County Green Democrats, a coalition of elected officials, candidates for office, and residents.[38] These groups were quite successful in helping local and state candidates win their races in the 1990 elections.[39]

As local environmental organizing heated up, Congress established a new transportation agenda to succeed the nearly completed interstate program established under the 1956 Highway Act. Despite the spending of hundreds of billions of dollars over thirty-five years, the nation's highways were decaying by the early 1990s and fostered sprawling patterns of development with traffic congestion and significant air pollution. Passage of the Intermodal Surface Transportation Efficiency Act of 1991 (ISTEA) reinforced the federal government's emphasis on auto-based mobility, devoting three-quarters of funding to highways. It also continued a decade-long trend of giving state and local officials more decision-making authority.[40]

Although ISTEA continued the long-standing tendency to privilege highways over mass transit, it had two significant innovations. The first was a requirement that transportation plans and programs be developed and approved at a regional level by metropolitan planning organizations (MPOs). MPOs had been around for a few decades—the Metropolitan Washington

Council of Governments dated back to the early 1960s—but they had previously been more of a coordinating organization rather than a regulatory
entity. Empowering MPOs offered the opportunity for coordinated transportation planning, but this was not a guarantee of certain outcomes. Indeed,
some regions saw strong regional planning in support of more compact and
equitable growth while others saw a perpetuation of sprawling development,
even as regional organizations exerted more influence.[41] ISTEA also included
expanded requirements for public participation in hearings for regional projects, which grassroots activists used to their advantage to gain political and
public support.[42]

Shortly after the passage of ISTEA, the Metro system was completed in
Greater Washington, one of the few regions to see construction of a mass
transit system during the second half of the twentieth century. Efforts to harness transit, however, varied across the region. Close-in communities and
those with traditions of robust land use planning were the most likely to align
transit with development, while highways dominated places where unmitigated development had taken hold.[43]

State officials relaunched the planning process for the ICC at a time when
highway projects dominated transportation planning but public concern
about their environmental impact was heightened. The Maryland Department of Transportation (DOT) began a three-year study that brought together
elected officials and planners in Montgomery and Prince George's and featured numerous meetings, television programs, and online bulletin boards and
other forums.[44] The state transportation secretary assured the public that this
more collaborative approach would yield "'a community-driven decision.'"[45]

State highway officials and elected leaders continued to support the ICC
as the best way to alleviate traffic congestion and compete for economic
development in the region.[46] Critics countered that the highway would induce
sprawl, harm natural resources, and only generate more traffic problems in
the future.[47] New groups such as ICC-SCAR (Save Communities Against This
Route) and STIR (Stop That Infernal Road!) expressed growing indignation
about political support for the highway. ICC opponents also began to do their
own research to refute the information provided in official reports. A 1996
consultant's study for a citizen-led "ICC Study Group," for example, disagreed
with findings that the ICC would improve traffic flow on local roads.[48] This
research coincided with recent national findings that travel forecasting procedures had overestimated the need for highways for decades while under-
estimating the negative impact of highways on air quality.[49] While some ICC

opponents challenged the integrity of state highway officials, most focused on advocating for road and intersection improvements on local roads and the Beltway as well as adding mass transit.[50] The formation of the Coalition for Smarter Growth in 1997, the first organization of its kind in the United States, reflected the heightened emphasis among grassroots activists in coordinating transportation with land use plans to concentrate development.[51]

The debate over the ICC highlighted a rift between elected officials and area residents, who generally supported the highway, and federal environmental agencies, which called for stronger protection measures. In a 1994 letter to the Maryland DOT, one EPA official concluded: "the original transportation corridor [for the ICC] remains unacceptable in light of the large waterway, wetland and parkland impacts. . . . The documentation of need does not warrant this level of destruction."[52] These concerns did not sit well with the state highway department, whose chief retorted: "We're not about to let EPA dismiss 30 to 40 years of local master planning."[53]

The comments above underscored the divergent missions of federal, state, and local officials in managing metropolitan development. Despite decades of national legislation that integrated environmental issues into transportation planning, state transportation officials focused on their traditional areas of expertise—alleviating traffic congestion and promoting economic development—which had earned them deference within the government bureaucracy. When they did address environmental issues, it was primarily at the project level, not the broader policy or planning levels. For these officials, there was no real question of *whether* to build the ICC. Instead, their goal was to figure out how the ICC should look and what environmental mitigation measures were necessary to secure its approval.[54]

As the ICC became tied up in administrative deadlock, its supporters grew tired of delay. One particular critic was Aaron Handler, a member of the Montgomery County Citizens Advisory Committee on the ICC and a homeowner in the town of Olney, which would become more accessible if the highway were built. In a letter to state representative Adrienne Mandel, herself an opponent of the ICC, Handler criticized the environmental review process that allowed residents and environmentalists to use NIMBY (Not in My Back Yard) rhetoric and other tactics to delay a decision. "Did the US Congress and the Maryland State Legislature pass laws to protect our environment to give tools to environmentalists to block highway and road construction? I think not," Handler responded.[55] The Greater Washington Board of Trade, a staunch advocate of highway construction that been silent in the case, now got involved as traffic congestion worsened and opportunities for development abounded in a booming economic climate. In 1996, it commissioned a survey that found two-thirds of voters in the project area favored the highway compared to 13 percent who opposed it.[56]

The prevailing civic and political climate, however, required the highway's supporters to address its environmental impact. "An environmentally sensitive and a community sensitive ICC can be designed and built," Aaron Handler explained. "The days of the large superhighway are long gone."[57] By the late 1990s, the environmental and fiscal costs of several years of rampant growth in Greater Washington had soured political and public interest in the ICC, giving the highway's opposition the upper hand in the debate.

A Groundswell of Opposition

In March 1997, the federal and Maryland highway administrations released a second draft EIS after their first version failed to receive necessary federal approvals. The new report estimated that between 1990 and 2020, the project area and surrounding region would see a 40 percent increase in households and a 43 percent increase in employment, which would produce a 44 percent increase in weekday vehicle trips. It used these estimates to justify the highway as a means to improve regional mobility and connect the I-270 and I-95 corridors to bolster economic development. The draft EIS featured a preferred seventeen-mile master plan alignment from Gaithersburg in Montgomery to U.S. Route 1 in Prince George's as well as several alternate routings, improvements to existing roads, and a no-build option, all required under NEPA and federal transportation policies. It insisted that the ICC could be built in a way to "support [the] social, natural and cultural environmental values of the region." On one hand, the statement acknowledged the influence of federal policies and local activists in pushing officials to seriously consider the impact of highways in the planning process. On the other hand, the draft EIS read like an endorsement for a single version of the ICC and a rationale of why other options would not work.[58]

Among the more vocal backers of the ICC were two former leaders of the Maryland National Capital Park and Planning Commission (M-NCPPC), Gus Bauman and Charles A. Dukes Jr., whose business backgrounds reinforced their support for large-scale, auto-dependent growth. Bauman, who chaired the Montgomery planning board of the commission from 1989 to

1993, had been a litigator for the National Association of Homebuilders and a land use lawyer at a Washington law firm, to which he returned after his tenure on the M-NCPPC. Dukes had built a career in commercial real estate in Prince George's, having chaired the county's planning board in the mid-1980s, and was now the leader of the county chamber of commerce and chair of the ICC Task Force for the Greater Washington Board of Trade. Bauman insisted that not building the ICC would allow traffic congestion to continue to increase on the Beltway and along the I-270 and I-95 corridors and thereby push businesses to locate in other communities with better mobility.[59] Dukes added, "The need for the connector is incontestable."[60] While highlighting issues of traffic congestion and economic development, ICC supporters downplayed how the highway would put pressure on localities to support rapid growth that tended to be less compact than that organized by transit.[61]

The new draft EIS faced widespread criticism from federal environmental agencies. The EPA and the Department of the Interior rejected the preferred project because it would destroy at least 145 acres of parkland, cut across 22 acres of wetlands, take away habitats for 27 species of migratory birds, and overheat streams where brown trout spawned.[62] While concluding that road improvements would not be sufficient to alleviate traffic congestion, they recommended an alternate route with less impact.[63] Maryland environmental agencies, on the other hand, expressed little concern, likely because they faced greater political pressures to support regional economic development than the EPA, which was not financed by or subject to state action and could therefore concentrate fully on environmental protection.[64]

The findings of the draft EIS also sparked sharp criticism among residents. Nearly two-thirds of those who delivered testimony at the first public meeting in Montgomery following the release of the report opposed the project.[65] After nearly a decade, public anger about routing the ICC through Paint Branch, the Washington area's only freshwater stream, was sufficient to convince the state highway department to shift the highway's path to avoid passing through the wetlands. Neil Pedersen, the state highway department's project manager for the ICC, interpreted the decision to require rethinking "the traditional way of approaching highway construction" that focused on the most direct routing and instead build a project that balanced transportation objectives with environmental protection.[66] Although the decision eliminated the preferred route for the ICC, it still left two alternatives that both tracked farther north.[67]

In the fall of 1997, the Montgomery delegation to the Maryland General Assembly held a public hearing on the ICC. Among those in attendance was Lois Sherman, who represented the Montgomery ICC Coalition, a group of five dozen local civic, environmental, and taxpayer watchdog groups. Sherman testified that much of the county's transportation problems were due to inadequate regulations on growth and development. She also cited evidence from the draft EIS in arguing that the ICC would do more harm than good, as 60 percent of affected intersections would experience worsened conditions if the highway were built.[68] Representatives from other groups agreed that the ICC would be a failure and instead advocated policies that would eliminate sprawling development and reduce dependence on automobiles.[69]

In the face of public pressure, the Montgomery County Council voted to reverse its long-standing support for the ICC. The council told state officials that it preferred a program of improvements to existing roads and mass transit to protect their constituents from a $1 billion highway that would likely not alleviate traffic congestion but instead induce sprawl. While Democrats had by now developed a reputation as the "environmental party," Nancy Dacek, a moderate Republican, joined her Democratic colleagues in opposing the highway because of its potential to create sprawl in the county's well-known Agricultural Reserve.[70]

For years, environmentalists had argued that highways induced sprawl, but it was only around the turn of the century that emerging research on the relationship between population growth and vehicle mileage in the Washington area confirmed this association.[71] Between 1982 and 1996, the population of Greater Washington grew by 28 percent while commuters' mileage on major roads increased 78 percent, both slightly higher than the national average.[72] The increase in vehicle miles traveled was associated with the ongoing decentralization of the region through highway building.[73] Despite broad acceptance of the idea that highways were vital to growth, some research suggested that metropolitan areas with lower rates of vehicle miles traveled actually featured "a larger amount of expected growth."[74] A study of Montgomery confirmed that county officials could accommodate more growth by clustering development near mass transit rather than building more roads.[75]

As the impact of sprawl became more serious, public interest in a new model for transportation planning grew. Local writer and environmentalist Mike Tidwell offered a frank assessment of the perils of auto-based growth: "To permanently reduce our traffic problems, and save what's left of our shrinking farmland and ecological treasures," he argued, "we must toss out our current development orientation . . . an orientation that forces us to drive, drive, drive."[76]

Tidwell's comments touched on the impetus for smart growth, which inspired the passage of Maryland's Smart Growth and Neighborhood Conservation initiative in 1997. While this policy, championed by former Prince George's county executive and now governor Parris Glendening, offered a model of more sustainable development compared to conventional suburbanization, its ability to curb highway construction proved quite limited in light of the influential role of national policies.[77] Discussions near the end of the century about federal transportation policy, for example, failed to alter prevailing practices that promoted sprawl, undercut environmental protection, and limited public participation in transportation planning. Moreover, the successor to ISTEA actually gave state highway departments more authority to determine transportation priorities, undermining an earlier commitment to regional planning.[78]

Many ICC opponents increasingly became convinced that the project's continued existence was a product of a rigged political system.[79] Edward Abramic was among those who lambasted a "pro-highway coalition" of "federal and state highway departments, congressional leaders, developers and businesses [who] have created their own institution [that] plows along of its own momentum, always for the singular purpose of 'relieving congestion.'"[80] Another environmentalist argued the state highway administration made a mockery of public involvement by engaging in "half-truths, obscuration of facts, denial of public access, and repeated arm-twisting."[81] Both claims underscored the distrust many environmentalists had of public officials, who they believed were often biased supporters of business and development interests.[82]

The Death and Life of the ICC

Rising public opposition to the ICC had persuaded many elected officials to reconsider their support for the highway. By spring 1999, most of the Prince George's and Montgomery county councils opposed the project, although their county executives—Wayne Curry and Douglas Duncan—still supported the ICC. The dominance on both councils of environmentally conscious Democrats, matched against growth-oriented top leaders who were also Democrats, offered an intriguing wrinkle in the growing partisanship associated with environmental issues over the past two decades.[83]

Following passage of Maryland's landmark smart growth legislation, Glendening established a Transportation Solutions Group in February 1999 to consider alternatives for resolving regional mobility in suburban Maryland. In June, the group endorsed the highway but recommended cutting it from six lanes to four and turning it into a toll road to reduce its fiscal costs, now over $1 billion. Three months later, Glendening rejected their recommendation and abandoned the ICC altogether. He blasted the project as "an environmental disaster" and proposed instead a program of road widenings and intersection improvements.[84]

Glendening's reversal was a dramatic event in a long struggle and provoked strong reactions. His announcement vindicated ICC opponents, who had insisted public support for the highway was limited. A survey several months earlier, for example, confirmed that 52 percent of Montgomery voters felt the best way to address local mobility issues was to make road improvements, while 66 percent also supported adding a Metrorail line.[85]

For ICC supporters, the decision was a rebuke of decades of planning to alleviate traffic congestion and advance a new wave of economic development. Douglas Duncan called it "a real slap in the face to the people who've been stuck in traffic for years."[86] He also worried about the fate of over thirty-two million square feet of development in various stages of planning and construction that might be lost if the ICC were not built.[87] State legislators, who tended to focus more on tax revenue from development than its local impact, spoke out against the decision. State Senate president Thomas V. Mike Miller and House speaker Casper R. Taylor Jr. argued that the ICC was not just a local issue but affected the entire state and that Montgomery, as a recipient of state funds, should consider the impact of the decision to abandon the ICC. The fact that Miller and Taylor represented jurisdictions— Prince George's County and Alleghany County in Western Maryland— thirsting for economic growth surely factored into their views.[88] Leaders of the Greater Washington Board of Trade agreed that disowning the ICC would harm the region.[89]

In 2000, state lawmakers struck a deal with the Montgomery Council to avoid a potentially nasty political fight over the disposition of land for the recently defunct ICC. The agreement required the county not to sell off the land, in exchange for which state lawmakers dropped legislation to bar the county from doing so.[90] The agreement deferred a decision on the ICC to the next council, which would be elected in 2002 along with a new governor as Glendening completed his final term in office.

As election season approached, traffic congestion displaced curbing growth as the central issue in local and state elections. There were several reasons for this. The first was the general economic decline after September 11, 2001, which made states and localities anxious to attract development.[91] The more crucial reason was that traffic conditions had worsened because of the rapid and scattered growth of the previous decade. In Montgomery, for example, the increase in total new lane miles (10 percent) and new state lane miles (7.6 percent) had not keep up with the growth in jobs (13 percent), population (15 percent), or vehicle mileage (21 percent).[92] With prospects for construction of a mass transit line marginal at best, many residents concluded that adding a highway would draw growth away from existing communities with traffic woes.[93] This logic, however, ignored the sprawling development that a new highway would create over the long term.

Voters pushed candidates to take strong positions on how to resolve traffic congestion. Incumbent county executive Douglas Duncan capitalized on voter frustration—one poll found that three-quarters of residents felt congestion to be a "major problem" or "crisis"—in offering a plan called "Go Montgomery!" that included a program of new roads to build the county's way out of its traffic woes, the centerpiece of which was the ICC. His counterpart on the county council, Blair Ewing, had been elected in 1998 on a slow-growth platform and argued "with more roads there will be more cars and more sprawl, and in three years, the roads will fill up and we'll be stuck again."[94] Special interest groups formed rapidly on each side, with Citizens for Quality Living forming a coalition of local and regional business interests in support of Duncan and like-minded candidates, and Neighbors for a Better Montgomery supporting Ewing and other slow-growth and environmentally minded candidates.

Duncan ran a vigorous campaign that resonated with voter sentiment not only in his race but across the state. Duncan's reelection team effectively shifted public conversation from slowing growth to congestion and the need to build roads by offering a massive $1 billion transportation plan, forming a coalition of like-minded candidates known as the End Gridlock team, and partnering with the business and development community.[95] Duncan helped oust Blair Ewing in the primaries by supporting a negative ad campaign that one former council member described as "relentless—day after day, after day—and it was hard to counteract and respond quickly."[96] Nancy Dacek, a moderate Republican who also opposed the ICC, met a similar fate in the general election.[97] Duncan was reelected to an unprecedented third term in 2002, winning 77 percent of the vote and playing a critical role in unseating a Democratic-majority council that opposed the ICC in favor of a Republican majority that supported it.[98]

The partisan shift in Montgomery was felt across the state as the election of Robert L. Ehrlich Jr. allowed Republicans to claim the governor's seat for the first time since the late 1960s. This coalition of partisan, pro-development leaders gave ICC advocates new hopes for the project's approval while serving as a big blow to ICC opponents.[99] The latter's worries came true when the Republican county council and Democrat Doug Duncan issued a joint resolution to revive the ICC in December 2002.

Even as public sentiment about the ICC shifted, the project still needed an approved final EIS for construction to begin. Just as a partisan shift at the state and local levels renewed political interest in the ICC, changes at the federal level helped to revive the project. In September 2002, President George W. Bush issued an executive order that established an interagency task force to solicit projects of regional or national significance that included innovative elements of environmental stewardship; in exchange, the task force would streamline the federal environmental review process.[100] The secretary of the national DOT selected the ICC in early 2003 after requests from Ehrlich and Duncan. A spokesman insisted that the expedited process would not curtail scrutiny of the project but instead reduce bureaucratic delays.[101]

One final political change that smoothed the way the ICC was Ehrlich's appointment of Neil Pedersen as Maryland's new state highway administrator. Pedersen not only had twenty years of experience as a state highway official but also had been the agency's longtime project manager for the ICC. Ehrlich cited both factors for making Pederson "uniquely qualified to lead our efforts to build the Intercounty Connector and address other critical road and congestion issues around the state."[102]

With pro-growth Republican leadership at all levels of government, a new environmental study of the ICC began in June 2003. There were twenty-one federal, state, regional, and local agencies involved, spanning the fields of transportation, environmental protection, and land use planning. More hearings, meetings, and workshops were held to solicit the public's input for a third EIS. In the first year, some two thousand residents attended public hearings or workshops. Over the next couple of years, Montgomery and Prince George's held four more hearings that were attended by nearly 1,900 people, with hundreds more providing testimony.[103] Compared to the late 1990s, the tenor of public conversations was far more focused on alleviating traffic congestion in the short term through highway construction than ensuring compact growth with a smaller environmental footprint over the long term.

The ICC now moved swiftly through the environmental review process. The Metropolitan Washington Council of Governments endorsed the highway after verifying it met federal air quality standards. From late 2004 through early 2006, the EIS moved through the rest of the approval process. Nearly four thousand comment letters from the public were submitted to government agencies after release of a new draft EIS.[104] Most supported the highway.

Only two and a half years after a third attempt to secure approval for an EIS had begun, the Federal Highway Administration (FHWA) and state transportation agencies signed off on it in January 2006.[105] The final EIS offered a broad view of the project's purpose, which was "to increase community mobility and safety; to facilitate the movement of goods and people to and from economic centers; to provide cost-effective transportation infrastructure to serve existing and future development patterns reflecting local land use planning objectives; to help restore the natural, human, and cultural environments from past development impacts in the project area; and to advance homeland security [assisting with evacuation and emergency vehicle access]."[106]

While the justification for the ICC was familiar, measures to mitigate its impact on the environment and local communities were far more ambitious than when it was first proposed. These took two basic forms. The first considered not only of the direct impact of the ICC but also indirect and cumulative impacts that emerged when added to past, present, and future activities.[107] The second required a spectrum of approaches for mitigating its environmental impact.[108] The ICC included sixty-three environmental stewardship activities to limit the impact of the project as well as remediate previous development.[109]

After publication of the final EIS, residents continued to present their views on the ICC in preparation for a final determination of the project's fate. Nearly eight hundred letters were sent to federal and state transportation agencies in the first few months of 2006. Many supported the project, with a number saying the ICC was "long overdue" and that people were frustrated with traffic congestion. Critics on the other hand argued that the project's impact had been marginalized and that the planning process was "crafted to produce a preordained outcome" that excluded "several better-performing and less environmentally harmful alternatives." Such comments struck a familiar chord about the influence of the growth imperative in driving support for the ICC.[110] The public responses to the final EIS, however, suggested that more people supported the ICC now than ever before, or at least that its supporters were more vocal than its detractors. Political support was now high and coordinated across all levels of government.[111]

As government agencies signed off on the final EIS, financing the growing costs of the ICC became a political challenge. In 1997, the estimated cost of the highway was $1 billion, but by 2005, it had ballooned to $2.2 billion. The traditional way of financing large-scale highways involved issuing bonds that were paid back with revenue from federal and state taxes on the purchase of gas. But the unpopularity of raising the tax, growing fuel efficiency, and the expensiveness of environmental safeguards for other highways created a shortfall. Maryland's transportation secretary recommended converting the highway into a distance-based toll road and using future revenue to pay back nearly the entire cost of the highway. In testimony to the state legislature, he reasserted the economic benefits of the ICC and cited costs of nearly $100 million in inflation for every year the project was delayed. Critics argued that committing a large percentage of federal transportation aid for a single highway was excessive given other issues in the state. Nonetheless, the unpopularity of raising taxes to finance the project led the General Assembly to endorse the toll plan and, moreover, committed to raising tolls on roads, bridges, and tunnels throughout the state if necessary to pay back the bonds and loans.[112]

The FHWA granted the last approval needed to build the ICC in May 2006. The final project was an eighteen-mile toll highway accessible through eight interchanges. It was six lanes wide in most places, extending from I-370/I-270 near the Shady Grove Metrorail station in Montgomery to US-1 between Beltsville and Laurel in Prince George's. The roads that connected to the ICC received funds for improvements to accommodate the new highway and increases in traffic flow. The project also included future commitments for express bus service and two Park-and-Ride lots for commuters.[113]

The approved proposal attempted to integrate the ICC into the surrounding area. The Federal Highway Administration used sweeping language to demonstrate its commitment and that of state transportation agencies to "balancing the need for safe and efficient transportation with national, state, and local environmental protection goals." This came with $370 million in funding for over one hundred environmental projects to mitigate the impact of the highway, repair the damage it would cause, and remediate the impact of past growth and development in the project area. The projects addressed a

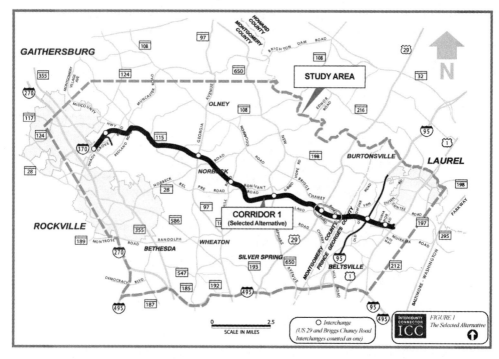

Figure 11. The Intercounty Connector. Source: FHWA.

wide range of environmental objectives including stream restoration, water quality improvements, and storm-water management; passages to protect fish and wildlife as well as special protection areas for a diverse range of species; and new parkland and pedestrian and bicycle routes.[114]

These safeguards suggested that government agencies were far more responsive in recent years to the concerns of civic activists than before 1970, when technical questions of traffic service and land accessibility for development prevailed. Environmental organizations tried to use the federal courts to argue that the decision-making process for the ICC was flawed. But a U.S. District Court judge rejected their claim, ruling that the project had offered a "seemingly open and deliberative process" that did not violate federal policies for public participation.[115]

With approval of the ICC final, the work of completing land acquisition and beginning construction began. Ground breaking for the project took place in May 2006 with Robert Ehrlich, Doug Duncan, and many other ICC supporters in attendance. The fierce campaign season four years earlier had kicked up support of the project to around 60 percent, where it now remained. The few protestors who attended the event continued to argue against the project's purported ability to alleviate traffic congestion and maintained that the toll prices would have to be set high to help finance the cost of the highway. "They should have had a manure fork out there," hissed Greg Smith, a longtime opponent.[116]

The ICC was built in five stages. In February 2011, the first portion opened to traffic. Two months later, the developers of the massive mixed-use Konterra project, which had been in the planning phases for nearly thirty years, reached an agreement with state and county officials to donate 240 acres of land as right-of-way for the final portion of ICC between I-95 and US-1 in Prince George's. In exchange, the state of Maryland paid $30 million toward the cost of extending the ICC to reach Konterra. By the summer of 2012, three of the five portions of the ICC were open to traffic, totaling seventeen of its eighteen miles and connecting the I-270 and I-95 corridors. The final portion from I-95 to US-1 opened in November 2014.[117]

Two and a half years after the first part of the ICC opened, the highway failed to meet expectations for its usage and toll revenue. In 2003, state consultants had conservatively estimated that 52,013 to 56,175 vehicles would use the ICC each day by 2012, but the actual use was nearly 20 percent lower. They had also projected that drivers would pay $58.9 million to $68 million a year in tolls by 2012, but during the fiscal year from July 1, 2012, to June 30, 2013, revenues amounted to only $39.6 million. It is not clear why usage of the road was so low; perhaps it was the $8 toll for a car making a full round trip, the recession that caused many people to cut their transportation costs, or changing lifestyles that reduced the need for long-distance commuting. Whatever the reasons, the Capital Beltway remains packed during the weekday rush hours while the ICC remains relatively uncongested.[118]

State officials have taken several steps to try to increase use of the ICC. First, they established and heavily subsidized several bus routes on the ICC, but these have not caught on. Second, the state raised the speed limit from 55 to 60 miles per hour, but this has not increased usage because police are aggressively issuing tickets for speeding. Moreover, the massive debt to pay for the ICC has impaired the state's ability to undertake other projects. As a result, the Maryland General Assembly increased tolls on the other roads, bridges, and tunnels in the state to generate enough revenue to service the

debt for the project. Still, there was no money for other projects as the state
tolling agency reached its debt limit and the state paid 15 percent of its
annual federal highway funds just to service the federal bonds for the ICC.
In a last-ditch effort, the General Assembly agreed to increase the gasoline
tax for the first time in twenty-one years to inject $880 million into the
Transportation Trust Fund.[119]

While its future is uncertain, the history of the ICC underscores the
crucial role of grassroots activists for bringing environmental protection to
the fore in transportation planning during the late twentieth century. Suburban sprawl, worsening traffic congestion, and intense competition for tax
revenue made highways appealing ways to improve traffic flow and open
land for revenue-generating development. Opponents of the ICC countered
that regional highways had instigated sprawl in the first place and that a resolution would come not from building more highways but instead through
promoting more compact growth that was connected to mass transit. Their
critique of both the environmental and financial cost of highway-centric
suburban development was, at its heart, the rhetoric of smart growth more
than a decade before that term gained widespread usage in metropolitan
America. For more than a quarter century, opponents of the ICC harnessed the procedural features of federal environmental policy to entangle
the highway in multilevel government and public review. Because of this
politicking, they could scale down the size of the highway project as well
as obtain an unusually robust package of environmental stewardship measures. As long as the public felt that the environmental and fiscal impact
of the highway would make their quality of life worse and decision makers
agreed, opponents of the ICC were successful in blocking the highway. But
they were overcome in the new century as regional mobility worsened, concerns about economic development emerged, and a slate of conservative
leaders took control at all levels of government. As a result, the debate over
the highway shifted from its harmful impact to its prospective benefits for
mobility and the economy.

Even with a federal environmental review process, the devolution of federal policies to the state and local levels after 1970 and the focus of national
policy on highways limited the options for enhancing mobility in metropolitan Washington. Because states and localities looked to federal investment for
regional projects such as major highways, they tended to follow national policy preferences. This put transportation priorities in conflict with local land
use planning. Supporters of the ICC, which included many elected officials,

members of the business and development community, and ordinary residents, insisted that the highway was not only necessary for alleviating traffic congestion associated with existing development but also vital for attracting additional jobs and investment. Alternatives that might have had less impact on the environment and local communities became untenable given financing options, prevailing patterns of dispersed growth, and public preferences for auto-based mobility.

The case of the ICC demonstrated a key lesson of late twentieth-century metropolitan politics: the right of the public to participate did not ensure effective representation. State and local officials may have fulfilled the procedural requirements of federal policies for informing and engaging the public in the planning process, but in substance, state highway officials did not develop a community-centered proposal. Instead they offered their own plan, added alternatives and modifications that reflected the most prominent public concerns, and allowed technical details to cloud the bigger picture of how to enhance regional mobility by creating complementary transportation and land use patterns. This hampered the ability of residents to stay engaged, voice their concerns, and have a demonstrable impact on projects. While easing traffic congestion and attracting future growth were major attractions of the ICC, it was approved largely because it outlasted public opposition long enough for coordinated political leadership and public consensus to guide it through the planning process.

The primary aim of the smart growth movement—securing more compact development that was environmentally sensitive—was inextricably tied to protecting agricultural and rural land from sprawl. Support for highways, like the ICC, that opened land to development thus made agricultural and rural land preservation on the urban edge a greater imperative during the late twentieth century. Land preservation in some ways proved even more challenging than managing the impact of suburban development. First, it was tied to state and local boundaries, which insulated it from federal environmental oversight that governed pollution and other environmental concerns that ranged across jurisdictions. Second, land preservation efforts came up against political and public interest in economic development that downplayed environmental protection. In Montgomery County, a tradition of progressive land use planning and public interest in rural land preservation combined to support a measured, effective approach to protecting a contiguous base of rural land. In Loudoun County, however, there were fewer planning tools available and a far more uneven commitment among both public officials and residents to land preservation. Perhaps even more critically, Loudoun and other counties in Northern Virginia struggled against unusually strong state involvement in decisions about growth and development. Rural land preservation, then, was a logical and integral component of a smart growth movement devoted to promoting compact development and protecting environmental resources for local communities.

CHAPTER 5

A Master Plan for Agriculture

On January 29, 2009, W. Drew Stabler stood in front of a harvesting machine and reminisced about his lifelong devotion to farming. "I feel that in my life I've been able to do what I love and make a living at it," Stabler said, "and I am thankful for that."[1] Stabler, aged seventy-one, was a sixth-generation farmer in Montgomery County whose children were not interested in carrying on the family business. Given the high costs of farming and the development pressures he faced in a large suburban county, he decided to sell the development rights on 75 acres of his 600-acre Sunny Ridge Farm, in Damascus. Using the county's Agricultural Easement Program, he received $591,532 in state and local funds to invest in his farm. While he retained ownership over the entire farm, a conservation easement was placed that protected a section of the farm from suburban development in perpetuity. Stabler's decision, one of dozens of similar agreements made over the years in Montgomery, concluded a thirty-year campaign to protect a 93,000-acre Agricultural Reserve that represented one of the greatest success stories of rural land preservation in metropolitan America during the late twentieth century.[2]

Beginning in the early 1960s, county officials drew upon expansive state authorization for growth and development regulations as well as financial incentives to preserve agriculture and rural land. When these came up short, officials initiated a master plan for rural land preservation. Its centerpiece was a transfer of development rights (TDR) program, which redirected growth pressures to areas better able to accommodate additional development, allowing TDR purchasers to develop these sites at higher densities than normally permitted. During the 1980s, officials implemented the plan with limited civic involvement, achieving significant gains even as rural land gave way to development at a rapid clip. By the early 1990s, a coalition of civic organizations formed in support of the Agricultural Reserve. Initially, they focused on protecting natural amenities, but over time they expanded their interests to include a broad range of ecological functions that farms offer, the lower costs of more limited services in rural areas, and greater support of rural economic development to enhance the viability of farming and other enterprises.

Montgomery County's success with redirecting growth pressures away from the countryside to closer-in areas made the Agricultural Reserve a nationally significant example of both rural land preservation and smart growth. Compared to localities in Virginia, Montgomery enjoyed substantial state support for growth management.[3] This included a mix of regulatory and market-based strategies, the most important of which was the TDR program. Given the difficulty that communities had in controlling metropolitan development, land preservation required a sustained commitment. Planning professionals and elected officials took the lead, but success would not have been possible had civic support and collaboration not increased over time.[4] Protecting the amenities of the Agricultural Reserve resonated with many suburban residents in an affluent county, where concerns about jobs, tax revenue, and economic development were less pressing than in, say, Prince George's.[5] The Agricultural Reserve would also not have been possible without the support of farmers and rural communities, whose commitment to land preservation curbed sprawl onto the urban edge.[6] The Agricultural Reserve showed how robust land use planning and civic engagement could put metropolitan localities on a stronger footing for smarter growth by preserving rural land.

Despite several public benefits, two major groups questioned the impact of rural land preservation. The first were residents whose communities faced increased traffic congestion and property taxes to support development from the TDR program. Although the ostensible purpose of the Agricultural Reserve was to support smart growth, that growth had to go somewhere and, in some cases, it went to communities that were paradoxically more rural than (sub)urban in nature. The second set of critics were some of the county's farmers, for whom the smart growth philosophy of rural land preservation undermined efforts to provide economic development in the community and for their businesses more particularly.[7] Protecting rural amenities conflicted with the demands of technologically intensive farming that required large machines, utility infrastructure, and bigger roads to move their equipment.[8] While farmers generally had utilitarian attitudes about the land—what worked well for farming as a business—the great majority valued an independent way of life, lack of intrusion, and the open space that land preservation supported.[9] At the turn of the century, environmentalists and farmers became closer allies as the push for smart growth called for fuller direct financial investment in farms.[10] Tensions remained, however, as some environmentalists sought to maintain rustic roads that farmers found tough to navigate and pressed farmers to offer more products for direct sale to consumers, which some argued was not economically feasible.

Early Planning and Preservation

Postwar suburbanization inaugurated the long-term loss of rural land and agriculture in Montgomery. Historically, local farming was based in livestock, dairy, and small grain operations that sold their products in Maryland and the mid-Atlantic more broadly. By World War II, close-in areas such as Bethesda and Silver Spring had begun suburbanizing. After the war, Montgomery experienced a building boom that lasted for more than two decades and tripled its population between 1950 and 1970.[11] As the county grew, officials drew on strong state support to develop the widely known wedges and corridors plan that concentrated development within suburban areas while keeping it out of rural communities. The plan laid a strong foundation for the county's reputation as Greater Washington's leader in reducing sprawl.

After reaching its postwar zenith in the early 1950s, the base of farmland in America began a steady decline of one million acres per year through the end of the century.[12] Even with local support for preserving rural land, Montgomery struggled against regional development pressures and agricultural consolidation at a national scale that left its rural communities at a severe disadvantage with large farming regions like the Midwest.[13] The number of farms in Montgomery dropped nearly 60 percent between 1949 and 1969 while their average size increased nearly 30 percent. With larger farms and greater yields, the market value of agricultural products per farm rose by almost 130 percent, but the ability of small farmers to survive economically or be heard politically in a suburbanizing county was more impaired.[14] Thus total farmland in the county declined from 213,000 acres in 1950 to 150,284 acres by 1971, a drop of 30 percent.[15]

After a quarter century of rampant growth, local officials entered office across Greater Washington in the late 1960s and early 1970s with a mandate to rein in the fiscal and environmental costs of sprawl. No county in the region took greater strides to advance rural land preservation than Montgomery. The new preservation movement owed its origins to Royce Hanson, who served as chair of Montgomery's planning board between 1972 and 1980. Born in the late 1920s into a farm family in Oklahoma, Hanson worked his way through college before moving to Washington to attend graduate school at American University. After graduating, he became a faculty member there and a leading civic activist in Montgomery. During the 1950s, Hanson led two major successful initiatives. The first was a local campaign to change the county government from a county manager to a council executive system to better accommodate the needs of a growing suburban population. The second was a reapportionment campaign that redrew legislative district boundaries in Maryland to embrace the "one person, one vote" doctrine of the U.S. Supreme Court, the net result of which shifted the locus of representation from rural to more urban and suburban communities. In 1972, the county council appointed Hanson, a national expert on urban affairs and planning, to chair its planning board.[16]

Over the next eight years, Hanson took the lead in positioning Montgomery County as a regional and, indeed, national leader in growth management. In 1973, the county council agreed to reduce the density of development on nearly one hundred thousand acres of rural land in a bid to curb the construction of small-lot residential subdivisions. A year later, a new county council and county executive pressed forward with Hanson's and the planning board's proposal for an adequate public facilities ordinance designed initially to block growth in outlying areas without existing facilities but later used to halt development by mid-decade.[17] While Fairfax and Loudoun Counties instituted similar ordinances, the state judiciary overturned them, unlike in Montgomery, where local officials had strong support from the state for growth management.

Hanson's strong, hands-on leadership as chief planner in a rapidly growing county endeared him to suburbanites fed up with sprawl. His approach, however, also initiated a shift in the county from supporting economic development in rural communities to preserving rural land from suburban encroachment. In 1975, the county council moved agricultural activities into the planning department, where planners were more apt to treat farming as open space rather than an industry.[18] For a county with a strong civic base of support for curbing sprawl, however, there was little interest at the time in a more comprehensive plan for rural preservation.[19] Instead, Hanson and the county planning board were pioneers in thinking through the connection between curbing sprawl and preserving rural land. In 1977, county planners asked Sugarloaf Regional Trails, a local hiking group, to prepare a report on the noneconomic values of land preservation. Their report focused on environmental benefits that farmland offered, including slowing runoff and filtering water; reducing air pollution by providing vegetation that captured carbon dioxide and produced oxygen; and preserving wildlife habitats.[20] Their desire to protect agricultural land as "a living historic landscape" underscored a shift among suburbanites toward preserving the amenities of rural land rather than sustaining local agriculture as a viable industry.

The transition in the approach of county officials to agriculture coincided with both the ongoing consolidation of American agriculture and regional growth pressures that worked against small farmers on the urban edge. In the early 1970s, secretary of agriculture Earl Butz famously advised farmers to "get bigger or get out." His comments reflected a reality that farming in metropolitan America was becoming less necessary for feeding the U.S. population and international consumers thanks to technological innovations that exponentially increased agricultural yields.[21] Even as Montgomery officials curbed development locally, regional growth pressures escalated the value of rural land, thereby encouraging farmers to sell their businesses. Total farmland in the county dropped 12 percent during the 1970s, nearly a third in the final year.[22] While average farm value increased by 10 percent between 1969 and 1974, it rose 66 percent from 1974 to 1978.[23] As the cost of property taxes, labor, land, and supplies increased, the farmers who remained sought opportunities to earn income from off-farm work.[24]

National studies showed that farmland was disappearing at a rapid rate and that the reserve of potential land for farming was smaller than previously thought.[25] Although planning regulations had helped stem the tide of suburbanization in some communities, they were not enough to help farmers on the urban edge. For agriculture to retain a significant presence, stronger efforts were need to manage growth and preserve rural land. Montgomery's status as an innovation leader in progressive land use planning in Greater Washington positioned it well in this regard. Drawing on the county's long-standing wedges and corridors plan, Royce Hanson commented in a 1978 article: "The key to the preservation of farmland in the [open space] wedges depends heavily on implementation of the general plan's recommendation that development be concentrated in the corridors and down-county activity centers."[26]

Hanson recognized that development regulations alone would not lead to long-term rural land preservation; instead, rural landholders also needed more direct economic supports to resist the pressures to sell out to developers and to sustain their businesses. In the late 1970s, Hanson helped implement a pilot TDR program around Olney, a town with twenty-two thousand residents, to redirect growth.[27] The program worked by allocating development rights that rural landholders could sell to developers for redemption in areas better suited for growth. A number of residents and civic leaders protested, arguing that the southern and eastern portions of their town were sacrificed to preserve land further north, near Montgomery's agricultural heartland. But the program was successful at protecting rural land and did so without any expenditure of public funds.[28]

By 1980, a plan to preserve agriculture and rural open space in Montgomery was coming together. Local planners had decided to link land preservation to a broader plan for growth management.[29] They had identified a critical mass of farmland in the upper part of the county as the base for an economically viable industry.[30] The trial TDR program showed it could exploit development pressures to preserve rural land without the high acquisition costs associated with outright public purchases of land or conservation easements. The pieces were in place. "This is the last chance we have," said Mable Granske, one of Hanson's planning colleagues in 1980. "If we do not do something now, there will be no farms in Montgomery County.[31]

A Plan for Farming

In October 1980, the Montgomery County Council approved a *Functional Master Plan for the Preservation of Agriculture and Rural Open Space*. It proposed an 110,000-acre Agricultural Reserve and 26,000-acre open space buffer that constituted over 40 percent of the county's land base. The plan insisted that preserving rural land was an extension of earlier policies intended to curb the environmental and fiscal burdens of sprawl, and a way to protect local food supplies and rural lifestyles.[32] Instead of only intensifying development regulations in rural areas, however, the plan sought to redirect growth to areas better able to accommodate it. As Royce Hanson, the plan's lead architect, affirmed: "There is adequate room for *both* development and agriculture in Montgomery County."[33] The plan first reduced allowable development from one house per five acres to one per twenty-five acres and then rezoned land for inclusion in the TDR program. Landowners in the reserve would receive one development right, equivalent to one housing unit, for every five acres of land.[34] They could sell one or more of these rights to be redeemed in a "receiving area" designated for additional development. As a condition of selling a TDR, a landowner agreed to have an easement placed on that section of the property that required it to remain undeveloped in perpetuity.[35]

Planners acknowledged that the master plan offered limited support for the agricultural industry, which depended on public policies and market forces outside of local control.[36] While national consolidation continued to work against metropolitan farmers, more recent events also had an impact. In 1979, the Federal Reserve raised interest rates to curb inflation, which not only increased the cost of borrowing for farmers but also made U.S. products more expensive internationally, sparking the worst economic crisis for farmers in half a century. A grain embargo instituted against the Soviet Union in 1980 had real consequences for Montgomery. Between 1978 and 1982, the number of cash grain operations dropped from 209 to 119.[37]

The most noticeable impact of suburbanization on farming was its erosion of the number of animal-based operations. During the late 1970s and early 1980s, the number of beef cattle farms in Montgomery dropped by two-thirds while poultry operations nearly disappeared.[38] Moreover, farmers increasingly lost political influence to suburban voters interested in open space amenities but unsupportive of farming operations that produced waste and odors. "People and livestock are not always compatible," as one county official wryly put it.[39] The decline of animal-based agriculture and its support services also eroded the commercial network for other sectors. In sum, farming was under siege. Even as county officials creatively aimed to reduce the impact of suburbanization, their plans to redirect growth were more suited to protecting rural land as open space than supporting farmers.[40]

Development interests were quick to criticize the 1980 master plan as they felt the new regulations on development unduly restricted property rights and undermined efforts to attract economic growth.[41] Frank Jamison, a realtor in western Poolesville, disagreed with reducing the density of development in the Agricultural Reserve. "I think they're crazy as hell," Jamison railed. "Everybody wants a couple of acres of ground for a horse or two and maybe a cow, and this effectively would slim down that American dream."[42] Jamison tapped into a sentimental view of small-time farming as a symbol of honest labor, property ownership, and stability in modern urban society.[43] His perspective also belied the long-term pattern of consolidation made small farms less viable. A zoning lawyer offered a more direct indictment of the plan as "an antigrowth ploy cloaked in the coat of agricultural preservation."[44] Given

that the plan's focus was based on curbing the reach and impact of suburbanization, this assessment was not wholly inaccurate.[45] But his comments
obscured the premise that private land had public value and that in some
cases preservation rather than development best served the common good.[46]
Even with its drawbacks, the 1980 master plan that Royce Hanson engineered
would take its place with the county's wedges and corridors plan as the twin
pillars for smarter growth in Montgomery.

Forming the Agricultural Reserve

County officials began to implement the TDR program—the key to Montgomery's new approach to rural land preservation—in the early 1980s. First,
officials reduced the buildable density of land in the northwestern third of
the county where the Agricultural Reserve would be created. Next, they allocated TDRs to landowners at the rate of one per every five acres, distributing
roughly half of the total TDRs by the first-year anniversary of the master
plan.[47] The county council then designated "receiving areas" in Olney, Fairland, Potomac, and Damascus for developers to apply purchased TDRs. At
the time, these areas were not heavily developed.

The first successful use of the TDR program occurred when planners
approved a 262-unit townhouse project in Fairland, about seven miles west
of Silver Spring, in June 1982. The project's developer purchased eighty-seven
TDRs from a turf farm at a cost of $4,750 each in order to build at a higher
density than regular zoning permitted. The developer leveraged this ability to
build extra units to offer a discount of more than 10 percent on the sales price.
Given Montgomery's high housing costs—a product of its strong economy,
public services, and natural amenities—using extra density to lower prices
offered an added benefit to rural land preservation. In return, conservation
easements were placed on 435 acres of land in the Agricultural Reserve.[48]

The designation of nearly 90,000 acres of land to protect in the reserve
meant that receiving areas could gain up to 18,000 extra housing units above
those permitted under existing zoning. As the TDR program became more
popular, residents such as Fairland inhabitant Gloria Marconi objected to the
encroachment of large-scale housing in their formerly bucolic communities.
"This area [Fairland] right now is lovely the way it is," Marconi railed, "and
they're [county planners] doing their damndest to wreck it."[49] Nearly two
hundred residents of Potomac, where Royce Hanson lived, protested plans

to allow an additional 1,500 houses. "We are not against agricultural preservation upcounty," one person explained. "We are against trying to reach that goal by disrupting long-standing zoning and environmental protection for downcounty areas."[50]

While local residents were understandably frustrated about being asked to accommodate new residents to protect the Agricultural Reserve, county planners resisted calls to dial down the TDR program. Although Hanson ended his tenure on the planning board two years earlier, his successor maintained the board's position. "There are going to be people raising questions narrowly focused on their neighborhood," he explained, "[but] we and the County Council are looking at it from a broader perspective."[51] The decision to protect a critical mass of farmland over scattered plots of land made sense based on the idea that a large contiguous landscape with a support network was more likely to survive than scattered plots of land. Progress, however, was slow for most of the 1980s not only as the TDR program was set up but also because the 1978 elections had ushered in more development-friendly officials who sought to appease a mini "tax revolt" that called for attracting more growth to ease residential property tax burdens.[52]

The Agricultural Reserve suffered a major setback in 1987 when the Maryland Court of Appeals invalidated Montgomery's TDR program because it had been implemented, without state approval, as a change to the local zoning code. The ruling put local land preservation in limbo as officials and residents debated what to do. While the county executive supported reinstating the program, county council president Rose Crenca, who cast the lone vote against the *Functional Master Plan* in 1980, and Mary Anne Thane, a member of the citizens' association that initiated the case, disagreed. They opposed the use of TDRs to develop farmland outside the reserve and the impact of extra density on residents in receiving areas such as Fairland and Potomac.[53]

The court ruling forced stakeholders to reconsider agricultural preservation to date, including the shortcomings of the TDR program. Margaret Coleman, who owned a farm in Boyds, had hoped to sell some of her TDRs to a developer to get money to clear land and restore a historic farmhouse but was unable to find buyers. She also sought to protect her land through a state preservation program but was unable to convince her neighbors to join with her to create an agricultural district large enough to meet the requirements. Charles Jamison, who owned over 3,000 acres in the reserve, did not sell any of his TDRs because he felt agriculture was on the decline and wanted to sell his land with its development rights intact. Statistical data seemed to confirm

Jamison's point. From 1979 to 1987, total farmland in the county declined over 19 percent from 132,233 to 106,667 acres.[54]

Even with this loss, the TDR program still protected a significant amount of rural land. Between 1980 and August 1987, nearly 20,000 acres of agricultural land had been preserved, three-quarters through the TDR program and the balance through statewide land purchase programs operated by the Maryland Environmental Trust (MET) and the Maryland Agricultural Land Preservation Foundation (MALPF).[55] A 1987 study revealed that farmers preferred the TDR program because it offered "greater flexibility in terms of when they sell their development rights, who they sell to, how much they sell, how quickly they get paid, and what rights they retain."[56] State programs were less popular because of their stricter regulations, focus on larger properties, lengthy process for approval, and low appraisal prices.[57] Given its voluntary nature, opportunity to earn income through the sale of development without leaving their land, and less restrictive criteria, the TDR program remained appealing to farmers.[58]

The focus of agricultural preservation on curbing development rather than sustaining rural businesses, however, frustrated many farmers. Austin Kiplinger, owner of a 382-acre farm, was not thrilled about keeping his land free from development: "'I've found that people in the city want everybody else to keep their land open—for them."[59] For Kiplinger and others, preserving "open space" went against the need to grow their businesses to remain profitable. As farmland continued to decline, the limitations of preserving rural land became more apparent. As one researcher explained, "Just because you limit development on land doesn't mean you're going to have a viable agricultural economy."[60] Montgomery's Office of Economic Development agreed that new strategies were needed to support rural economic development.[61]

In December 1987, three county council members introduced a bill to reinstate the TDR program and increase the county's share in tax revenue derived from the sale of agricultural land for nonrural uses. At the time, Montgomery had to give two-thirds of the 5 percent tax back to a state land preservation foundation and lose its own portion if the funds were not used within five years to purchase conservation easements.[62] The council bill enabled county officials to purchase easements with their own share of the agricultural land transfer tax directly from landholders, thereby avoiding the cumbersome state regulations on easement acquisition and potentially accelerating land preservation in the process.

A public hearing on the bill in early 1988 suggested that civic interest in the Agricultural Reserve was on the rise as suburbanization intensified.

One of its foremost advocates was Edward Thompson Jr., who lived in the Agricultural Reserve and served as chair of the county's citizen-led Agricultural Preservation Advisory Board from 1986 to 1997. Thompson worked as a staff attorney for the Environmental Defense Fund during the 1970s and then as director of the Agricultural Lands Project for the National Association of Counties before cofounding the American Farmland Trust (AFT) in 1981. The AFT became a leading national advocate for curbing the loss of farmland from metropolitan development, encouraging environmentally friendly agricultural practices, and using a mix of regulations and financial incentives to balance the costs of farmland preservation between agriculturalists and the public. Thompson and the AFT endorsed the Agricultural Reserve as an innovative model of farmland preservation in metropolitan America. On behalf of the group, Thompson endorsed the bill "to retain and put to good use millions of dollars of its own revenue that otherwise would be lost to other counties" to protect "the only significant chunk of fertile open space within a 50-mile radius of Washington that anyone is actively trying to preserve."[63]

With strong political and public support, the county council reinstated the TDR program in February 1988 and created an Agricultural Easement Program (AEP) to purchase easements with its share of the agricultural transfer tax directly from farmland owners. A year later, additional state regulations enabled the county to purchase easements on ten acres or more of land zoned as rural so long as the development rights had not already been sold.[64] They also created a formula that rated farmland for preservation, including aspects such as "size, land quality, land tenure, road frontage, and location in the Agricultural Reserve."[65] This made assessment straightforward and allowed the county to focus on preserving the best and/or most threatened farmland.[66] In 1991, Maryland increased the percentage of the agricultural land transfer tax that Montgomery could keep from 66 percent to 75 percent. This offered more funds for local officials administering the AEP to buy easements in the reserve. Later, the county was able to give TDRs, through local ordinance, to landowners who participated in the AEP program, which could then be sold for additional revenue.[67]

Between August 1987 and June 1991, the reinstituted TDR program preserved nearly ten thousand acres of land while the recently created AEP program preserved over two thousand acres, more than either the MET or MALPF programs had since their inception in the 1970s.[68] The success of the local programs suggested that rural land preservation worked best with flexible guidelines, worthwhile financial incentives, and quick response times

to applications. Strong growth management regulations, including limiting
the extension of infrastructure, also proved critical, especially as suburban
development pressures heated up in the 1990s.

Growing the Agricultural Reserve

Local officials were the main advocates of the Agricultural Reserve during the
1980s, but civic and environmental activists became its most vocal champi-
ons over the next quarter century. In addition to Sugarloaf Citizens Association, a number of groups became active, including For a Rural Montgomery
(FARM) and Citizens to Preserve the Reserve, as well as local chapters of
the Sierra Club and Audubon Naturalist Society. The increase in local organizing came from two currents. The first was the escalation of suburban
development in Greater Washington during the 1990s that intensified conversion pressures on rural areas and spawned greater environmental organizing against large-scale projects like the ICC. The second was a longer-term
redirection of advocacy from national lobbying to state and local activism in
light of the gridlock in national policy making and the devolution of environmental politics associated with the Reagan Revolution.[69] Over time, more
residents became convinced of the benefits of farmland preservation, which
included the protection of food sources and open space, less pollution, and
fewer demands for expensive public services like schools and public utilities
that came with it.[70]

What really sparked civic organizing was an announcement in 1993 that
the Saudi government wanted to build an Islamic school for 1,500 students to
replace an overcrowded facility in Northern Virginia and a mosque to serve
over two hundred congregants on a 525-acre parcel in the town of Poolesville.
Development regulations had helped protect the reserve from suburbanization, but large private institutions, particularly churches, were largely exempted
because this would violate the free exercise clause of the First Amendment;
instead, regulations only affected sewage and parking. Nancy Dacek, a state
representative for western Montgomery who later opposed the ICC as a county
council member, sensed a conflict: "We're not opposed to religious groups, but
the question is whether you would be able to build a school in the middle of
land that has been carefully preserved for agriculture for years."[71]

Because it was the first major case of large-scale institutional development
in the reserve, local environmentalists scrambled to respond. They included

Caroline Taylor, who lived in Poolesville and worked for the National Wildlife Federation. Taylor was concerned that the Saudi project would impair the replenishment of the only aquifer in the reserve due to runoff from rooftops and spaces for cars, curtailing access to well water for local residents. Given this possibility, along with the potential for erosion and the loss of open space, Taylor helped form FARM and became part of a coalition that set out to break the "complacency and a general lack of information" about the project and the reserve more broadly. Taylor and others argued that the Saudi project was too big, would promote sprawl, and would harm the only aquifer in the reserve.[72] These critiques resonated with those made in the Burling case more than two decades earlier as well as those that opponents of the ICC were making in the Montgomery at the time.

A year after unveiling their proposal, the Saudi government asked Poolesville officials to annex their property from the county, which would confer local control for planning development. As an incentive, the landowners offered $5 million to help develop a water supply and sewage treatment infrastructure, a tempting offer. Town officials considered annexation positively as a way to counteract the tendency for county officials to put undesirable land uses such as landfills or prisons in small towns, where working-class and poor residents were less able to marshal political opposition than middle- and upper-class suburbanites. County officials in turn worried that town officials would dilute the development process and leave the county to pay for public facilities. County executive Neal Potter, along with members of the Montgomery County Agricultural Preservation Advisory Board, was among those who felt the Saudi facilities were incompatible with the reserve. Deep disagreement over the project led town officials to put the question of annexation to a public vote.[73]

Over 1,350 people jammed into a middle and high school auditorium in Poolesville in late October 1994 for two hearings on the proposed annexation, not unlike the crowds who went to meetings about the ICC. Attorneys for the Saudi property owners insisted that they would not exceed the density limits in the Agricultural Reserve and reiterated their commitment to building water and sewage infrastructure. The project not only instigated questions over the scale of development and its prospects for opening the door to sprawl, but also sparked a cultural backlash tied to the religious and international affiliation of the students and mosque congregants. One resident worried that the student body would be "from all over other countries and none would be American." School officials responded that many students were children of U.S. citizens while others were children of foreign diplomats and businessmen. But this did not assuage many and ultimately provoked a heated debate that tore the fabric of the community.[74]

Between the two hearings and the annexation referendum in February 1995, politics and social relations in Poolesville unraveled. Representatives for the Saudi government insisted that they wanted to be a good neighbor and that opponents were acting on unfounded cultural fears. Edward Kuhlman was voted off of Poolesville's town commission and reportedly lost friends over his support. Supporters reported receiving hate mail and being shouted down at public meetings, including Robert Ladd, a horse breeder who maintained the project would be better than a county incinerator and police firing range that was proposed nearby. A small contingent of annexation opponents took an unsavory view of the cultural background of the Saudi project's constituents. John Stringer, a retired federal official with the National Oceanic and Atmospheric Administration, argued that the proposal would allow "one of the most intolerant, bigoted kingdoms in the Middle East," whom he also labeled terrorists, "to infiltrate businesses and education facilities." Opponents of the project also faced verbal barrages and in some cases threats of violence. Dolores Milmoe, a friend of Caroline Taylor's and fellow member of FARM, reported a shotgun being fired through her bedroom window after her name appeared in a local newspaper opposing annexation. Things got so bad that public events at churches and schools were ruled off-limits for debating the project, while people avoided running into those with whom they disagreed.[75] Such vehemence was an unusual departure for suburban politics but set a noticeable precedent for when property rights advocates and environmentalists battled a few years later over the future of growth and rural land preservation in Loudoun County.

On February 11, 1995, Poolesville voters rejected annexation. Anti-Saudi sentiments had led to accusations that some opponents were acting out of bigotry rather than concern about the environmental impact of the project. Environmentalists, however, insisted people had gotten involved not to criticize Islamic adherents but to oppose the location of the facilities. While the referendum defeat only precluded the town of Poolesville from reviewing the project on its own, the rising tide of opposition pushed Saudi officials to give up on their plans. They instead acquired a site in eastern Loudoun north of Dulles Airport and near two large planned residential communities, hoping that they would find a friendlier environment to build an even larger residential school campus to serve 3,500 students and 275 faculty and staff.

Loudoun's Board of Supervisors approved the project in 1998 after months of debate that replayed the clashes in Montgomery. A barrage of political and public scrutiny, however, led Saudi representatives to withdraw their proposal and reinvest in their two existing schools in Fairfax.[76]

The protest over the Saudi school and mosque was a formative moment for local environmentalists and the Agricultural Reserve. The case raised public consciousness about the threats of suburbanization and laid the foundation for an upswing in opposition to the ICC a couple of years later. For Caroline Taylor, the Saudi project "was what really got me going" in local rural land preservation. As a result, she decided to leave the National Wildlife Federation to work on the local level, where felt environmentalists could "really affect longstanding change."[77] Taylor thus became part of a large and growing group of environmentalists across the United States who turned their attention from national to local and state concerns after more than a decade of environmental deregulation and devolution of political authority.[78]

Rampant exurbanization across Greater Washington during the 1990s, particularly across the Potomac in Loudoun County, helped many farmers in Montgomery become more appreciative of the county's land preservation efforts. "If we didn't have farm preservation," one grain farmer remarked, "you would see development down every road in this county, and there wouldn't be a farm economy."[79] Strong development regulations combined with effective market-based incentives such as the TDR program helped Montgomery connect agricultural preservation to a broader program of growth management. Nearly two decades after crafting the master plan for the Agricultural Reserve, Royce Hanson underscored the crucial role of the TDR program for promoting the "conservation of a rural area that was to be a kind of cultural resource, and higher-density housing where we had the public facilities to support it."[80]

Even as support for the Agricultural Reserve expanded, the TDR program generated significant opposition in small communities that received high shares of additional development too quickly without the provision of adequate public services. By 1997, Gaithersburg and Fairland had the second and third largest shares of housing built under the program, but this constituted a low percentage of their total housing, at 1.9 percent and 2.8 percent respectively. On the other hand, TDR housing represented 16.7 percent of Olney's total housing and 15.1 percent of the housing stock in Damascus. While the TDR program created a framework to support high-density transit-oriented development, few developers built close to Metro stations. Instead, they continued the trend of building housing farther out in communities that were dependent on the automobile, which undercut the ethos of growth management governing the wedges and corridors plan and the master plan for the Agricultural Reserve.[81]

Another contentious issue for the reserve involved plans to preserve old rural roads. Historically, farmers depended on roads to bring products to market, but roads and highways also fostered suburban encroachment. By the early 1990s, there was significant public interest in preserving rustic roads, defined by a task force as "a road within the Agricultural Reserve or adjoining rural areas in Montgomery County, which enhances the rural character of the area due to its particular configuration, alignment, scenic quality, landscaping, adjacent views, and historic interest, and which exemplifies the rural and agricultural landscape of the county."[82] In 1993, the county council approved an ordinance limiting alterations to designated rustic roads and in 1996 adopted a long-range plan for that purpose. Because many roads were in farming areas, the plan urged "that their designation as rustic roads not preclude providing adequate roads for the farming community." A decade later, the county had designated 106 rustic roads.[83]

Local environmental advocates supported the rustic roads program as an extension of protecting the county's rural landscape and heritage. Dolores Milmoe explained, "We're trying to maintain some sort of physical reference, visual reference, to try to keep the county's heritage intact."[84] Her comments reflected desires for stability in the midst of suburbia, particularly among middle- and upper-middle-class environmentalists who were the main supporters of the Agricultural Reserve.[85] They also defined the preservation of private property as being in the public interest because of the natural features and local heritage it protected.[86]

Despite homage to protecting farms as businesses, the criteria to designate rustic roads were mostly aesthetic and cultural. According to Jeremy Criss, who had headed the county's Office of Agriculture since its creation in 1996, farmers were told they should scale down the size of their equipment to be able to traverse narrow roads with overhanging trees. This, however, was antithetical to the economies of scale in the industry, which pressed farmers to mechanize and expand their operations. The rustic roads program, Criss charged, led the county to renege on its obligations to maintain roads for the residents and businesses that depended on them. A farmer in Brookville highlighted the tensions between public interest in rural land preservation and the business needs of local farmers: "The county says we need to keep agriculture in the area, but we're not going to give you the roads you need to do it."[87]

Figure 12. A farm in Boyds/Clarksburg, Maryland. Source: Andrew Bossi, Wikimedia Commons.

Local officials, residents, and environmentalists made substantial strides in protecting the Agricultural Reserve during the 1990s. Plans for a Saudi academy and mosque had mobilized a grassroots coalition in support of rural preservation. The TDR and AEP programs continued their success with securing conservation easements on rural land. The state government also became more invested in protecting rural communities. In 1997, the Maryland General Assembly enacted the Rural Legacy Program (RLP). This program, which provided money to local jurisdictions, transcended conventional preservation concerns by directly protecting natural habitats, creating greenbelts around rural communities, and promoting rural economic development of farming, tourism, and related industries.[88] Montgomery was among several jurisdictions that used the program, which created a TDR system like the county's AEP.[89] The RLP became the third most popular option in Montgomery for preserving rural land, after the TDR program and AEP.[90] Maryland also passed the Smart Growth and Neighborhood Conservation Act in 1997, which attempted to redirect growth pressures from rural areas to existing communities along major transportation routes.[91] This reinforced Montgomery's long-standing wedges and corridors plan as well as its master plan for agricultural and rural land, although the inner wedges had mostly been developed and attention was now on preserving the outer wedges.[92]

As growth pressures intensified across metropolitan America at the turn of the century, public interest in land preservation reached a level not seen since the early 1970s. Between 1998 and 2002, American voters approved over five hundred ballot measures to provide more than $20 billion for land preservation.[93] Land trusts such as the Potomac Conservancy also became more prominent as citizens turned to direct action strategies to curb the impact of sprawl.[94] By 2009, Maryland had nearly four dozen land trusts.[95] Given Montgomery's robust development regulations and preservation programs, however, land trusts played a limited role in the reserve. As the twenty-first century dawned, a growing coalition of officials, residents, and environmental activists worked to finish assembling the 93,000-acre Agricultural Reserve.

The Possibilities and Limitations
of Agricultural Preservation

By 2000, Montgomery's Agricultural Reserve already represented a major achievement in Greater Washington. With a collection of local and state land preservation programs, a coalition of civic and environmental organizations, and successes in both preserving land and opposing intensive development, the possibilities for permanently protecting most of its land looked promising. Development pressures continued to pose threats in the early twenty-first century, but strong collaborations between officials and environmentalists further restricted suburbanization and widened interest in preserving rural amenities.

In 2001, local officials reached an agreement with Bethesda developer Mike Rubin for the largest single property purchase in the Agricultural Reserve's history. Rubin agreed to buy and sell at a discounted rate a 1,700-acre tract of land owned by a British mining company. The land was situated in Boyds between the Potomac and Patuxent Rivers at the gateway to the reserve. Despite its potential for development, Rubin wanted to preserve the land as open space to avoid "the death of an environmental resource."[96] Rubin's commitment to land preservation was unusual for developers, but demonstrated how pervasive support for rural land preservation was in an affluent county with a tradition of progressive land use planning. Rubin purchased the land with financial support from the national Trust for Public Land.[97] Once the sale was finalized, a state-held easement was placed on the land. Afterward, the state and county purchased the land in sections to incorporate it into a park system. Rubin later became a founder, with Caroline Taylor, of the Montgomery Countryside Alliance, whose work focused on blocking suburban development in the reserve and supporting local investment in agriculture.[98]

The single biggest threat to the Agricultural Reserve in the early twenty-first century were several local megachurches interested in building facilities for their expanding congregations. Three of the most prominent were the Bethel World Outreach Church in Silver Spring, which had 2,500 members; the Seneca Creek Community Church in Germantown, which had 2,000; and the Derwood Bible Church, with 1,500. Each purchased land with the expectation that their projects would not be blocked because private institutions were exempted from the county's ban on public water and sewerage service in the Agricultural Reserve. Such an exemption had opened the door to the Saudi academy and mosque project in the 1990s.

Civic and environmental activists criticized the scale and ecological footprint of the projects as their predecessors had with the Saudi project in Poolesville a few years earlier. Residents in Laytonsville, which had a population of only two hundred, objected to the plans of the Derwood Bible Church. "The size and scope of what they plan on doing," one resident argued, "does not fit with what else is out here."[99] While church officials promised to use well and septic systems to limit the scope of development, many residents worried that the church would dry up groundwater resources.[100] Town residents soon organized a Committee to Preserve the Reserve to protest the project and the broader threat that large institutions posed to the environmental goods and services of the reserve.[101] The president of the Montgomery chapter of the Sierra Club was blunt about the megachurches as a test of political will for protecting the reserve. As she told local officials, "The time has come to put your vote where your mouth is."[102]

Representatives of the churches saw their desire to relocate as enhancing their ability to serve existing congregants and attract new members. The leader of the Bethel church told the county council: "To say no to a church is to say no to individuals and families, children and senior citizens."[103] Council members, however, were more sympathetic to environmentalists' concerns, as they were a key base of support for Democrats and even some Republicans. Church officials grew frustrated. The pastor of the Bethel church said, "We're disappointed because it's a political game that is being played, and we happen to be pawns in this game."[104]

At the twenty-fifth anniversary of the Agricultural Reserve, local officials reaffirmed their commitment to protecting rural land in the county. After a public hearing in 2005, the county's planning board unanimously recommended the county council limit the extension of public utilities for, and the size of, private institutions in the reserve.[105] Later that year, the council also voted unanimously to close the utilities loophole for federal tax-exempt private institutions, effectively blocking the churches' plans to build.[106] Church officials were taken aback, while public officials and environmentalist residents endorsed the decision. Derrick P. Berlage, chair of the county's planning board noted, "This is the first time the county has made an unequivocal statement that sewer service has no place in the agricultural reserve."[107]

Blocking the extension of public sewerage service put in place the last major piece of the puzzle for managing suburban encroachment in the Agricultural Reserve. Three years after the council vote, local officials purchased an easement on 75 acres of W. Drew Stabler's Sunny Ridge Farm. The transaction capped the county's assembly of a 93,000-acre Agricultural Reserve, over 70,000 acres of which were permanently protected. The significance of the event was not lost on county officials, as county executive Isaiah Leggett drove out on a snow-covered, unpaved road in January 2009 to commemorate the decision.

In an interesting twist, Royce Hanson, the lead architect of the master plan for the reserve, was serving out a second tenure as chair of the county's planning board after being recalled by the county council in 2006. With terms bookending the creation and completion of the reserve, Hanson could take pride in his serving as "the institutional trustee for the future of the county" through his work in support of growth management and rural land preservation.[108]

The Agricultural Reserve represented an unparalleled success in agricultural preservation in metropolitan America. Thanks to the work of visionary planners, committed elected officials, and a coalition of residents, environmentalists, and farmers, Montgomery created the second highest number of acres of preserved farmland of any locality in the nation and the highest percentage of its total land base preserved for agricultural use, at nearly one-third.[109] Of the 71,353 acres protected by conservation easements, nearly three-quarters were preserved through the TDR program. That program's flexibility, and its ability to turn the development potential of rural land into a source of revenue for farmers, made it widely popular with landholders. The AEP was the second most popular program in the Agricultural Reserve, preserving 8,060 acres. Unlike the TDR program, the AEP used public funds, in this case from a tax on farmland outside the reserve that was sold for nonagricultural use. The two advantages of the AEP was that it allowed the county to prioritize the acquisition of certain properties while it also enabled rural landholders to avoid tense negotiations with a prospective buyer as the county established the price for the TDR. The state-sponsored RLP was similar to the AEP, although a more recent innovation that preserved about half of the acreage. The least popular programs were run by state agencies and which tended to have stricter criteria for easement acquisition and less financial benefits compared to the locally administered programs.[110] Given that land preservation was most directly a local and community concern, it made sense that local programs would be more responsive and appealing.

One of the distinctive features of the Agricultural Reserve was that the bulk of its rural land preservation was privately financed. While the total public investment through state and local preservation programs to acquire easements totaled $46 million, the private sector spent $115 million for the development rights of rural land through the TDR program.[111] True to the aim of the county's 1980 master plan, the TDR program harnessed growth pressures to pay for most (75 percent) of the county's land preservation. As many

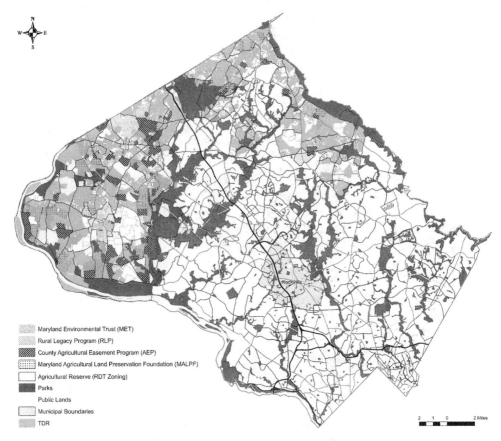

Figure 13. The Agricultural Reserve in Montgomery County, Maryland. Source: Montgomery County Office of Agriculture.

communities experienced a general decline in local support of land preservation after 1980, Montgomery County overcame political hurdles and development pressures to become a national leader in rural land preservation.[112]

While Montgomery became a success story for rural land preservation, the benefits for local agriculture were more uneven. The county's total farmland, including that in reserve, slipped nearly 40 percent between 1979 and 2009, about the same percentage as the three decades prior to the master plan. Its agricultural industry also consolidated. From 1978 to 2007, the number of operations declined 16 percent, but this was a small drop compared to the 60 percent decrease during the three decades prior to 1980. This was even more remarkable given the growth pressures that rural Montgomery faced during the late twentieth and early twenty-first century, especially with exurbanization.[113]

As farm acreage and the number of operations declined, Montgomery's agricultural industry adjusted to life on the urban fringe after 1980. The most noticeable trend was the decline in traditional livestock operations such as dairy farms and beef cattle as well as cash grain operations.[114] The biggest increases were in horticulture, which included plants and produce, and operations supporting horses for riding and competitions. These changes mirrored those in Loudoun, where suburbanization sparked declines in operations considered less "people-friendly" and gains in sectors that catered to more affluent populations through direct sales. In 2007, the 561 farms and 350 horticultural operations in Montgomery contributed over $243 million to the local economy. Horticultural operations made up half of that, while the equine industry contributed another third. Traditional agriculture provided just over $33 million, a decline from nearly $42 million only five years earlier.[115]

These changes yielded mixed responses. For elected officials, who had invested significant political capital in the reserve, the decline in traditional agriculture and growth of other sectors was not a sign of failure. "It doesn't mean that we are abandoning agriculture," explained the county council president in 2004, "It means we are expanding the definition of agriculture."[116] For residents, changes in local farming enabled greater access to buy local produce and miscellaneous farm products. By 2011, over a dozen farmers' markets and a dozen more on-farm markets in the county served residents in Montgomery and beyond.[117] An annual summer Farm Tour and Harvest Sale, then in its twenty-second year, and a more recent Fall Festival of Farms were among several special events for residents to buy local.[118]

Community supported agriculture (CSA) also established a foothold in the county, with ten operations by 2012. For producers, CSAs offered a much greater return per acre versus bulk prices from processing operations while providing financial stability at the beginning of the growing season through subscribers' fees. For consumers, CSAs offered access to locally grown products that were fresher and often grown using fewer chemicals and pesticides, an alternative to mainstream agriculture. The greater expense of local food, however, limited its accessibility, to more affluent consumers.[119]

Even with rising public support of local farming, the officials who managed local agricultural matters worried about the decline in commodity

agriculture. Jeremy Criss and John Zawitoski, who led the county's Office of
Agriculture, were responsible for advocating for farmers politically, helping
them navigate local planning and land use issues, and offering technical assistance.[120] They reported hearing often from local suburban residents that they
wanted farmers to grow more produce and organic foods for direct local consumption; however, Criss and Zawitoski believed that producers should be
free to make decisions about what to grow.[121] According to them, several factors undermined the sustainability of CSAs and related direct-to-consumer
sales models including costs for land, housing, and labor; regulations for
farming generally and for organic certification in particular; energy costs; the
cost of chemicals and other methods to control pests, diseases, and encroach-
ing animals; and a lack of technical assistance for farmers.[122] Such concerns
challenged how prevailing methods of retaining farmland in metropolitan
areas. The longtime focus in Montgomery was to protect farmland as rural
open space, but it became clear that a more effective method was to support
rural economic development that ensured the profitability of farming.[123]

On a more positive note, the tensions between land preservation and
direct public investment in local agriculture have eased recently. When
long-time local environmentalist Caroline Taylor joined the Montgomery
Countryside Alliance in 2009 as its executive director, she wanted to shift
the attention of the group from reactive battles against development toward
greater collaboration with local producers. In an interview, Taylor reported
the surprise that a group of livestock farmers felt after expressing frustration about the lack of local support facilities. "All of the sudden, people
who had historically thought of us as only tree-hugging dirt worshippers"
realized that she and her organization were genuinely interested in their
concerns. Recently, her organization has tried to get on-farm markets to
accept payment from food assistance programs to make local food more
accessible to Montgomery's lower-income residents. Although the effort
has had limited success to date, it offers possibilities for greater collaboration between farmers and environmentalists to enhance the public benefits
of the Agricultural Reserve as an area with rural land amenities and viable
local farming.[124]

Over the last four decades, Montgomery County developed a nationally
recognized model of how to protect agricultural and rural land from suburban encroachment in metropolitan America. When conventional development regulations and financial incentives were not enough and national

agricultural policies worked against them, stakeholders in Montgomery took bold steps on its own. In 1980, officials led by Royce Hanson endorsed a plan to create an Agricultural Reserve that included a program to direct growth pressures away from rural areas and enhance long-term land preservation. While the first decade of the reserve's history was mainly the creation of local officials, residents stepped forward to block land development and promote its environmental benefits as growth pressures intensified beginning in the early 1990s.

Although tens of thousands of acres of rural land were protected, there were several drawbacks with the Agricultural Reserve. For residents who received extra development from the TDR program, land preservation came at the expense of inadequate public services in their communities. For farmers, land preservation was not the same as rural economic development to ensure the profitability of agriculture. In some ways, rural land preservation was better suited for protecting open space for suburban residents than for sustaining farming and other rural enterprises. The rustic roads program was but one example.

The example of the Agricultural Reserve confirmed that the most effective approaches to curbing suburban encroachment on farmland required a mix of regulations to sufficiently limit the scale of development as well as market-based incentives to encourage adoption of preservation tools. Together, these measures redirected growth pressures and generated support among landholders who wanted outside investment to support their work and the value of rural land.[125] Much of this success, however, depended on expansive support from the state for authorizing localities to use tools like the TDR program to redirect growth and public support for their use. Communities in Maryland that already enjoyed large-scale development geared to the middle and upper classes, like Montgomery County, were more likely to see local public and political support for rural land preservation. By contrast, residents and officials in Prince George's were legally empowered to use the same tools as their neighbor to support land preservation but were far less inclined to do so because they felt there was an insufficient level of upscale development.

In suburban Maryland, the question of rural land preservation often centered on whether the public and its local officials wanted to use growth management tools made available by the state. In Northern Virginia, however, the default position of the state government was to offer strong support for property rights in support of development. Not only did localities lack access to many regulatory tools, they also had limited market-based incentives to offer in support of rural land preservation. For places like Loudoun County, where there was widespread public support for agriculture but not necessarily land preservation, environmentalists depended heavily on mobilizing support when suburban sprawl acutely impacted the public's quality of life. The experiences of both Montgomery and Loudoun Counties underscored that rural land preservation was an integral part of a broader effort to manage the environmental, fiscal, and social impact of suburban development during the late twentieth century.

CHAPTER 6

Saving Farms from Development

Metropolitan America exploded during the 1990s as sprawling development ran full throttle into the countryside. This rampant expansion of the population, activities, and boundaries of large regions left many communities struggling with how to curb development pressures. Loudoun County, Virginia, was the epicenter of this trend in Greater Washington and one of the most remarked-upon cases in the United States. At the turn of the century, public frustrations over the environmental impact of scattered development and sharp increases in taxes to pay for public services in outlying areas had reached a boiling point. The clashes between suburban growth and the county's rural character were chronicled in newspaper headlines and played out in public hearings, where environmentalists denounced developers as "landscape rapists" for wanting to build on rural land, and growth supporters cast environmentalists as "frog-kissing Stalinists" who wanted to turn private property into open space for the masses.[1]

In Loudoun County, Virginia, local environmentalists formulated a smart growth movement in the face of sharp opposition to regulating suburban growth in support of rural land preservation. Democrats representing the western two-thirds of the county and county planners began to protect rural land in the 1970s using the limited regulations and financial incentives that the state permitted. The prospective residential development of Beacon Hill outside of Leesburg during the 1980s tested these efforts by threatening to open the door to sprawl in the rural west of the county and increase taxes to pay for public services. In the early 1990s, voters ousted a long-standing preservation-oriented Democratic majority on the board of supervisors in favor of a Republican-led board that supported rapid exurban growth. Near the end of the decade, however, civic frustration with the environmental and financial impact of sprawl led to the formation of smart growth groups, such as Voters to Stop Sprawl and the Loudoun County Taxpayers Alliance, which helped elect a new slate of leaders to enhance agricultural preservation. These and other groups collided with the state legislature, local judges, and Citizens for Property Rights, who argued that limiting development undermined property rights. Despite some setbacks, local officials and residents made significant investments in agricultural preservation and rural tourism in the early twenty-first century.

Rural land preservation was generally left to local communities as national policies focused instead on price-support programs for agriculture, addressing the impact of large-scale projects like highways, and pollution. This posed real challenges for many communities and leaders because of the imperative to continually attract revenue-generating development to pay for existing and future commitments. Rural land preservation varied widely across metropolitan areas depending on perceptions of the existing state of development and the availability of tools to manage growth. While Montgomery County, for example, had substantial state and local support for a mix of regulatory and market-based strategies to protect rural land, Loudoun faced extensive opposition from stakeholders who supported extensive protections of property rights and insisted that curbing development would increase housing costs by reducing the supply of land.[2] Over time, political and civic opposition in Loudoun resulted in piecemeal land preservation compared to the Agricultural Reserve in Montgomery.

Although smart growth advocates sought to preserve the countryside as a shared asset, many rural residents considered development regulations as infringing on property rights, their ability to operate active farms and related businesses, and the saleable value of their land.[3] Over time, rural landholders in Loudoun, albeit to a lesser degree than their counterparts in Montgomery, recognized that unmitigated suburbanization threatened their independent way of life and livelihoods while environmentalists came to realize that preservation required supporting rural businesses.[4] As Loudoun's farmland base declined, new opportunities for smaller and more specialized operations such as organic and pick-your-own food emerged alongside new rural tourism options including wineries and bed-and-breakfasts.[5] This chapter and the previous one offer two different cases for exploring how rural inhabitants were not simply objects of metropolitan growth but actively shaped regional development through farming and land preservation.[6]

The Context for Land Preservation

Loudoun experienced little postwar suburbanization compared to neighboring Fairfax and Montgomery Counties. While the population of Fairfax, for example, increased tenfold between 1940 and 1970, Loudoun's did not even double.[7] Small towns such as Leesburg dotted an otherwise rural landscape that featured some of Virginia's most productive farmland, with corn, hay, and dairy as major products and a thriving equestrian culture among affluent residents.[8] Things began to change in the 1960s when eight thousand acres of farmland were purchased to build Washington Dulles International Airport and water and sewer lines were extended through the eastern third of the county. Over the next decade, thousands of residents moved into Sterling and other communities. Suburban growth combined with national agricultural policies and regional development pressures to consolidate farming in Loudoun, as farmhands left for better jobs and landholders looked to capitalize on rising land prices by selling to developers.[9]

Suburban pressures bore down more fully in the 1970s, disrupting an agrarian and small-town way of life that many residents enjoyed, and pushing officials to act. One of the earliest advocates for growth management in Loudoun was Frank Raflo. Born in 1919, Raflo lived in Leesburg and ran a dress shop with his wife. He served four years on the Leesburg Town Council in the 1950s and two years as mayor before winning a seat on Loudoun's Board of Supervisors in 1972. A fiery personality, he was well-known for his "cheese speech," in which he cut a block of Swiss cheese into smaller and smaller pieces. The block was a metaphor for growth, with the lesson being that if intense development were allowed, no one would enjoy the bucolic environment that attracted people to a community in the first place. During the 1970s, Raflo and his colleagues in the rural west could institute an adequate public facilities ordinance to put a moratorium on growth as well as reduce the density of development to ease the pressures on landowners, just as their counterparts in Montgomery did.[10]

Unlike Montgomery, where there was strong state support for allowing localities to make decisions to curb growth, Loudoun saw the state judiciary overturn its development moratorium. The court's decision was one of fifteen state supreme court rulings between 1954 and 1978 that maintained that local government had a duty to provide public infrastructure and that it should not reduce the profitability of development.[11] Such rulings underscored the tendency for Virginia officials to privilege the private interests of landholders over the public costs of suburbanization.[12] Although Loudoun's population increased 50 percent during the 1970s, from 37,150 to 57,427, that number would surely have been higher if not for the development moratorium, which blocked the construction of an estimated twenty thousand homes.[13]

Given the legal barriers to robust development regulations, officials in Loudoun sought to maximize the use of state-authorized programs. Nearly fifteen years later than Maryland, Virginia allowed localities to assess farmland at use value rather than its full market value for development.[14] By the early 1980s, Loudoun had applied the tool to 220,000 acres of rural land, which, depending on one's view, either eliminated $3 million in annual tax revenue or helped rural landholders stay on their land.[15] In 1977, Virginia permitted localities to create agricultural and forestal districts. Membership was voluntary, established for a defined period, and conferred use-value assessment if a locality did not have it. The program also required state and local service providers to limit their activities, although it did not permit blocking them as in Maryland. Four years after it adopted the program, Loudoun had over 60,000 acres of land in agricultural districts, more than the rest of Virginia combined.[16] While these voluntary tools helped protect rural land, the lack of regulation left private landholders, who often undervalued environmental resources, to take the initiative on land preservation.[17]

By 1980, Loudoun led Northern Virginia in rural land management. One study lauded it as an example of how "to promote the conservation of the very qualities that often attract suburbanization and other growth: open spaces, clean air and streams, wildlife, fields and pastures, forests and a sense of place created by the farms and villages built in years past."[18] It also noted that much of Loudoun's conservation was tied to historic preservation, through which it protected the eighteenth-century village of Waterford and ten thousand acres of mostly agricultural land. Civic interest among affluent residents was critical for defining rural land preservation as a public concern.[19]

Another motive involved recognition of the contributions of agriculture and rural amenities to the local economy. In 1978, the total value of local agricultural products was $29 million while tourism contributed another $20 million.[20] For a county with an annual budget of $50 million, protecting rural land was economically smart. Given public support for farming, the county's relative safety from suburban pressures, and the availability of land preservation programs, one researcher concluded: "It would appear that Loudoun is in a good position to take the kind of effective political action that could lead to a permanent agricultural reserve."[21] The researcher was right—but about a different county.

Development pressures intensified across Greater Washington during the early 1980s. Rising taxes to pay for infrastructure and public services in core suburbs like Fairfax pushed development outward to Loudoun.[22] Evidence could be found in the spike in recent land subdivisions, which presaged development, as well as in the political influence of the Loudoun Business Alliance (LBA), a group of eighty members concentrated in the real estate and development industry. Concerns about large-scale projects in the east encouraged a group of landowners, business owners, and preservationists to form the Coalition for Loudoun in 1983. Commenting about the situation and the influence of the LBA, the vice president of the Coalition for Loudoun remarked: "The county is essentially under siege right now and there are a lot of people who want to make a quick buck and take advantage of the county's vulnerability to development."[23] Bruce Brownell of the LBA accentuated the differences between the groups, using a partisan metaphor to make his point: "LBA and the coalition are so far apart it's like putting Carter and Reagan in the same room and asking them what to do" about a problem.[24]

The Coalition for Loudoun joined with local officials to support strengthening the county's growth management policies. This included creating a rural land management plan.[25] Work began when the board of supervisors authorized a civic committee to explore the issue and offer recommendations.[26] The committee's report, submitted in July 1983, featured several recommendations, the centerpiece of which was a transfer of development rights (TDR) program like that used in Montgomery.[27] County planners approved a rural land management plan in 1984 to maintain the rural west as an "agricultural conservation area" while allowing existing towns to receive some development. Two years later, the board of supervisors approved its use.[28]

Even with local approval, Loudoun needed authorization for the plan and TDR program from the state legislature. It did not receive this approval, for two reasons.[29] First, areas poorer than Loudoun dominated the state legislature and were concerned that a TDR program might downshift the engine of development in Northern Virginia that helped fund the rest of the state. Second, most legislators supported extensive protections of property rights.[30] "The concept of property rights is very dear to the hearts of Virginians and the members of the General Assembly," one legislator noted. "They love the soil and don't want anyone tampering with their development rights."[31] Loudoun officials periodically renewed their petitions over the next two decades, but were unsuccessful with convincing the state legislature.[32]

Despite these setbacks, Loudoun officials pressed ahead with rural land preservation through reducing tax burdens on rural landowners and encouraging them to join voluntary agricultural districts.[33] While these measures were helpful, local agriculture was already in the midst of a longer-term evolution. That evolution involved a decline of 10 percent in the number of traditional dairy and grain operations between 1982 and 1987, and the emergence of direct-to-consumer operations for produce as well as seasonal items including Halloween pumpkins and Christmas trees.[34] With a recent spike in property taxes that presaged growth pressures, Loudoun faced its first case of a major development project in the rural west.[35]

A Test for Rural Land Preservation

The first major test case for land preservation in western Loudoun involved the two-thousand-acre Beacon Hill estate. Located in the foothills of the Catoctin Mountains just west of Leesburg, the property featured a lavish Tudor-style mansion built in 1912 and a farm with four hundred cattle, a facility to house racehorses, and a collection of exotic animals. Its owner, radio and television personality Arthur Godfrey, sold Beacon Hill to a Saudi prince for $5.15 million in 1979. As a condition of the sale, the new owner agreed to maintain the estate's rural character. Over the next five years, he converted part of it into a vacation resort and spent $10 million to restore the mansion, although no one lived in it. In 1985, a partnership known as Beacon Hill Farm Associates (BHFA) purchased Beacon Hill with plans to develop it.[36]

In September 1985, BHFA proposed building a private golf resort and luxury residential community on part of the estate. Loudoun officials rejected the application as incompatible with the surrounding landscape. Several months later, after reviewing a scaled-down version of the proposal, the board of zoning appeals approved the golf course. In announcing the decision, county planner Joseph Davis encouraged the developer to preserve the site's natural features. "We care a lot about the future well-being of this place," he declared.[37] Davis's comments were prescient, as environmentalists began to monitor the developer's proposals in an effort to protect the estate's rural amenities and avoid likely tax increases to pay for services at a remote site.[38]

The leading activist to protect Beacon Hill from large-scale suburbanization was Burr Powell Harrison, one of Loudoun's most prominent residents. Harrison, born in 1911, was an insurance agent who worked in Leesburg. He had organized a trip to England for Frank Raflo and other local leaders in the early 1970s to learn about countryside preservation. He founded the Piedmont Environmental Council (PEC) shortly after their return, which became a major civic lobby in Loudoun and western Virginia during the late twentieth century. He also had an affinity for historic preservation, serving as president of Oatlands, an early nineteenth-century estate, from 1965 to 1987 and as an advisor for the National Trust for Historic Preservation in the 1970s and early 1980s. After serving as PEC president for a decade and retiring from his job, Harrison turned his attention to local preservation and environmental issues, helping to form the Coalition for Loudoun. He took a quick and keen interest in Beacon Hill, which was across the street from his home.[39] He urged nearby residents to be involved in the planning process to ensure that the development of Beacon Hill did not raise taxes or destroy the area's rural character.[40]

Over the next several years, the public became more involved as Harrison organized the Catoctin Mountain Alliance (CMA) in June 1987.[41] A few months after the formation of CMA, Loudoun's planning commission held a public meeting on a proposal to build fifteen houses on a 130-acre parcel. A standing-room-only crowd of 250 residents attended the boisterous two-hour hearing. Harrison was among the majority of attendees, who argued that the project would open the door to sprawl in western Loudoun. Arguing in favor of preserving the estate, he asked, "Shall the Catoctin Mountains become a billboard to developments or an inspiration to the public?" The developer rejected the idea that it had to satisfy the interests of residents who wanted to preserve the estate's bucolic landscape. Their representative explained: "I understand that a lot of people would prefer nothing happens to this farm. But, as property owners, we have the right to do what we want with our property."[42]

These differing views reflected enduring debates over the public's investment in private property. The developer held a traditional view that property should benefit its owner and that in nearly all cases its best use was for growth and development. This did not mean that developers ignored the public welfare. Indeed, they claimed that the housing, employment, leisure opportunities, and tax revenue that suburbanization offered had widespread benefits. Local police powers and zoning also protected the public by promoting orderly development. The environmental impact of postwar suburbanization, however, had highlighted the deficiencies of these tools. The BHFA was not opposed to conventional zoning but to newer environmental regulations that sharply reduced the developable value of land in favor of land preservation. Its ideas also presaged a property rights movement that emerged in the Washington area by 1990.[43]

After a lively hearing, the planning commission rejected the developer's proposal. It cited the lack of access roads, inadequate drainage for sewage, and a desire to see plans for the entire estate first to ensure compatible development. Two years earlier, the county's zoning board had granted a special exception for a golf course on the estate. Now the planning commission took a harder line as it reviewed the master plans that guided the county's long-term development and tried to stem a decline in farming operations by curbing growth into the rural west.[44]

The commission also endorsed an ordinance to protect mountainsides, the first in the Washington area, which was inspired by the Beacon Hill case and which the board of supervisors adopted two weeks later. Its purpose was to ensure that development would not substantially harm the topography, soil conditions, or flora and fauna of hilly terrain. It included several provisions. First, it forbade housing on slopes of more than 25 percent; second, it limited grading and clearing on smaller slopes; third, it required uses other than "agriculture, forestry, [or] fisheries" to receive a special exception directly from the board.[45] As a supervisor in one of the western districts explained, "With this ordinance, we're setting apart this area as being the most critical environmentally sensitive area in Loudoun County."[46] Because the BHFA had not received approval for a residential subdivision before the ordinance went into effect, the group was now subject to its terms.

In early 1988, the CMA, local civic and historic preservation organizations, and the PEC wrote to the board of supervisors to urge fuller public review of Beacon's Hill's prospective development. Frank Raflo's retirement from the board a couple of years earlier was part of a shift in the political base of the county from the preservation-oriented west to the more growth-inclined east. This included the election of Betty Tatum, a Democrat representing a district in eastern Loudoun, who joined the board of supervisors in 1981 and served as its chair from 1987 to 1991. Keeping a low profile, Tatum took development proposals on a case-by-case basis rather than being predisposed to preservation like Raflo.[47] Feeling that county officials were disinterested in their concerns about Beacon Hill, Harrison concluded that the county had lost interest in curbing suburbanization. A couple of years later, he said of Tatum in particular: "She would do anything to get development."[48]

Harrison's characterization was not exactly accurate. Tatum supported preserving Beacon Hill, explaining that it "captures the scenic beauty and heritage of Loudoun County."[49] But, she explained, the county's hands were tied. Because the BHFA had followed zoning and planning guidelines, and Virginia state law did not allow officials to withhold public facilities, unlike in Maryland, the supervisors could not block development. Instead, Harrison's criticism reflected a distrust of elected leaders as predisposed to supporting growth—a common refrain of many environmentalists. Curbing development in a comprehensive way over the long term was rare given the growth imperative that forged enduring coalitions among public officials, residents, business interests, and special interest groups around the opportunities and revenue it offered.[50]

In April 1988, the BHFA filed two lawsuits to push ahead with development. The first involved plans for two hundred homes on part of the site that were rejected for being too dense. In response, Loudoun officials promised "to fulfill the traditional government role of aggressive leadership in protecting public assets and guiding development in the public interest." This declaration, which was also a jab against the state's refusal to authorize stronger development regulations, convinced the BHFA to withdraw its lawsuit.[51] Its second lawsuit, filed in federal district court, alleged that Loudoun's mountainside ordinance violated the due process and equal protection clauses of the Fourteenth Amendment. More specifically, it maintained that the ordinance overstepped the use of zoning as a valid government interest in maintaining the character and land uses in a community as established in the *Euclid* case because its application to property of a certain elevation and slope was "arbitrary, discriminatory, unreasonable, and [bore] no reasonable or substantial relation to a legitimate governmental interest."[52] The federal district court disagreed with the developer, thereby upholding the ordinance.[53]

As development pressures intensified, the board of supervisors sought to strengthen rural land management. Adopted in 1989, *The Vision for Rural Loudoun County* criticized "rapid, scattered growth" for threatening environmental resources, overburdening roads, increasing housing costs, and making the provision of county services more difficult and costly.[54] It called for concentrating development in the east while permitting a traditional pattern of towns and villages surrounded by agricultural land and open space in the west. After having several of its proposals rejected previously, the BHFA applied in 1989 to have the property removed from the county's primary rural land preservation zoning category to allow residential clustering in a rural village pattern. The BHFA maintained that such a change would still "preserve agricultural operations and rural vistas in Western Loudoun County."[55] A member of the county's planning and zoning division disagreed, finding it would "set a precedent for future haphazard and possibly higher density rural development throughout the county."[56] Members of the CMA and the PEC agreed, underscoring the likely tax increases to support development rather than environmental concerns to cultivate public support.[57]

After years of controversy over Beacon Hill, the developer reached an agreement with the Loudoun County Board of Supervisors and the CMA on May 27, 1992, for a small project. The proposal allowed for development of half of the estate on seventy lots ranging from four to fifty acres. It also required that lots and open spaces be placed under permanent easements to avoid further subdivision, and landscaping measures that minimized erosion.[58] On one hand, the agreement helped maintain the rural character of Beacon Hill by avoiding a higher-density residential development that would have been more expensive to support and come with a greater environmental footprint. On the other hand, the approved proposal foreshadowed the wave of exurban growth that made Loudoun a headline story during the 1990s in Metropolitan Washington and nationally.[59]

Exurban Growth Heats Up

The foundations for Loudoun's explosive growth at the end of the century were now visible. The county's population increased 50 percent during the 1980s as high housing costs in Fairfax pushed residents westward and development spun off from Sterling and surrounding communities in eastern Loudoun. This put heavy pressures on the county government to review development applications, provide infrastructure, and build schools. The resulting delays and frustration over the development process led people to question the leadership of Philip Bolen, the county administrator. Before becoming the county's chief executive in 1971, he had been a physical education teacher and the county's first director of parks and recreation. Bolen had a casual, personal leadership style that worked well for a rural county but that proved increasingly ineffective as Loudoun underwent major changes and needed a stronger leader. In 1991, he resigned amid rumors he would be fired.[60] His departure was not the only shakeup. The same year, voters in eastern Loudoun unseated a preservation-oriented Democratic majority on the board of supervisors in favor of development-driven Republicans.[61]

The result was rampant and scattered growth.[62] Loudoun added three thousand homes and seven thousand people per year during the 1990s, nearly doubling its population compared to the 14 percent increase in the broader Washington area. It added seventeen million square feet of commercial space, more than that already built in Washington, D.C., and Arlington combined. The county added tens of thousands of jobs, boosting its share of employment in Northern Virginia from 4.6 percent to 8.5 percent. Its average household income rose as affluent residents moved into "McMansions" dotting the rural landscape, but was slightly lower than the regional average because of the construction of a significant amount of affordable housing and the presence of lower-income rural residents.[63]

Construction of the Dulles Greenway was a major enabler of exurban growth. In the early 1990s, officials wanted to build a highway to open up rural land for development. Lacking public funds, they turned to private investors, who obtained approval for a four-lane, fourteen-mile toll road. There were mixed opinions about the project as it underwent construction to connect Dulles Airport with Leesburg. One landowner who sold property for it highlighted the shorter and faster route to Washington that it provided. A lawyer who owned a farm, however, saw it as a precursor to sprawl that he likened to "the Fairfaxing of Loudoun County."[64] This jab at Loudoun's neighbor highlighted two issues of concern. The first was a general reminder about the perils of highway-oriented scattered growth that had dominated postwar America and that still retained heavy influence during the late twentieth century. The second was a more specific contrast between the large-scale suburban feel of Fairfax and the more bucolic type of environment that many residents of Loudoun hoped would remain in the county. After opening in 1993, the Dulles Greenway was by the end of the decade a "double-edged sword" that attracted revenue-generating commercial development, especially in telecommunications, but also promoted residential construction that often cost more in services than it yielded in taxes.[65]

As western Loudoun took on a suburban feel, newcomers undermined the political influence of rural residents and the character of rural communities. Many were attracted to the bucolic landscape but also wanted suburban services, major highways, substantial retail facilities, and high-performing schools. Consequently, they aggressively lobbied public officials for development.[66] In

Figure 14. Sprawl in Middleburg, Virginia. Source: La Citta Vita, Wikimedia Commons.

the process, officials aimed to satisfy their new constituents' interests as the county's small towns struggled to adjust.[67] "On the one hand, growth brings new business and jobs," one longtime resident of Leesburg explained, "but on the other hand, it could also threaten the very reasons why Leesburg is such a nice little town."[68] A newspaper headline aptly captured the tensions: "County's Explosive Growth Clashes with Traditions of Its Rural Past."[69]

As public officials approved thousands of homes and commercial projects, Loudoun's agrarian landscape eroded. From 1992 to 2002, farmland acreage dropped from 195,476 to 164,753. The number of traditional operations such as dairy and grains declined significantly. For many, this loss came with a sense of resignation. "'Farming is dying here. I don't think it will ever come back," lamented a resident of the historic village of Waterford. Given the lack of available and affordable labor, rising property taxes, offers from developers to buy, and a lack of public investment, it was little wonder that Loudoun farmers were discouraged.[70]

A closer look, however, revealed that farming was not dying per se but adjusting to new conditions that were conducive to the proliferation of part-time farmers in specialized sectors such as plant nurseries and vineyards. [71] Local agriculture bucked a half-century trend toward consolidation as the number of farms increased 50 percent, from 942 to 1,516, between 1992 and 2002. After a small drop earlier in the decade, sales of agricultural products rose from $26 million in 1997 to nearly $39 million by 2002.[72] Loudoun assisted part-time farmers moving into and working in the county by reducing property taxes for those who sold at least $1,000 worth of products annually. They also benefited from financial and technical support from the USDA's Office for Small-Scale Agriculture, created in the early 1980s to help farmers on the urban fringe. As local agriculture adapted, the number of livestock and poultry operations even increased by several dozen, upending the tendency for animal-based agriculture to decline in suburbanizing areas.[73] Nonetheless, the decline in acreage and farm size made farming difficult due to rising land prices, which curtailed the activities that would be profitable and eroded county political support for investment.

In adapting to life on the urban fringe, some farmers looked to more directly market to the public. Suzanne Unger left her job as a lawyer to work with her husband on a farm in Lovettsville. In 1993, the couple, both in their late thirties, became the first in Loudoun to adopt a community supported agriculture (CSA) model of production. They reserved one acre of land for organic produce for people who paid an annual subscription fee, which provided financial stability for their operations. Although produce was not a large sector of farming in the county, the CSA enabled the Ungers to engage a growing base of consumers interested in local food grown using environmentally conscious practices.[74] As Suzanne explained, "There is a real demand out there for this kind of relationship between fresh food and reliability."[75]

CSAs became a popular alternative to industrial agriculture over the next two decades, particularly for suburbanites seeking a more direct connection to their food. In the process, some people argued that CSAs were somewhat of a misnomer as local residents generally did not work the land as part of the program and because these kinds of farms tended to cater to residents who were able to pay for food that was generally more expensive.[76] While both criticisms had some truth to them, CSAs offered a viable means of counteracting suburban growth pressures by fostering public support for preserving rural land.[77]

After several years of rapid suburbanization, many residents began to feel that their quality of life was declining. New housing, which generally costs more to support than it generates in tax revenue, more than tripled the county's debt for infrastructure and schools.[78] Consequently, the tax rate rose 7 percent between 1995 and 1997.[79] With tax bills up, school construction lagging, and local roads more congested, opposition to rampant growth coalesced. "People on a massive scale are now understanding that development equals tax increases," noted Tim Powers, the founder of the Loudoun County Taxpayers Alliance.[80] Citizens turned out in greater force at public hearings to promote slow growth and reassert public control over the use of private land. Pro-development forces were surprised and frustrated: "There is almost an anger, a passion to stop development," one land use lawyer remarked.[81]

In 1999, Loudoun voters prepared to choose a board of supervisors that would carry the county into the next century. The campaign saw unprecedented support for slowing growth in order to reduce property taxes and improve services, a platform popular in many exurban communities at the time.[82] This included the formation of a political action committee known as Voters to Stop Sprawl. Many group members had recently moved to Loudoun, which was ironic given their desire to now curb development. The group was quite successful in its efforts, raising nearly $100,000 and seeing eight of the nine candidates it endorsed win election to the board of supervisors, which shifted its majority from Republican back to Democratic.[83]

Loudoun would see multiple partisan shifts over the next fifteen years as voters wavered between supporting strong growth and curbing it. These shifts, however, did not always align as one might expect. For example, Scott York, a Republican representing Loudoun's major suburban district of Sterling, became chair of the board in 2000 by riding the tide of slow-growth sentiment.[84] His counterpart in Montgomery, county executive Doug Duncan, who was a staunch advocate of suburban growth, survived a reelection campaign despite most the newly elected county council winning on a platform to slow growth.

A Push for Land Preservation

As a new board of supervisors took their seats in 2000, frustrations over the costs of sprawl, aided by a strong economy, translated into stronger support for rural land preservation. Research and experience confirmed that supporting agriculture ensured an adequate food supply, produced lower levels of pollution than suburbia, offered scenic open space, and required fewer expensive public services like schools and major highways.[85] In light of the benefits that agriculture offered, advocates of rural land preservation insisted that the costs should be shared between landholders and the public through programs that provided financial incentives that complemented development regulations.[86] This support was warranted. A 1998 survey found that two-thirds of landholding farmers in Loudoun wanted to continue their businesses but had experienced declining profits over the past few years because the low prices at market did not match their higher tax rates and the costs of equipment and labor.[87]

One of the board's first actions was to revive plans for a purchase of development rights (PDR) program that was proposed two years earlier by a task force of farming, civic, and environmental stakeholders.[88] Unlike a TDR program, where private interests paid landowners for their development rights, a PDR program used public funds. The proposal, however, had run into strident opposition from developers, one of whom railed that it smacked of "the socialistic power that they might have over in Maryland," because, in his view, it used cash incentives to push landholders to permanently relinquish the right of selling their land for development.[89] In April 2000, the supervisors allotted $4 million for a PDR program designed to help preserve rural land, reduce the costs of dispersed development, and improve environmental quality.[90]

But it had two liabilities. The first was that the amount of money was a pittance given the county's high land prices, meaning that only a small number of landholders could benefit.[91] Second, the county also needed to apply comprehensive regulations to cool down inflated land prices that encouraged landholders to sell to developers.[92] For that, the board of supervisors needed state authorization to limit development in places where adequate facilities did not exist or would be too expensive to provide, as well as to assess impact fees on developers to offset the soaring costs of public services. The state legislature, however, rejected both measures, which Maryland counties enjoyed, leaving Loudoun to find other tools to curb growth.[93]

The PDR program suggested a return to more vigorous rural land preservation with wide support. A 2001 survey found nearly 81 percent of residents supported the program with nearly half strongly supporting it. Support was strongest and most prevalent in western Loudoun, where exurbanization had moved in the past several years.[94] Between 2001 and 2004, the board of supervisors used the PDR program to protect over 2,500 acres of land.[95] One of the most noteworthy cases was the preservation of Sage Hill Farm in Leesburg, a 125-acre property that was the last piece of land needed to preserve two contiguous miles of parks and open space along the Potomac River, at a cost of $1.7 million.[96]

Just as slow growth advocates were gaining strength, however, property rights advocates mobilized to oppose regulations that reduced the developable value of their property. In early 2000, a group of farmers, rural landowners, and developers, led by a retired federal accountant named Jack Shockey, formed Citizens for Property Rights (CPR). The organization was one of a number of similar groups that had emerged in the United States over the previous two decades, mainly in the West.[97] Such groups were not found in Montgomery, which was more liberal than Loudoun and more inclined to accept development regulations as part of supporting their quality of life. While the group had a conservative political ideology that was critical of regulations that limited their property rights, its primary focus was on maximizing the developable value of their land for future sale. Shockey, for example, helped form the group because he wanted to protect the value of his mother's eight-hundred-acre farm.[98] A married couple in their mid-seventies who owned a farm near Lovettsville had similar concerns about the economic impact of slow growth policies. They railed against slow growth advocates for not understanding that older farmers depended on selling their land for retirement income: "You can't get through to these people what that means. All they want to see is their open space preserved."[99] A study commissioned by the county confirmed these frustrations, revealing the value of rural land would drop between 18 and 55 percent if proposals to reduce the density of development were adopted.[100]

The couple's testimony underscored competing interpretations of the countryside. For suburbanites and environmentalists, it was idealized as a healthful, aesthetically pleasing place of leisure, while for farmers the land was a working landscape that grew food or other products only with drainage, irrigation, and the application of chemicals.[101] Strong differences also existed over the fiscal impact of development. For rural landholders, development pressures increased their property taxes, but also the value of their land. For suburbanites, however, the previous few years of exurban growth had come with a high price tag for financing infrastructure and public services, inspiring support for development regulations and land preservation.

In mid-2000, Loudoun officials began revising the county's general plan in order to guide development for the next two decades. Initial plans for the west called for reducing development from one house per three acres to no more than one house per ten acres. They also advocated more investment in farming and rural tourism to better support public demand for local food and rural gateways.[102] "They [voters] highly value natural resources and they want them retained," one county official said, "and that's why they voted for the supervisors."[103]

CPR members and environmentalists soon clashed over plans to regulate growth in western Loudoun. Dozens of CPR members, including some who arrived on their tractors, attended a hearing in early June 2000 at which the board of supervisors were considering plans to reduce the density of development by taking back the power to change the zoning of a piece of land without the owner's consent, which they had relinquished in the early 1990s to cater to growth. Although such a basic zoning power was common in Virginia, members of the organization argued that it "took away their God-given rights" to own and use property as they saw fit. Barbara Churan rebuked the supervisors for being lackeys of environmentalists: "We all know you are owned and operated by the PECkers," she argued, making a snide reference to the long-term political influence of the citizen-led Piedmont Environmental Council. The group, who collectively owned thirty thousand acres, warned against an ordinance that might reduce the value of their land. James Clarke, a Christmas tree farmer, avowed, "If the equity or value of our land is damaged by this action, I cannot predict what the consequences will be or how loud the cry will be, but I can tell you it will be heard far and wide." At one point, CPR members became so unruly that board chair Scott York threatened to clear the meeting room.[104]

Other attendees supported the proposal for ensuring that private development did not harm the public. Resident Valerie Kelly framed the issue pointedly. "Why can't I put apartments all over the land? Why can't I put up a sports stadium?," she asked. "Because planning and zoning for the good of the community allow you to say no to me." Kelly's comments defined the community's stake in provisioning public services: "The cost of that person over there developing their land is going to cost me as a taxpayer. Property owners' rights have to be controlled.[105] At this hearing and others, supporters of curbing growth wore stickers that cautioned "Sprawl Costs US All."[106] They insisted that unhampered growth would drive up taxes, degrade environmental resources, and accelerate the loss of rural land. The lower costs of supporting farmland, according to this logic, warranted its preservation.[107] Over time, environmentalists and allies developed a biting slogan, "Don't Fairfax Loudoun," that cautioned against allowing suburbanization to overtake the bucolic landscape of western Loudoun, as happened with its neighbor to the east, with some exceptions like the Burling case.[108]

Following a tense three-hour public meeting, the board of supervisors took back the power to zone property without a landowner's consent. Over the next year, county officials continued working on plans to limit growth and development in the western part of the county over the next decade. As they did, they faced fierce opposition.[109]

While CPR members continued to stress their property rights, over time they broadened the appeal of their message. At one hearing the group carried signs that read, "Say No to Snob Zoning," making the case that lowering the density of permitted development would drive up housing costs by increasing demand for scarcer land and the natural amenities that attracted many residents.[110] As one member explained, "It's when you only have big tracts of land that only rich people can buy and build on."[111] Not only did CPR make a persuasive point about the tendency for farmland preservation to increase housing costs in metropolitan areas, they also lambasted specific environmentalists as elitists for moving into the county and then wanting to exclude others so they could enjoy open space.[112] Their advocacy underscored the ability of growth politics to unite a broad swath of the electorate—including conservative farmers in Loudoun and liberal African American residents in Prince George's—who endorsed the material benefits of development and were less inclined to support strong environmental protection safeguards that limited their access.

On the other hand, the tide of public opinion in Loudoun was squarely in favor of curbing growth. One survey of residents revealed that two-thirds found the issue to be the most important facing the county, not including another 17 percent who indicated that traffic congestion, largely associated with development patterns, was a problem. Seventy-nine percent felt that the pace of residential development was too fast, including 91 percent in the epicenter of the county's exurban growth in the rural west.[113]

In July 2001, the board of supervisors held its final hearing on the general plan after eighteen months of heated debate. Interest groups had spent over $1 million, or about $33 per Loudoun voter, to advance their positions. The debate also garnered national attention, as the National Association of Realtors gave $55,000 and promotional materials to its 1,600 local affiliates on how to combat slow-growth movements. The tone of the debate had also became acrimonious, with media outlets reporting on hearings "where real estate interests are denounced as landscape rapists [for wanting to develop rural land] and environmentalists cast as frog-kissing Stalinists" who wanted to turn private property into publicly held open space.[114] A crowd of two hundred packed the final hearing, requiring four sheriff's deputies to keep order.

The contentious meeting recalled the fierce debates in Poolesville over the Saudi school and mosque project in the Agricultural Reserve a few years earlier, as well as meetings about the Intercounty Connector.[115]

At this hearing, the supervisors approved a general plan that cut over eighty thousand homes permitted in earlier plans and abandoned a major highway that would have crisscrossed the rural west. The plan offered a strong framework for supporting well-planned, compact growth that had a lower environmental and fiscal cost than unhampered sprawl. It divided the county into three zones: a "suburban" area of higher-density development in the east; a "rural" area covering the western two-thirds of the county, where public utilities would not be available and housing would be limited; and a "transition" or buffer zone. The primary aim of the rural area was to preserve its "green infrastructure," which included over sixty thousand acres of land, hillside and mountain landscapes, hundreds of miles of scenic and historic rural roads, and several local historic districts.[116]

The new general plan reflected a growing trend in metropolitan communities to preserve rural land through growth and development regulations. It also acknowledged that sustaining rural communities required not just land preservation but also ensuring the profitability of farms through support for economic development, which included nontraditional agriculture and rural tourism.[117] In a place with a strong property rights movement like Loudoun, economic incentives proved far more palatable than development regulations.

The plan sharply divided county stakeholders. In an interview, Scott York joined environmentalists in praising it, as it sought "to ensure that, as development does occur, that it's done in a way that protects the environment, protects many of the historic features that we have in Loudoun County and goes further to hopefully address the many concerns we have had with growth, particularly building schools and roads and the funding issues that are associated.[118] Property rights advocates and the business and development communities opposed it. CPR leader Jack Shockey argued that county officials were "creating open space that's going to be a no-man's land."[119] The development community railed that the cutbacks in permitted development suggested the county "is closed for business" and would lose the opportunities and tax revenue that growth brought.[120] A month after the decision, residents and some of the county's largest business interests had filed two hundred lawsuits claiming that the new regulations were an unconstitutional taking of private property because they deprived landowners of the full value and use of their land. Other lawsuits, from major employers such as the Xerox Corporation, sought exemptions from environmental regulations that prohibited construction near sensitive natural features like floodplains or waterways.[121]

One year after Loudoun officials adopted a new general plan, the election season for the board of supervisors began. Local groups invested more energy and money than ever in trying to influence the outcome. Between July 2002 and October 2003, real estate and development interests contributed over $460,000 to candidates, seven times more than in the 1999 elections. Voters to Stop Sprawl, a major influence in the 1999 elections, raised $115,400 in 2002 alone. Partisan differences also hardened, with Democrats advocating for more public investment in agriculture and rural land preservation and Republicans calling for easing land use restrictions.[122]

After a heated election season, voters split their ballots. Eastern voters chose Republicans for their six seats, all of whom promised to retract recent development regulations and enhance support for growth. Voters in the west returned board chairman Scott York, who had run as independent after the county Republican Party had taken up arms with CPR and other conservatives, and two other supervisors who promised to regulate growth.[123]

In March 2005, Loudoun's preservation efforts suffered a major setback when the Virginia Supreme Court invalidated the new zoning regulations to curb home building in western Loudoun in support of the general plan. They maintained that local officials had not provided adequate notice for hearings based on two technical issues. The first was that the county had not met state requirements for defining the areas affected by the proposals, while the second was that a hearing announcement's mention of a "Provision to implement Conservation Design policies in the Revised general plan" did not offer sufficient detail about the purpose.[124] The decision opened up the possibility for widespread development until new policies were adopted.[125]

Public opinion about the decision was sharply divided. A sizeable coalition of residents, real estate interests, property owners, and conservative former and current officials praised the invalidation as a "victory for property rights."[126] Others were less pleased. The Coalition for Smarter Growth, PEC, and moderate and liberal officials were among those who criticized the ruling, citing the open and transparent decision-making process that had involved numerous mailings and hearings.[127] "If [the ruling] is allowed to stand," one supervisor said, "it probably means the end of rural western Loudoun as we know it."[128]

Following the rebuke of the general plan and its zoning measures, the board of supervisors asked planning officials to review the county's rural land use policies in preparation for new hearings. Seventy people testified at the first hearing in June 2006, while hundreds more testified or submitted comments at other hearings. Supporters of regulating development focused on the fiscal and environmental benefits of rural land. According to the Campaign for Loudoun's Future, a coalition of environmentalist citizens and organizations, residential development cost the county $6,000 per house per year for public services above what the households contributed in property and other taxes, not to mention increasing traffic congestion, impinging on rural amenities, and eroding hilly terrain.[129] As one resident explained, "We aren't supporting the infrastructure and the number of people and the overcrowding of schools as it is. I just don't see how in good conscious we can accept more development"[130] The biggest opposition came from the residents who had taken advantage of the Virginia Supreme Court's striking down of rural zoning to subdivide their land either for sale to increase cash flow or to create residences for family members live nearby. They wanted their applications to be grandfathered in to avoid losing the money they spent and the loss of value if density of development was reduced.[131]

The other major topic of discussion involved how to support a rural economy. Plans for the Rural Policy Area included capitalizing on the potential for rural tourism, which made sense given that Greater Washington had the highest median income of any metropolitan area in the United States.[132] At the time, Loudoun had over one hundred produce, horticulture, and nursery operations, many of which offered goods for direct consumer purchase, along with thirty wineries, and several outlets for local foods.[133] One rural business owner who supported the rural plan noted, "As a winemaker, my business depends upon customers who want to visit the rural setting that is western Loudoun County."[134] Compared to their counterparts in Montgomery, supporters of rural land preservation in Loudoun tended to focus more on the importance of rural economic development than on environmental objectives to support farms and communities.[135]

Given the strong legal and political sway of property rights advocates and development interests in the county, elected officials revised the zoning and subdivision ordinances in late 2006 for the county's Rural Policy Area to balance support for rural economic development with more flexible options for housing.[136] They divided western Loudoun into two districts. Each supported adding businesses with a light ecological footprint, such as telecommunications; facilities for tourism, recreation, and entertainment; and support services for agriculture. Both featured more flexible development options, including clustering homes. The biggest difference was the density of development. The northern tier, AR-1, featured a mix of small lots and larger agricultural parcels that permitted twenty-acre minimum lot sizes, while AR-2, which was mostly agricultural and the base of the county's equine industry, had minimum lots of forty acres. The plan also limited improvements to highways and over three hundred miles of rustic roads to safety upgrades. Several of the county's environmental overlay districts, including those for river and stream corridors, however, were eliminated, while the mountainside ordinance, dating back to the Beacon Hill case, was reinstated.[137] Compared to the plans rejected by the state judiciary, the revised zoning code was a reasonable compromise, particularly given the growth-oriented leadership that now governed the county.

Soon thereafter, another round of elections for the board of supervisors approached. After a four-year interlude of a development-driven board, eight of the nine candidates who won in 2007 supported a slow-growth platform. Voters' unhappiness with vigorous growth came with a mandate for protecting Loudoun's rural character and reducing the fiscal impact of sprawl. According to one civic lobby, the elections suggested that voters "know that the best way to deal with problems like traffic and taxes is to get a handle on where and how we grow."[138]

Strong pro-development forces had saddled Loudoun's agriculture industry with major challenges. Although farmland continued its long-term decline, dropping from 164,753 acres in 2002 to 142,452 by 2007, more troubling was the loss of agricultural operations and reduced profitability. After reaching a high of 1,516 farms in 2002, that number dropped to 1,427 five years later, while the value of agricultural products sold per farm dropped 7 percent per farm. One of the factors responsible was a drop in federal government subsidies by 59 percent during the early 2000s, which left cash-strapped farmers harder pressed to remain viable. Because more than half of the county's farmers did not farm full-time, the decline might also have reflected a high percentage of hobby farmers scaling back or ending their operations.[139]

Loudoun's major mechanism for rural land preservation in the early twenty-first century continued to be the state's voluntary and temporary agricultural and forestal district program. As of January 2012, it included 47,818 acres.[140] By 2014, Loudoun had 65,000 acres of land protected under conservation from this and other program, which totaled 19 percent of the county's land base.[141] Although recent policies have supported rural land preservation, the protected land was scattered across the county instead of concentrated in a reserve as in Montgomery. Without being able to use stronger tools such as

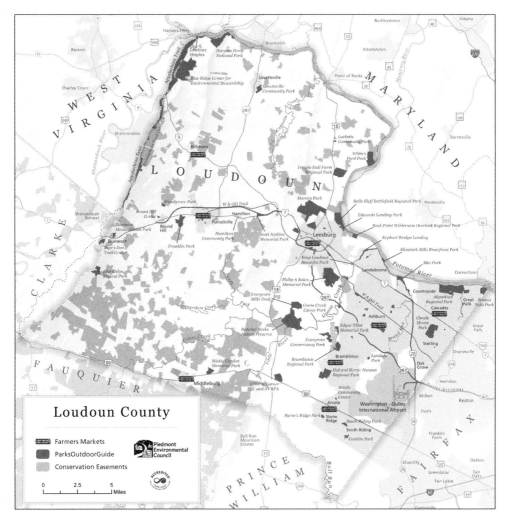

Figure 15. Rural land preservation and farmers markets in Loudoun County. Source:
Piedmont Environmental Council.

an adequate public facilities ordinance or TDR program, Loudoun has been
hard pressed to maintain a critical mass of farmland with an institutional
base that could help support farming over the long term.

The growth of metropolitan America after 1970 transformed many rural
communities. Rural land preservation was an extension of efforts to manage
the environmental and fiscal impact of suburbanization by limiting large-scale

development. Loudoun was one of many places in Greater Washington that struggled to balance the benefits of suburbanization with protection of its rural landscape and agriculture. During the 1970s and 1980s, preservation-minded officials and a small cadre of residents attempted to regulate growth and preserve rural land but encountered chronic opposition from the state and a lack of civic interest. In the 1990s, voters in the eastern part of Loudoun elected officials who vigorously pursued suburban development for the rural west. As the impact mounted, a sizeable contingent of residents pressured officials to curb growth and preserve rural land. In the early twenty-first century, however, local civic groups such as CPR, development-minded elected officials, and the state government continued to stymie comprehensive development regulations and more aggressive tools for rural land preservation.

Land preservation in metropolitan America has depended on local responses to regional growth pressures. Although federal policies provided an environmental review process to mitigate the impact of some development projects, protecting rural land was dependent on state and local initiatives. Within Greater Washington, support for growth and protecting property rights tended to be higher in Virginia than in Maryland. Where this was the case, local actors had to explain how rural land preservation offered economic benefits, not just environmental ones. The argument that they made was that rural land uses often cost less to support with public services than suburban development, but they also insisted that investing in rural economic development for farming and tourism could pay off.

Supporting environmental protection in metropolitan America during the late twentieth century, then, depended more on sustained political and civic commitments at the state and local levels than on federal policy making. Advancing these commitments proved challenging over the long term as regional growth pressures created a short-term horizon through which the longer-term value of development regulations, land preservation, and pollution cleanup were harder to appreciate. For these environmental strategies to be successful, communities not only needed planning tools but also a sufficient level of development to convince stakeholders that additional growth would be a detriment to their quality of life. Balancing growth and environmental protection has been, and will continue to be, a fundamental dilemma of metropolitan America.

Conclusion

The rapid and expansive development of Greater Washington after 1970 transformed the landscape and the environment. By 2015, the region's population stood at more than six million people as its geographical reach extended over six thousand square miles, both more than double those of 1970. As the Washington area expanded, so too did the environmental footprint of suburbanization. The construction of homes, businesses, and institutions that were signs of economic prosperity also eroded the presence of agriculture on the urban edge and polluted the air, water, and soil.

Addressing the environmental impact of growth in metropolitan America after 1970 depended primarily on what types of regulations, incentives, and other tools communities could and should use to manage growth without unduly infringing upon private property rights. Federal policies offered a robust environmental review process for major development projects and mandated strict standards to clean up pollution, but they were insufficient. The environmental impact statement (EIS) process, for example, only applied to a small percentage of development projects and when it did, federal agencies acted more as gatekeepers than as strong regulators. Over time, federal policies also devolved political authority to the state and local levels, where commitments to environmental protection varied widely according to political and public interest. Even strong federal policies such as the Clean Water Act depended heavily on public engagement and public-private partnerships to achieve lasting and significant environmental gains. Finally, federal policies did little to protect metropolitan farms from growth pressures. Instead, they supported the consolidation of the industry, leaving states and localities to develop tools for agricultural and rural land preservation with quite different approaches and results. Ultimately, federal policies were just one part of a decision-making process for managing growth that depended on leadership in politics and planning; existing laws, policies, and patterns of development; the work of civic actors; and the relative dominance of business and private property rights interests.

The uneven development of metropolitan America guided commitments to environmental protection during the late twentieth century. As Greater Washington transitioned from a central city and dependent suburbs to a more diffuse and diverse collection of communities, suburbanization stratified the population and escalated the competition for development that could offset the costs of providing an ever-widening array of services to residents who settled farther and farther out. More socioeconomically diverse communities inside the Beltway struggled with this, sacrificing strong environmental safeguards to compensate as Prince George's County did with National Harbor. More affluent counties with greater resources and appeal for developers, like Fairfax and Montgomery, were better positioned to advance strong growth management and environmental protection, but politics and public preferences determined if and how they did so. The material benefits of development and the competition for it, however, created an imperative for growth that resonated with many. As a result, communities across Greater Washington and beyond offered variable and incomplete commitments to environmental protection locally and in relation to regional issues such as pollution cleanup, transportation, and economic development.

Differences in state and local political leadership played a critical role in the pursuit of growth and environmental protection. Communities in Maryland had substantial support from state officials for growth management and environmental protection, including permission to use strong development regulations, market-based land preservation programs, and significant funding for state-based land preservation programs. Montgomery's Agricultural Reserve was a testament to local leadership willing and able to use tools to support rural land preservation, although the approval and construction of the Intercounty Connector (ICC) in the same county suggested enduring support for auto-based mobility and economic development. Legislative and judicial actions at the state level in Virginia often elevated protections for property rights above regulations and incentives to curb growth and preserve rural land. Officials and civic activists in Fairfax County during the early 1970s and off and on in Loudoun County from that time on were able to advance environmental protection, but faced more intransigence than their counterparts in Montgomery. This state-based divide, however, was not absolute. Support for growth was far more robust in Prince George's, which had access to many of the same tools as Montgomery, but did not use them because having a more socially diverse population than their suburban peers put them at a chronic disadvantage for attracting large-scale development catering to the middle-class.

While political decision making has continued to stress growth, grass-roots activism gradually improved environmental protection in Greater Washington. The troubling legacies of postwar suburbanization inspired a generation of environmentalists to help slow down growth, preserve agricultural land, and protect the air and water from pollution. The results of their work could be found in a rich history of projects that were not built or where the environmental impact was mitigated through measures to limit the size, type, and location of development. The broader success of their efforts was in their ability to position environmental protection as an ever more important component of the political and public discourse of metropolitan development, even as the imperatives of growth remained powerful into the early twenty-first century.

The primary aim of the smart growth movement—securing more compact development that was environmentally sensitive—was inextricably tied to protecting agricultural and rural land from sprawl. That movement enjoyed several major successes in Greater Washington at the turn of the century because its supporters made a persuasive case that compact development was both environmentally and fiscally beneficial. The first milestone was passage of the Smart Growth and Neighborhood Conservation Initiative in Maryland in 1997, a first-of-its-kind policy that supported reinvestment in closer neighborhoods and rural land preservation through tax incentives and public-private partnerships. Two years later, the bill's chief supporter, Governor Parris Glendening, garnered widespread publicity for abandoning the ICC highway, which he argued would open the door to sprawl in Montgomery and Prince George's Counties. On the other side of the nation's capital, voters and officials in Northern Virginia eased off of the accelerator for growth. In Loudoun County, Voters to Stop Sprawl played a major role in electing local leaders in 1999 and 2003 who reduced plans for development south of Dulles Airport and curbed suburban projects in the western two-thirds of the county. Even places not known for curbing growth did so. Residents persuaded officials in Prince William County, for example, to cut nearly thirty thousand homes from future development plans, limit public infrastructure in certain areas, and create an eighty-thousand-acre rural crescent to be protected from large-scale development.

As Greater Washington tried to rein in sprawl, the nation's capital underwent a wave of redevelopment that capitalized on its central location and tourist appeal. The National Capital Planning Commission's 1997 plan for the city, *Extending the Legacy,* laid the groundwork, even though its authority was confined to areas and projects involving federal lands or monies. *Extending the Legacy* shifted attention from the monumental core and preservation to developing neighborhoods, commercial districts, and the waterfronts along the Potomac and Anacostia Rivers. In Southeast Washington, the poorest section of the city, two major projects were built to replace derelict federal facilities. The first was a stadium for the Washington Nationals, bringing major league baseball back to the city after a more than thirty-year absence. The second renovated an old building nearby into a mixed-use complex of three thousand housing units, stores and restaurants, and office space. Later, more recreational facilities were added along the waterfronts as well as a new convention center downtown, part of the turn to a tourist-driven economy in the new century.

While smart growth blossomed at the high tide of suburban sprawl in the late 1990s, the new century saw a bit of a retrenchment. Worsening traffic congestion, a product of decades of sprawl, frustrated the region's drivers, who faced the longest commutes of any major metropolis by 2009 even though 14 percent of commuters—the third highest percentage in the United States—used public transportation. In Maryland, residents and a new slate of conservative officials renewed the push for the ICC highway, while the construction of National Harbor in Prince George's brought numerous shopping and leisure opportunities to the county's large African American middle-class population. In Loudoun, Citizens for Property Rights helped roll back recently adopted development regulations on rural land.

Even with some setbacks, the early twenty-first century witnessed significant progress with promoting compact growth and improving environmental quality. Around 2005, slow growth leadership regained control in much of Maryland and Virginia. In Loudoun, leaders overcame challenges at the local and state levels to craft a robust rural land preservation plan for the western half of the county in 2006. The Citizens to Preserve the Reserve and the Montgomery Countryside Alliance were among the local groups that came together to complete a thirty-year campaign to protect the ninety-three-thousand-acre Agricultural Reserve in 2009. Many localities also began to directly invest in agriculture, wineries, and other businesses to enhance rural tourism. At a regional level, the efforts of the Interstate Commission on the Potomac River Basin, environmental organizations, and civic-led clean-up campaigns left the "nation's river" with far less pollution than fifty years earlier.

Over time, coalitions of residents, officials, and organized interests debated—at times quite fiercely—how to balance growth and environmental protection. In the process, they laid the foundation for pursuing smarter growth that included adjustments in the scale, location, and other impacts of development projects; regulations and incentives to preserve rural land and open space from suburbanization; and efforts to curb pollution through infrastructure and public awareness campaigns. One of the most crucial strategies that advocates of smarter growth adopted was to argue that sprawl was not just harmful to public health, ecological resources, or mobility but was also fiscally expensive. This argument inspired places that experienced rapid sprawl to initiate stronger development regulations and a renewed push for land preservation.

This study highlights three major challenges for advancing development that is environmentally sustainable, fiscally sound, and socially equitable. The first is the continued presumption by most officials, residents, and organized interests that economic prosperity occurs through growth that involves more development, more expansion, and more individual and collective consumption. Under this model, environmental protection is seen as too expensive because it either discourages economic development or raises the costs of it by requiring greater financial investments in sustainable development practices. This is especially problematic given that the payoff of environmental goods and services tends to be over the longer term and their contribution to people's quality of life is harder to calculate in terms of tax revenue, jobs or leisure opportunities for residents.

Over the past two decades, there has been a wide-ranging debate about whether the sprawl so-often associated with suburban America was on the decline or on the rise. Analysis of census data suggested that suburban sprawl actually began to slow during the 1990s in the United States as geographical barriers and quality-of-life concerns limited expansion, and as older suburbs morphed into cities, although this was truer for the West and Northeast than the South.[1] Those looking to highlight the contributing factors behind the decline of sprawl have pointed to smaller families, the preference of "millennials" for living and working in urban areas, the rising costs of transportation, and the lack of access to high-paying jobs in the urban core that comes from living in far-out suburbs.[2] On the other hand, there is also significant research that suggests that people are continuing to move to suburban communities farther away that offer larger and more affordable housing, good schools, open space, and other features that have tended to make suburban living desirable.[3]

While the question of whether sprawl is on the decline continues to be debated, there are increasingly more opportunities to promote compact, transit-oriented development. Indeed, Greater Washington has inaugurated a new chapter in its national leadership of mass transit with construction of the Dulles Corridor Metrorail Project. The twenty-three-mile project, to be known as the Silver Line upon its completion, will proceed west from East Falls Church through Washington Dulles International Airport to Ashburn in Loudoun, running mostly along the median of the Dulles Toll Road / Dulles Airport Access Highway. At present, half of the track mileage is complete and open to the public with the other half slated to open in 2020. Although the Silver Line connects communities in Northern Virginia, where sprawl has already become the prevailing development, it has the opportunity to promote denser, more compact, transit-oriented development if closer-in locations become more sought after.[4]

The second major challenge for advancing smarter growth is that political decision making provides at best incomplete attention to the impact of growth. Competition between localities and states for development has produced complex class and racial divisions, leaving poorer communities struggling to attract jobs, investment, and commercial opportunities while more affluent communities are chronically concerned that pressing for strong environmental safeguards will push away development opportunities. Communities trying to balance development with environmental protection face a herculean task. Thus, when residents, public officials, and organized interests do support strong environmental protection and curbs on growth, it tends to be mostly on a project-by-project basis rather than at the broader policy or planning levels, where it could have a far more significant impact. This reinforces a piecemeal approach to environmental protection based on acceptable levels of pollution or reducing the loss of agricultural and rural land, rather than creating a context for decision making that begins with the full integration of concerns about the environment into the pursuit of development. It also undermines building public-private partnerships across communities to address concerns that operate at a regional level, particularly watershed protection and the relationship between mobility and development patterns.

Finally, even with the expansion of state regulation and civic engagement, political processes surrounding the use of property continues to prioritize private gain over environmental protection for the public good. Local elected officials and the business community continue to heavily influence community decision making in support of short-term interests in tax revenue and commercial expansion rather than longer-term quality-of-life issues like smarter growth and environmental protection. The existing political milieu of endless meetings, complex planning and environmental regulations, and an imperative for growth can thus bury fundamental public concerns under a pile of small revisions to a project whose merits have already been decided. As a result, communities where efforts to support environmental protection are more successful usually depend on a base of active middle- and upper-income residents who have the time, energy, and resources to be politically active and are willing to pay the higher costs of living in communities where significant environmental resources are protected. In poorer or working-class communities, the growth machine of resource-intensive economic development often prevails. While the success of smart growth advocates could be found in projects built or not built, or land protected and preserved, to have a broader impact depended on changes in planning, policy, and—without overstating—philosophy about the "highest and best use" of land. Montgomery County was perhaps the best example of smart growth in Metropolitan Washington, but it was not the only one, and it certainly had its limitations.

With these concerns in mind, I would offer three prospective recommendations to build on historical gains to enhance environmental protection in metropolitan America going forward. The first is to shift the conversation about how people think about growth and environmental protection so that they are less focused on a short-term horizon, "fighting fires" over particular projects and technical details, and more attuned to a long-term holistic view about how to balance growth and environmental protection to support a high quality of life. As an example, while the long-term impact of the ICC is not clear, early indications are that the expensiveness and underuse of the highway has made a financial mess for transportation in the state of Maryland that could last for years. Over the longer term, the direct environmental impact of the highway as well as the development it will facilitate along its corridor will likely grow. National Harbor, on the other hand, has become a major source of economic development and a site for commerce and leisure in Prince George's. Going forward, though, the two long-term issues the latter project faces are how to accommodate greater traffic—through auto-based mobility or mass transit—and the instability of the tourism industry, which can affect the tenancy of merchants and create pressures to use public subsidies to support the convention center. As suburbanization continues apace, supporting rural communities will become ever more challenging. Over the long term, this will require a forward-looking commitment to provide regulations, incentives, and direct economic investment to support farms and other rural businesses.

The second recommendation is for greater political coordination and flexible public-private partnerships in support of managing growth and advancing environmental protection. Few issues in metropolitan America over recent decades have seen as much progress on this front as water pollution. A regulatory framework for controlling water pollution already exists, but additional regulations to address nonpoint pollution are not likely forthcoming anytime soon, given the persistent trend toward deregulation and devolution. Instead, states and localities, often at the prompting of civic activists, will continue to play critical roles in cleaning up pollution. Older political organizations like the Interstate Commission on the Potomac River Basin offer much in the way of expertise and regional relationships, but nonprofit organizations and public-private partnerships have become more important in lobbying, monitoring conditions, and undertaking cleanup and restoration activities in many communities. Environmental education and a shift from mitigating impacts to ecosystem restoration, locally and writ large, will play a critical role in shaping the next generation of environmental stewardship.

The final recommendation is to reinvigorate public participation in decision making. Although existing policies mandate public input, the public faces many challenges in having its concerns heard and addressed. Ordinary Americans often have a greater sensitivity to the long-term impact of a project than do elected officials or business interests, who often take a short-term view of the immediate fiscal payoffs. Many Americans, however, are not effective in making their voices heard given the broken and biased decision-making process that currently exists. When people understand environmental issues in ways that are concrete and that can be interpreted in terms of how they affect their quality of life, they are more likely to support environmental protection. Charrettes are one way of enhancing public engagement. They start not from a predetermined solution to a problem but by identifying an array of issues and concerns among diverse parties, considering a range of possible solutions, and then having parties work closely together to design a project that serves a community. While charrettes have been a valuable tool at the project level, they are not yet widely used at the policy and planning levels.

Making large strides to support environmental protection in metropolitan America will depend on more than technical and bureaucratic solutions: it requires challenging existing notions about the relationship between growth and the environment. It took a social movement in the postwar period to create the paradigm for environmental protection that prevailed during the late twentieth century. The usefulness of that model is reaching its endpoint in an era of more complex environmental issues, tighter budgets, and greater awareness of more sustainable living.

In sum, a new social movement is necessary if we are to better reconcile the conflict between growth and development, on the one hand, and environmental protection, on the other. As citizens come to better understand the environmental and fiscal costs of sprawling, resource-intensive development, they can mobilize to elect officials who are less beholden to private property rights, more willing to integrate environmental protection into plans and projects for growth and development, and more inclined to open the decision-making process more fully to the public. The net result can support growth that is environmentally, fiscally, and socially equitable—in a word, smarter.

NOTES

Introduction

1. Timothy Egan, "Urban Sprawl Strains Western States," *New York Times* [*NYT*], December 29, 1996.

2. For one of the early accounts of exurbanization near the end of the century, which includes a dedicated chapter on Tysons Corner in Fairfax County, Virginia, see Joel Garreau, *The Edge City: Life on the New Frontier* (New York: Doubleday, 1991).

3. Glenn Frankel and Peter Pae, "In Loudoun, Two Worlds Collide; County's Explosive Growth Clashes with Traditions of Its Rural Past," *Washington Post* [*WP*], March 24, 1997; Michael Laris and Peter Whoriskey, "Loudoun's Ambitious Plan to Create a Perfect Suburb," *WP*, July 22, 2001.

4. Carlton Wade Basmajian, *Atlanta Unbound: Enabling Sprawl Through Policy and Planning* (Philadelphia: Temple University Press, 2015).

5. Alan Ehrenhalt, "New Recruits in the War on Sprawl," *NYT*, April 13, 1999.

6. Ibid.

7. Minneapolis–Saint Paul saw a large coalition form during the 1990s to address regional sprawl and the resulting inequalities. For an account, see Myron Orfield, *Metropolitics: A Regional Agenda for Community and Stability* (Washington, D.C.: Brookings Institution Press, 1997).

8. For an overview of the region, see Carl Abbott, *Greater Portland: Urban Life and Landscape in the Pacific Northwest* (Philadelphia: University of Pennsylvania Press, 2001). On the Metro Council and the urban growth boundary, see Metro Council, http://www.oregonmetro .gov/ (accessed February 5, 2017). For a contrast of Portland and other western metropolises, see Timothy Egan, "Drawing a Hard Line Against Urban Sprawl," *NYT*, December 30, 1996.

9. United States (U.S.) Census Bureau, Metropolitan and Micropolitan Statistical Areas Main, *People and Households*, http://www.census.gov/population/metro/ (accessed October 13, 2015).

10. For a study of federal involvement in urban and planning history in the region in the postwar period, see Howard Gillette Jr., *Between Justice and Beauty: Race, Planning, and the Failure of Urban Policy in Washington, D.C.* (Philadelphia: University of Pennsylvania Press, 2006).

11. Orfield, *Metropolitics*; Basmajian, *Atlanta Unbound*.

12. Samuel P. Hays, *Beauty, Health, and Permanence: Environmental Politics in the United States, 1955–1985* (New York: Cambridge University Press, 1987); Adam Rome, *The Bulldozer in the Countryside: Suburban Sprawl and the Rise of American Environmentalism* (New York: Cambridge University Press, 2001); Charles Milazzo, *Unlikely Environmentalists: Congress and Clean Water, 1945–1972* (Lawrence: University Press of Kansas, 2006); Karl Boyd Brooks, *Before*

Earth Day: The Origins of American Environmental Law, 1945–1970 (Lawrence: University Press of Kansas, 2009); Sarah Elkind, *How Local Politics Shape Federal Policy: Business, Power, and the Environment in Twentieth-Century Los Angeles* (Chapel Hill: University of North Carolina Press, 2011); Christopher C. Sellers, *Crabgrass Crucible: Suburban Nature and the Rise of Modern Environmentalism in Twentieth-Century America* (Chapel Hill: University of North Carolina Press, 2012).

13. Hays, *Beauty, Health, and Permanence;* Walter A. Rosenbaum, *Environmental Politics and Policy*, 4th ed. (Washington, D.C.: CQ Press, 1998); Richard J. Lazarus, *The Making of Environmental Law* (Chicago: University of Chicago Press, 2004); Christopher J. Bosso, *Environment, Inc.* (Lawrence: University Press of Kansas, 2005); James Longhurst, *Citizen Environmentalists* (Medford, MA: Tufts University Press, pub. by University Press of New England, 2010).

14. Matthew J. Lindstrom and Zachary A. Smith, *The National Environmental Policy Act: Judicial Misconstruction, Legislative Indifference and Executive Neglect* (College Station: Texas A&M University Press, 2001), 9–12; Michael R. Greenberg, *The Environmental Impact Statement After Two Generations: Managing Environment Power* (New York: Routledge, 2012), 11–16; Basmajian, *Atlanta Unbound*; Thomas J. Sugrue, "All Politics Is Local: The Persistence of Localism in Twentieth-Century America," in *The Democratic Experiment: New Directions in American Political History*, ed. Meg Jacobs, William J. Novak, and Julian Zelizer (Princeton, NJ: Princeton University Press, 2003), 301–326; Sidney M. Milkis, "Remaking Government Institutions in the 1970s: Participatory Democracy and the Triumph of Administrative Politics," *Journal of Policy History* 10, no. 1 (1998): 51–74.

15. William L. Andreen, "Water Quality Today—Has the Clean Water Act Been a Success?" *Alabama Law Review* 55 (2003–2004): 537–594.

16. Edward Weiner, *Urban Transportation Planning in the United States: An Historical Overview*, 5th ed. (Washington. D.C.: U.S. Department of Transportation, 1997); Tim Lehman, *Public Values, Private Lands: Farmland Preservation Policy, 1933–1985* (Chapel Hill: University of North Carolina Press, 1995), 70–81, 93–95, 133.

17. Orfield, *Metropolitics;* Basmajian, *Atlanta Unbound. Smarter Growth* is situated as a contribution to the "new political history" historiography. On this field, see Meg Jacobs, William J. Novak, and Julian E. Zelizer, eds., *The Democratic Experiment: New Directions in American Political History* (Princeton, NJ: Princeton University Press, 2003).

18. Zachary M. Schrag, *The Great Society Subway: A History of the Washington Metro* (Baltimore: Johns Hopkins University Press, 2006), 222.

19. Lucille Harrigan and Alexander von Hoffman, *Forty Years of Fighting Sprawl: Montgomery County, Maryland, and Growth Control Planning in the Metropolitan Region of Washington, D.C.* (Cambridge, MA: Joint Center for Housing Studies of Harvard University, 2002), http://www/jchs.harvard.edu/publications/communitydevelopment/W02-6_von_hoffman.pdf; Lucille Harrigan and Alexander von Hoffman, *Happy to Grow: Development and Planning in Fairfax County, Virginia* (Cambridge, MA: Joint Center for Housing Studies, Harvard University, 2004), http://www.jchs.harvard.edu/sites/jchs.harvard.edu/files/w04-2_von_hoffman.pdf (accessed August 12, 2017); Frederick Gutheim and Antoinette Lee, *Worthy of the Nation: Washington, DC, from L'Enfant to the National Capital Planning Commission*, 2nd ed. (Baltimore: Johns Hopkins University Press, 2006).

20. For an overview of the "growth imperative," see Phil Hubbard et al., "Geographies of Governance," *Thinking Geographically: Space, Theory, and Contemporary Human Geography* (New York: Continuum, 2002), 175–203; Jonathan S. Davies and David L. Imbroscio, eds.,

Theories of Urban Politics, 2nd ed. (Thousand Oaks, CA: Sage, 2009). For the post–World War II era, see Robert O. Self, *American Babylon: Race and the Struggle for Postwar Oakland* (Princeton, NJ: Princeton University Press, 2003).

21. Self, *American Babylon*; John E. Anderson and Robert W. Wassmer, *Bidding for Business: The Efficacy of Local Economic Development Incentives in a Metropolitan Area* (Kalamazoo, MI: W. E. Upjohn Institute for Employment Research, 2000); Edward J. Malecki, "Jockeying for Position: What It Means and Why It Matters to Regional Development Policy When Places Compete," *Regional Studies* 38, no. 9 (December 2004): 1104–1108.

22. On the postwar period, see Matthew D. Lassiter, *The Silent Majority: Suburban Politics in the Sunbelt South* (Princeton, NJ: Princeton University Press, 2006); Self, *American Babylon*; Kevin Fox Gotham, *Race, Real Estate, and Uneven Development: The Kansas City Experience, 1900–2000* (Albany: State University of New York, 2002), 53–63. On the late twentieth century, see Carolyn Adams et al., *Restructuring the Philadelphia Region: Metropolitan Divisions and Inequality* (Philadelphia: Temple University Press, 2008); Jon C. Teaford, *The Metropolitan Revolution: The Rise of Post-Urban America* (New York: Columbia University Press, 2006).

23. Paul G. Lewis, *Shaping Suburbia: How Political Institutions Organize Urban Development* (Pittsburgh: University of Pittsburgh Press, 1996); David K. Hamilton, "Organizing Government Structure and Governance Functions in Metropolitan Areas in Response to Growth and Change: A Critical Overview," *Journal of Urban Affairs* 22, no. 1 (2000): 65–84; David S. T. Matkin and H. George Frederickson, "Metropolitan Governance: Institutional Roles and Interjurisdictional Cooperation," *Journal of Urban Affairs* 31, no. 1 (2009): 45–66.

24. Richard Hogan, *The Failure of Planning: Permitting Sprawl in San Diego Suburbs, 1970–1999* (Columbus: Ohio State University Press, 2003), 89.

25. Edward P. Weber, *Pluralism by the Rules: Conflict and Cooperation in Environmental Regulation* (Washington. D.C.: Georgetown University Press, 1998); Thomas C. Beierle and Jerry Cayford, *Democracy in Practice: Public Participation in Environmental Decisions* (Washington. D.C.: Resources for the Future, 2002); Walter F. Baber and Robert V. Bartlett, *Deliberative Environmental Politics: Democracy and Ecological Rationality* (Cambridge, MA: MIT Press, 2005); Carmen Sirianni, *Investing in Democracy: Engaging Citizens in Collaborative Governance* (Washington. D.C.: Brookings Institution Press, 2009); Richard D. Magerum, *Beyond Consensus: Improving Collaborative Planning and Management* (Cambridge, MA: MIT Press, 2011).

26. On charges of elitism and self-serving advocacy among environmentalists, see Denton E. Morrison and Riley E. Dunlap, "Environmentalism and Elitism: A Conceptual and Empirical Analysis," *Environmental Management* 10, no. 5 (1986): 581–589; Diane M. Samdahl, "Social Determinants of Environmental Concern," *Environment and Behavior* 21, no. 1 (January 1989): 57–81.

27. Gutheim and Lee, *Worthy of the Nation*, 230–233, 237–241.

28. Schrag, *The Great Society Subway*.

29. U.S. Census Bureau, *Census of Population and Housing*, 1940–1970, in Minnesota Population Center, *National Historic Geographic Information System: Version 2.0* (Minneapolis: University of Minnesota, 2011), http://www.nhgis.org (accessed November 3, 2012).

30. Gutheim and Lee, *Worthy of the Nation*, 235–255, 281–282; Kenneth T. Jackson, *Crabgrass Frontier: The Suburbanization of the United States* (New York: Oxford University Press, 1985), 203–218, 232–240.

31. Weiner, *Urban Transportation Planning*, 5–11.

32. U.S. Census Bureau, *Census of Population and Housing,* 1940–1970 https://www.census.gov/prod/www/decennial.html (accessed August 12, 2017).

33. Mark H. Rose, *Interstate: Express Highway Politics*, rev. ed. (Knoxville: University of Tennessee Press, 1990); Tom Lewis, *Divided Highways: Building the Interstate Highways, Transforming American Life* (New York: Viking, 1997).

34. Gutheim and Lee, *Worthy of the Nation*, 281–282.

35. Ibid., 259–275. On postwar urban revitalization, see Jon C. Teaford, *The Rough Road to Renaissance: Urban Revitalization in America, 1940–1985* (Baltimore: Johns Hopkins University Press, 1990); June Manning Thomas, *Redevelopment and Race: Planning a Finer City in Postwar Detroit* (Baltimore: Johns Hopkins University Press, 1997); Howard Gillette Jr., *Camden After the Fall: Decline and Renewal in a Post-Industrial City* (Philadelphia: University of Pennsylvania Press, 2005); Colin Gordon, *Mapping Decline: St. Louis and the Fate of the American City* (Philadelphia: University of Pennsylvania, 2008).

36. Census Bureau, *Census*, 1970; United States Commission on Civil Rights, *A Long Day's Journey Into Light: School Desegregation in Prince George's County*, Clearinghouse Publication 52 (Washington. D.C.: Government Printing Office, 1976), 1–16, 52–69.

37. Jackson, *Crabgrass Frontier*, 203–218; Lizabeth A. Cohen, *A Consumers' Republic: The Politics of Mass Consumption in Postwar America* (New York: Alfred A. Knopf, 2003), 8–9, 11, 289; Lassiter, *The Silent Majority*, 7, 11–14; David M. P. Freund, *Colored Property: State Policy and White Racial Politics in Suburban America* (Chicago: University of Chicago Press, 2007), 18–19, 216–217; Gotham, *Race, Real Estate, and Uneven Development*; Self, *American Babylon*; Kevin M. Kruse, *White Flight: Atlanta and the Making of Modern Conservatism* (Princeton, NJ: Princeton University Press, 2005), 6–10.

38. Gutheim and Lee, *Worthy of the Nation*, 247–251, 283–284, 293–296, 305–307.

39. Rome, *The Bulldozer in the Countryside*; Bruce L. Gardner, *American Agriculture in the Twentieth Century: How It Flourished and What It Cost* (Cambridge, MA: Harvard University Press, 2002); Lehman, *Public Values, Private Lands*.

40. Interstate Commission on the Potomac River Basin, *Teamwork on the Potomac: A Report on the Activities of the Interstate Commission on the Potomac River Basin"* (Rockville, MD: Interstate Commission on the Potomac River Basin, 1958), 38, 56.

41. Richard L. Lyons, "3d of River Is Sewage in Dry Spell; TV Series Sees Area-Wide Plan Badly Needed in Fight on Pollution," *WP*, August 31, 1955; "Tons of Soil Choke Area Streams; Engineer Blames Building Projects for Sediment," *WP*, November 5, 1960.

42. Milazzo, *Unlikely Environmentalists*, 6–7, 18–19.

43. Hays, *Beauty, Health, and Permanence*, 13–39, 71–98, 137–158; Brooks, *Before Earth Day*, 94; Sellers, *Crabgrass Crucible*; Rome, *The Bulldozer in the Countryside*, 120, 123.

44. "Low-Density Shorelines," editorial, *WP*, January 27, 1966.

45. Morrison and Dunlap, "Environmentalism and Elitism"; Samdahl, "Social Determinants of Environmental Concern."

46. Hays, *Beauty, Health, and Permanence*, 13–39; Sellers, *Crabgrass Crucible*.

47. Laura Richardson Kolar, "Conserving the Country in Postwar America: Federal Conservation Policy from Eisenhower to Nixon" (Ph.D. diss., University of Virginia, 2011), 148–190.

48. Milkis, "Remaking Government Institutions"; Sugrue, "All Politics Is Local"; Lindstrom and Smith, *The National Environmental Policy Act*, 16–52; Greenberg, *The Environmental Impact Statement*, 4–7; Longhurst, *Citizen Environmentalists*.

49. Lazarus, *The Making of Environmental Law*, 67–97.

50. Meg Jacobs, "The Politics of Environmental Regulations: Business-Government Relations in the 1970s and Beyond," in *What's Good for Business: Business and American Politics Since*

World War II, ed. Kim Phillips-Fein and Julian E. Zelizer (New York: Oxford University Press, 2012), 212–232.

51. Bosso, *Environment, Inc.*

52. Adam Rome, *The Genius of Earth Day: How a 1970 Teach-In Unexpectedly Made the First Green Generation* (New York: Hill and Wang, 2013).

53. Milkis, "Remaking Government Institutions"; Sugrue, "All Politics Is Local"; Jacobs, "The Politics of Environmental Regulations." Jacobs argues environmental protection served as a counterexample to 1970s deregulation because it imposed major checks on business power.

54. Milazzo, *Unlikely Environmentalists*; Joel M. Gross and Lynn Dodge, *Clean Water Act* (Chicago: American Bar Association, 2005); Loretta Tofani, "'Sewer Ladies' Keep Officials in Line," *WP*, March 1, 1980.

55. Greenberg, *The Environmental Impact Statement*, 11–16; Lindstrom and Smith, *The National Environmental Policy Act*, 9–12; Lehman, *Public Values, Private Lands*, 43–44, 70–81, 93–95, 133.

56. Peter Siskind, "Growth and Its Discontents: Localism, Protest and the Politics of Development on the Postwar Northeast Corridor" (Ph.D. diss., University of Pennsylvania, 2002), 94–95, 152–161, 215–219.

57. Grace Dawson, *No Little Plans: Fairfax County's PLUS Program for Managing Growth* (Washington. D.C.: Urban Institute, 1977).

58. Maryland-National Capital Park and Planning Commission, *On Wedges and Corridors; General Plan for the Physical Development of the Maryland-Washington Regional District in Montgomery and Prince George's Counties* (Silver Spring, MD: M-NCPPC, 1964).

59. Maryland-National Capital Park and Planning Commission, *Functional Master Plan for the Preservation of Agriculture and Rural Open Space in Montgomery County* (Rockville, MD: M-NCPPC, 1980).

60. Census Bureau, *Census of Population and Housing,* 1970 and 1980.

61. Virginia maintained unusual control over its localities under the Dillon Rule.

62. Department of Natural Resources (MD), *Program Open Space: Ten Year Report 1969–1979* [n.d.], box 3, Series II, Collection No. 87-8, Maryland Conservation Council Archives, 1970–1986, University of Maryland, College Park, MD; Virginia General Assembly, Agricultural and Forestal Districts Act, §§15.2-4300–15.2-4314 (1977); Virginia Outdoors Foundation, "Mission and History of the Virginia Outdoors Foundation," http://www.virginiaoutdoorsfoundation.org/about/mission-history/ (accessed August 12, 2017).

63. Karyn R. Lacy, *Blue-Chip Black: Race, Class, and Status in the New Black Middle Class* (Berkeley: University of California Press, 2007), 194–197. On other property tax revolts, see Lisa McGirr, *Suburban Warriors: The Origins of the New American Right* (Princeton, NJ: Princeton University Press, 2001), 237–239; Self, *American Babylon*, 317–326.

64. Gutheim and Lee, *Worthy of the Nation*, 313–328.

65. The delay with congressional financing was mostly the product of the obstructionism of the long-time chair of the D.C. appropriations subcommittee, Representative William Natcher (R-KY). On the history and construction of Metro, see Schrag, *The Great Society Subway.*

66. Hays, *Beauty, Health, and Permanence*, 287–328, 491–526; Judith A. Layzer, *Open for Business: Conservatives' Opposition to Environmental Regulation* (Cambridge, MA: MIT Press, 2012), especially chapter 4; Bosso, *Environment, Inc.*, 86–95; Patrick Allitt, *A Climate of Crisis: America in the Age of Environmentalism* (New York: Penguin Press, 2014), 156–165.

67. Census Bureau, Metropolitan and Micropolitan Statistical Areas Main.

68. Census Bureau, *Census of Population and Housing*, 1970–2000, https://www.census.gov /prod/www/decennial.html (accessed August 12, 2017); Arthur C. Nelson, "The Exurban Battleground," in *Contested Countryside: The Rural Urban Fringe in North America*, ed. Owen J. Furuseth and Mark B. Lapping (Surrey, United Kingdom: Ashgate, 1999): 137–149; Mark Friedberger, "The Rural-Urban Fringe in the Late Twentieth Century," *Agricultural History* 74, no. 2 (Spring 2000): 502–514; J. G. Masek, F. E. Lindsay, and S. N. Goward, "Dynamics of Urban Growth in the Washington DC Metropolitan Area, 1973–1996, from Landsat Observations," *International Journal of Remote Sensing* 21, no. 18 (2000): 3482–3483.

69. Audrey Singer, *The Rise of New Immigrant Gateways* (Washington, D.C.: Brookings Institution, 2004), 9, 21–29, https://www.brookings.edu/wp-content/uploads/2016/06/20040301 _gateways.pdf (accessed August 12, 2017); George Mason University Center for Regional Analysis, *Update from the 2010 Census: Population Change in the Washington DC Metropolitan Area* (April 2011), http://cra.gmu.edu/pdfs/researach_reports/recent_reports/Population_Change _in_the_Washington_Metropolitan_Area.pdf (accessed August 12, 2017); George Mason University Center for Regional Analysis, *The Washington DC Metropolitan Area Rental Market*, Update from the American Community Survey (March 2011), http://cra.gmu.edu/pdfs/CRA _Census_Series_RentalMarket.pdf / (accessed August 12, 2017).

70. Metropolitan Washington Council of Governments, *Regional Activity Centers and Clusters* (Washington, D.C.: Council of Governments, 2007), http://www.mwcog.org/uploads/pub -documents/ylhZVw20070828145020.pdf (accessed August 12, 2017).

71. Andrew Wiese, *Places of Their Own: African American Suburbanization in the Twentieth Century* (Chicago: University of Chicago Press, 2003), 274–281; Lacy, *Blue-Chip Black*, 2–3, 9–17, 48–49; Malecki, "Jockeying for Position," 1104–1108; Daphne T. Greenwood and Richard P. F. Holt, *Local Economic Development in the 21st Century* (Armonk, NY: M. E. Sharpe, 2010), 8–9, 14–25.

72. Schrag, *The Great Society Subway*, 222.

73. Joel Achenbach, "A Loopy Birthday to the Beltway at 30," *WP*, August 17, 1994.

74. Brooke A. Masters, "The Final N. Va. Frontier; Western Pr. William Eyed for Development," *WP*, February 16, 1990; Stephen C. Fehr, "Highway Links Loudoun to Region's Growing Pains," *WP*, September 24, 1995; Justin Blum, "Dulles Greenway a 'Double-Edged Sword'; Road Brings Business Loudoun Wants and the Housing Development It Doesn't," *WP*, July 26, 1999; Masek, Lindsay, and Goward, "Dynamics of Urban Growth."

75. Weiner, *Urban Transportation Planning*, 140–152; Richard F. Weingroff, "Creating a Landmark: The Intermodal Surface Transportation Act of 1991," *Public Roads* 65, no. 3 (November/December 2001).

76. Ann O'Hanlon, "But Who Will Tend to the Farm? No Man's Land: Many Outer-County Farmers Struggle on Property That Is Too Rural, Yet Too Urban," *WP*, April 7, 1996.

77. Peter Pae, "In Loudoun, Growing Steady; New Farmers and Methods Help Acreage Remain Constant Despite Development," *WP*, June 30, 1997; Graeme Zielinski, "Residents Raise a Stink over Chicken Manure; Odor from Nearby Farm Causes a Clash," *WP*, May 21, 2000; Raymond McCaffrey, "A Mild and Woolly Adventure; 'Hobbyist' Farmers Tend Flocks in Effort to Reconnect with Land," *WP*, March 24, 2001.

78. Brian Roe, Elena G. Irwin, and Hazel A. Morrow-Jones, "The Effects of Farmland, Farmland Preservation, and Other Neighborhood Amenities on Housing Values and Residential Growth," *Land Economics* 80, no. 1 (February 2004): 55–75; Thomas Harvey and Martha A. Works, *The Rural Landscape as Urban Amenity: Land Use on the Rural-Urban Interface in the*

Portland, Oregon, Metropolitan Area, Working Paper (Cambridge, MA: Lincoln Institute of Land Policy, 2001), http://www.lincolninst.edu/pubs/dl/92_Harvey01.pdf (accessed March 18, 2012).

79. Dan Eggen, "Attempt to Preserve Rural Flavor Leaves Some with a Bitter Taste," *WP*, February 1, 1998.

80. Justin Blum, "Panel Urges Protection County's Rural Character," *WP*, November 12, 1998; Amy Joyce, "Down on the Farm, a New Focus Takes Root; County Agency Aims to Redirect Rural Economy," *WP*, August 30, 2001.

81. Jennifer Ordonez, "Just a Little Reminder About Who Feeds You; Farm Tour Aims to Teach Locals, Draw Tourists," *WP*, September 25, 1997; Jennifer Lenhart, "Bumper Crop of Markets Is Paying Off for Farmers; Produce Vendors Find Fertile Ground at Variety of Area Sites," *WP*, June 20, 1999; Peter Pae, "Urbanites Explore Loudoun Farms," *WP*, October 17, 1999; Stephanie Stoughton, "N. Va. Suburbs Show Tourists a Rustic Face; 7 Counties Join Forces to Promote Rural Appeal," *WP*, February 26, 1998; Maria Glod, "Report Touts History's Riches; Rural Preservation Efforts Help Economy, Coalition Says," *WP*, May 4, 2000.

82. Rudolph A. Pyatt Jr., "Toss the Old Cures and Find a New Traffic Decongestant," *WP*, March 22, 1999; Mike Tidwell, "A Look at . . . Sprawl; Escaping L.A. on the Potomac," *WP*, May 3, 1998; Glenn Frankel and Stephen C. Fehr, "As the Economy Grows, the Trees Fall; D.C. Area's Green Space Is Shrinking Fast Because of Development's Ongoing March," *WP*, March 23, 1997; Richard K. Olson and Thomas A. Lyson, *Under the Blade: The Conversion of Agricultural Landscapes* (Boulder, CO: Westview Press, 1999), 147–160; Daniel Press, *Saving Open Space: The Politics of Local Preservation in California* (Berkeley: University of California Press, 2002), 59–60, 74; Dan Eggen and Peter Pae, "Anti-Development Forces Massing Along Home Front; Traffic, Taxes, Crowded Schools Rouse Suburbs," *WP*, December 14, 1997; Dan Eggen, "Suburban Developers Find Public Anger Building," *WP*, July 19, 1998.

Chapter 1. A River Revived

1. Darryl Fears, "Guardian of the Potomac Ed Merrifield Is Sailing Toward the End of His Job as Riverkeeper," *Washington Post* [*WP*], December 30, 2012.

2. Joel M. Gross and Lynn Dodge, *Clean Water Act* (Chicago: American Bar Association, 2005); Charles Milazzo, *Unlikely Environmentalists: Congress and Clean Water, 1945–1972* (Lawrence: University Press of Kansas, 2006); William L. Andreen, "Water Quality Today—Has the Clean Water Act Been a Success?" *Alabama Law Review* 55 (2003–2004): 537–594; John A. Hoornbeek, *Water Pollution Policies and the American States: Runaway Bureaucracies or Congressional Control?* (Albany: State University of New York Press, 2011); Dietrich Earnhart and Robert L. Glicksman, *Pollution Limits and Polluters' Efforts to Comply: The Role of Government Monitoring and Enforcement* (Stanford, CA: Stanford Economics and Finance, 2011); Andrew W. Stoddard, Jon B. Harcum, Jonathan T. Simpson, et al., *Municipal Wastewater Treatment: Evaluating Improvements in National Water Quality* (Hoboken, NJ: John Wiley and Sons, 2002).

3. Norbert A. Jaworski, Bill Romano, and Claire Buchanan, *The Potomac River Basin and Its Estuary: Landscape Loadings and Water Quality Trends, 1895–2005* (Rockville, MD: Interstate Commission on the Potomac River Basin, 2015), https://www.potomacriver.org/focus-areas /water-quality/the-potomac-river-basin-and-its-estuary-landscape-loadings-and-water-quality -trends-1895-2005/ (accessed August 11, 2017).

4. Myron F. Uman, "Blue Plains: Saga of a Treatment Plant," *EPA Journal* 20 (1994): 20–21.

5. Adam Rome, *The Bulldozer in the Countryside: Suburban Sprawl and the Rise of American Environmentalism* (New York: Cambridge University Press, 2001), 47, 117; Aubrey Graves,

"Fairfax County Moves Ahead to Reduce Pollution," *WP*, October 1, 1955; "Tons of Soil Choke Area Streams; Engineer Blames Building Projects for Sediment," *WP*, November 5, 1960.

6. The Interstate Commission began publishing its monthly *Potomac River Basin Reporter* in 1950, a large run of which is available at the Special Collections Research Center at the George Washington University in Washington, D.C. See also Interstate Commission on the Potomac River Basin, *Teamwork on the Potomac: A Report on the Activities of the Interstate Commission on the Potomac River Basin* (Washington. D.C.: Interstate Commission, 1958).

7. "Plan to Tap Potomac Is Revealed by WSSC; Rockville Informed by Utility That It Hopes to Use River as Water Supply," *WP*, August 16, 1956; Muriel Guinn, "New Move Is Revealed for Tapping Potomac; Fairfax Official Plans Construction of Filter Plant at Great Falls," *WP*, August 25, 1956; "Suburbs to Get Potomac Water," *WP*, May 9, 1957.

8. Richard L. Lyons, "3d of River Is Sewage in Dry Spell; TV Series Sees Area-Wide Plan Badly Needed in Fight on Pollution," *WP*, August 31, 1955.

9. Milazzo, *Unlikely Environmentalists*, 6–7, 18–19.

10. U.S. Congress, An Act to Authorize the Commissioners of the District of Columbia to Plan, Construction, Operate, and Maintain a Sanitary Sewer to Connect the Dulles International Airport with the District of Columbia System, 86th Cong., 2nd sess., Public Law 86-515, June 12, 1960.

11. For a collection of primary and secondary materials, see Samuel E. Neel Collection, MSS 06-02, Fairfax Public Library, Fairfax, Virginia. Stewart L. Udall Oral History Interview, Transcript, December 16, 1969, Lyndon Baines Johnson Library and Museum, http://www.lbjlibrary.net/assets/documents/archives/oral_histories/udall/UDALL05.PDF (accessed August 11, 2017).

12. Daniel Press, *Saving Open Space: The Politics of Local Preservation in California* (Berkeley: University of California Press, 2002), 69–74.

13. John B. Willmann, "5 Town Houses Under Way at Merrywood," *WP*, March 4, 1978.

14. Lyndon Baines Johnson, "Special Message to the Congress on Conservation and Restoration of Natural Beauty," *Public Papers of the Presidents of the United States: Lyndon B. Johnson, 1965*, vol. 1, entry 54 (Washington. D.C.: Government Printing Office, 1966), http://www.lbjlibrary.net/collections/selected-speeches/1965/02-08-1965.html (accessed August 11, 2017).

15. Alan L. Dessoff, "U.S. Fights Officialdom to Save Potomac Basin," *WP*, January 4, 1967.

16. William Nye Curry, "Suit Is Urged Against Md. Water Board," *WP*, August 15, 1971.

17. Norman M. Cole, "A River Revived," *WP*, May 18, 1980.

18. Environmental Protection Agency (EPA), *National Capital Region Water and Waste Management Report* (Washington. D.C.: EPA, 1971), II-1-2, box E10, Verlin W. Smith Business Collection, unprocessed, Virginia Historical Society, Richmond, VA; "The Politics of Pollution," editorial, *WP*, June 25, 1971; Henry Aubin, "Potomac Cleanup Efforts Mired in Red Tape: Lots of Promise, Little Cooperation," *WP*, January 16, 1971; Cole, "A River Revived."

19. Joseph W. Penfold, untitled, *WP*, December 12, 1971; Henry Aubin, "At Blue Plains: Sludge Is Piling Up, No Place to Put It," *WP*, January 2, 1971.

20. EPA, *National Capital Region Water and Waste Management Report*.

21. Matt Schudel, "Gilbert Gude, 84; GOP Legislator, Environmentalist," *WP*, June 9, 2007; "Perusing the Potomac," editorial, *WP*, August 8, 1975.

22. On the CWA, see Milazzo, *Unlikely Environmentalists*, 224–228; Gross and Dodge, *Clean Water Act*; Stoddard et al., *Municipal Wastewater Treatment*, 2–3, 27–41; Earnhart and Glicksman, *Pollution Limits and Polluters' Efforts*, 6–39. One major deficiency involved toxic pollutants. Following passage of the CWA, the EPA was supposed to develop a list of pollutants

to regulate within 90 days and propose standards within 180 days. But it took fifteen years and several lawsuits to get the regulations established. Rosemary O'Leary, *Environmental Change: Federal Courts and the EPA* (Philadelphia: Temple University Press, 1993), 23–44.

23. Cole, "A River Revived."

24. Ibid.; William N. Curry, "Fairfax Judge Lifts Ban on Sewer Links," *WP*, July 29, 1970; William N. Curry, "Fairfax Reduces Pollution of River," *WP*, November 7, 1970.

25. William N. Curry, "Holton to Name Three Activists to Water Board; Big Impact on Pollution Is Expected," *WP*, August 16, 1970; Cole, "A River Revived."

26. Curry, "Suit Is Urged." The WSSC was allotted 88 mgd but sent 124 mgd on average.

27. Cole, "A River Revived."

28. Ibid.; Aubin, "Lots of Promise, Little Cooperation"; Jim Landers, "WSSC Sewage Plant Delay Assailed: Pollution 'Time Bomb' Cited," *WP*, December 29, 1971.

29. Norman J. Cole Jr. to Johanna S. Norris, letter, December 31, 1971, in box 12, Call No. 32820, Subject Files of the Virginia State Water Control Board, Office of the Executive Director, 1946–1986, Library of Virginia, State Records Center, Richmond, VA.

30. Leon Dash, "Sewage Pollution in Montgomery Rises Despite Hookup Moratorium," *WP*, May 16, 1973.

31. Cole, "A River Revived."

32. Jay Mathews, "Va. Agency Asks Congress to Fight Potomac Pollution," *WP*, February 20, 1972; Jay Mathews, "U.S. Policing of the Potomac Opposed," *WP*, June 13, 1972.

33. *Poisoned Waters*, directed by Rick Young, Frontline (Boston: WGBH Educational Foundation, 2009), http://www.pbs.org/wgbh/pages/frontline/poisonedwaters/ (accessed April 21, 2014); Angus Phillips, "Nose Deep in Figures, GAO Can't See the River for the Cesspool," *WP*, February 14, 1982; Stephen J. Lynton, "Ol' Man Potomac, He Just Keeps Getting Cleaner: The Cleansing of the Potomac," *WP*, November 8, 1982; Interstate Commission on the Potomac River Basin, *Potomac River Basin Reporter* 47, no. 7 (July 1991).

34. Gross and Dodge, *Clean Water Act*; Stoddard et al., *Municipal Wastewater Treatment*, 27–41; Earnhart and Glicksman, *Pollution Limits and Polluters' Efforts*; Colin Crawford, "Wastewater Resources: Rethinking Centralized Wastewater Treatment Systems, Land Use Planning and Water Conservation," *Urban Lawyer* 42/43, no. 4/1 (Fall 2010/Winter 2011): 155–178.

35. State Water Control Board v. Washington Suburban Sanitary Commission, No. 1813-73, U.S. District Court for the District of Columbia (1974); Douglas B. Feaver, "Potomac Filth Pact Is Signed," *WP*, June 14, 1974. For more on Norman Cole, see Norman M. Cole Jr. Papers, 1962–1966, C0066, George Mason University Special Collections and Archives, Fairfax, VA.

36. Washington Post Editorial Board, "Norman Monroe Cole Jr.," *WP*, February 9, 1997.

37. Marian Agnew collected a wealth of materials on water issues in the Washington area during the 1970s, including a collection of interviews with the sewer ladies. See box 17, Marian K. Agnew Papers, ca. 1967–1993, MSS1 Ag635 a FA2, Virginia Historical Society, Richmond, VA.

38. Loretta Tofani, "'Sewer Ladies' Keep Officials in Line," *WP*, March 1, 1980; "Leader in Fight Against Pollution Dies," *WP*, February 25, 1979; Sewer Ladies–Fred Gannett Oral History with COG, July 12, 1999, box 17, Agnew Papers.

39. Sewer Ladies—Enid Miles Oral History with COG, February 20, 1999, box 17, Agnew Papers.

40. Tofani, "'Sewer Ladies.'"

41. Sewer Ladies—Enid Miles; Marian Agnew, Testimony on WMA (June 1977), folder 305, box 10, Agnew Papers.

42. Cole, "A River Revived."

43. Brian Balogh, *Chain Reaction: Expert Debate and Public Participation in American Commercial Nuclear Power, 1945–1975* (New York: Cambridge University Press, 1991), 16–20, 260, 271. In 1972, the EPA published a pamphlet encouraging citizen participation in environmental issues. Environmental Protection Agency, *Don't Leave It All to the Experts: The Citizen's Role in Environmental Decision Making* (Washington. D.C.: EPA, 1972).

44. Sewer Ladies—Ruth H. Allen Oral History Report with COG, February 19, 1999, box 17, Agnew Papers.

45. Thomas Grubisich, "Dickerson Plant Veto Is Upheld by U.S. Court: Montgomery County Has No Specific Alternative," *WP*, April 27, 1978.

46. The Safe Drinking Water Act of 1974 expanded federal authority to every public or private system that supplied water at least sixty days a year to twenty-five people or more, but monitoring and reporting was hard to enforce.

47. LaBarbara Bowman, "Sewage Facility Site Set; Montgomery Plant Slated at Dickerson," *WP*, October 16, 1973.

48. Sewer Ladies—Enid Miles; Environmental Protection Agency, Region III, NEPA Review of the Proposed Montgomery County, Maryland 60 MGD AWT Facility, Philadelphia, PA, March 31, 1976, folder 1860, box 62, Agnew Papers; Environmental Protection Agency, Administrator's Decision on the Proposed Dickerson Wastewater Treatment Plant Grant Application (August 20, 1976), folder 1860, box 62, Agnew Papers.

49. Montgomery Environmental Coalition, testimony, May 28, 1975, folder 1861, box 62, Agnew Papers; "Opponents Charge Insufficient Study Made on Dickerson Plant," *Frederick* [MD] *Post*, May 29, 1975. For an earlier statement, see Montgomery Environmental Coalition, Dollars Down the Drain: An Economic Critique of the Montgomery County Advanced Waste Treatment Study (n.p.), February 22, 1973, folder 1861, box 62, Agnew Papers.

50. Montgomery County Civic Federation, Testimony Regarding the Proposal for an Advanced Wastewater Treatment Plant at Dickerson, Maryland, May 28, 1975, folder 1861, box 62, Agnew Papers.

51. Sewer Ladies—Louise Chesnut Oral History with COG, February 18, 1999, box 17, Agnew Papers; Sewer Ladies—Patty Mohler Oral History with COG, March 25, 1999, box 17, Agnew Papers.

52. EPA, Administrator's Decision on the Proposed Dickerson Wastewater Treatment Plant.

53. Montgomery County Civic Federation, "Advanced Waste Treatment Plant Dickerson," letter to the editor, April 18, 1976, folder 1860, box 62, Agnew Papers; Montgomery Environmental Coalition, "MEC Supports EPA Dickerson Decision, Calls for Alternatives," press release, August 23, 1976, folder 1861, box 62, Agnew Papers; Milton Coleman, "EPA Urged to Clear Dickerson Sewage Plant," *WP*, July 16, 1976; Milton Coleman, "EPA Urged to Clear Dickerson Sewage Plant," *WP*, July 16, 1976.

54. Grubisich, "Dickerson Plant Veto Is Upheld by U.S. Court."

55. Maryland ex rel. Burch v. Costle, No. 76–1779 (D.D.C.), April 27, 1978, http://elr.info /sites/default/files/litigation/8.20442.htm (accessed October 26, 2015); Grubisich, "Dickerson Plant Veto Is Upheld by U.S. Court."

56. A permanent composting facility operated in Montgomery from the early 1980s until 1999, when officials closed it to avoid the costs of adding filters to reduce odors that drew complaints of incoming residents. Debbie Praeger, "Desperate Search: As Prime Land Is Filled with Sludge, Officials Say, 'There's No Place Left to Go,'" *WP*, May 17, 1979; United States v. District

of Columbia et al., 654 f2d 802, July 29, 1981; Montgomery County, MD, "County Relieved of Financial Obligation to Sludge Composting Facility Grants; Way Paved for Permanent Closure Of 'Site II' in East County," news release, June 5, 2001, http://www2.montgomerycountymd.gov /mcgportalapps/Press_Detail.aspx?Item_ID=8192 (accessed August 11, 2017).

57. Blair T. Bower and Anne M. Blackburn, *Dollars & Sense: A Report on Water Quality Management in the Washington Metropolitan Area* (Bethesda, MD: Interstate Commission on the Potomac River Basin, 1975), box 39, Agnew Papers; Phillips, "GAO Can't See the River for the Cesspool"; Lynton, "Ol' Man Potomac, He Just Keeps Getting Cleaner"; Paul Hodge, "Good News for Turtles: Potomac Plants Reviving," *WP*, September 2, 1983; Associated Press, "Potomac Gets Mixed Review on Pollution," *WP*, March 28, 1985; John Lancaster, "The Potomac's 'Remarkable Improvement': Plants, Fish Come Back and Some Spots Are Clean Enough for Swimming, COG Says," *WP*, May 14, 1987; Cole, "A River Revived."

58. J. Dicken Kirschten, "Plunging the Problems from the Sewage Treatment Grant System," *National Journal*, February 5, 1977; Bower and Blackburn, *Dollars & Sense*.

59. United States EPA, In the Matter of Blue Plains Sewage Treatment Plant NPDES Permit No. DC0021199, Docket No. DC-AH-102, esp. 74–108, box 4, Virginia State Water Control Board, Administrative Hearing and Legal Files, 1978–1983, Accession 38493, State Government Records Collection, Library of Virginia, Richmond, VA.

60. Keith M. Brooks, *208 Planning in the Potomac River Basin: The Key to the Clean Water Act or More Plans for the Shelf?* (Rockville, MD: Interstate Commission on the Potomac River Basin, 1979); Sewer Ladies—Ruth H. Allen.

61. Gross and Dodge, *Clean Water Act*; Andreen, "Water Quality Today"; Hoornbeek, *Water Pollution Policies and the American States*; Martin V. Melosi, *Precious Commodity: Providing Water for America's Cities* (Pittsburgh, PA: University of Pittsburgh Press, 2011), 71–75. On the issue of sprawl, see Thomas Grubisich, "Sewer Grants: The Pipelines to Urban Sprawl," *WP*, January 31, 1980.

62. O'Leary, *Environmental Change*, 45, 160, 170.

63. Blue Plains Technical Committee and Metropolitan Washington Council of Governments, "Annotated Version" of the Blue Plains Intermunicipal Agreement of 1985 (Washington, DC, January 2005), https://www.mwcog.org/environment/water/blueplains/documents /Annotated%20IMA-Jan%202005_final.pdf (accessed March 13, 2014).

64. Samuel Hays, *Beauty, Health, and Permanence: Environmental Politics in the United States, 1955–1985* (New York: Cambridge University Press, 1987), 491–526; *Poisoned Waters*, online transcript, http://www.pbs.org/wgbh/pages/frontline/poisonedwaters/etc/script.html (accessed August 11, 2017); Judith Layzer, *Open for Business: Conservatives Opposition to Environmental Regulation* (Cambridge, MA: MIT Press, 2014), 83–134.

65. Interstate Commission on the Potomac River Basin, "Chesapeake Bay Cleanup Gets into Gear," *Potomac River Basin Reporter* 39, no. 6 (July 1983); Interstate Commission on the Potomac River Basin, *Potomac River Basin Reporter* 39, no. 9 (November/December 1983); Interstate Commission on the Potomac River Basin, "'Summer Summit': New Chesapeake Bay Agreement Draft," *Potomac River Basin Reporter* 43, no. 8 (August/September 1987); Andrew H. Macdonald, "A Look at . . . the State of the Chesapeake: Bay Watch: Safer, But Still Not Saved," *WP*, February 23, 1997.

66. Susan DeFord, "District Is Part of Watershed Plan to Save the Anacostia: Plan Seeks to Revive Anacostia," *WP*, August 1, 1989; Angus Phillips, "Righting the Wrongs to the Anacostia," *WP*, June 12, 1990.

67. Gross and Dodge, *Clean Water Act*, 11, 101–111.

68. Thomas Bell, "Group Envisions a Clean Anacostia," *WP*, April 19, 1990.

69. Interstate Commission on the Potomac River Basin, "Md., D.C. Sign Anacostia Cleanup Bill," *Potomac River Basin Reporter* 40, no. 7 (July 1984); DeFord, "District Is Part of Watershed Plan."

70. Blake Gumprecht, *The Los Angeles River: Its Life, Death, and Possible Rebirth* (Baltimore: Johns Hopkins University Press), 2001.

71. Ellen Hoffman, "'The Anacostia Has Become 'Back Door to the Capital,'" *WP*, May 19, 1969.

72. Elizabeth Eiener, "City Environmentalists Join Forces at Conference," *WP*, November 21, 1991.

73. D'Vera Cohn, "Boone: Anacostia Is Worth Saving; 'Ugly' River Needs Friends," *WP*, September 16, 1990.

74. David A. Fahrenthold, "Waste-Deep in the Big Muddy; Advocate for the Anacostia Worked to Clean Up the Long-Fouled River. Now, as Robert Boone Steps Back, the Waterway Is Being Rediscovered," *WP*, June 17, 2008.

75. D'Vera Cohn, "In the Anacostia, Signs of Revival," *WP*, June 9, 1994.

76. D'Vera Cohn, "Leaders Set Goals for Ailing River: Anacostia Cleanup Already Underway," *WP*, November 14, 1991; Wiener, "City's Environmentalists Join Forces"; "Saturday Cleanup on Anacostia River," *WP*, April 27, 1989; Thomas Bell, "Group Envisions a Clean Anacostia," *WP*, April 19, 1990; D'Vera Cohn, "River Being Put Back on Course: Public and Private Efforts Coming Together to Restore the Anacostia to Health," *WP*, July 26, 1990; D'Vera Cohn, "Restored Marsh Dedicated at Aquatic Gardens," *WP*, September 22, 1993; Anacostia Watershed Society, "History," website of the AWS, http://www.anacostiaws.org/about/history (accessed January 19, 2015).

77. D'Vera Cohn, "Environmentalists East of River: Poll Finds Widespread Concern About Pollution in Wards Seven and Eight," *WP*, April 18, 1996.

78. Jamison E. Colburn, "Localism's Ecology: Protecting and Restoring Habitat in the Suburban Nation," *Ecology Law Quarterly* 33 (2006): 945–1014.

79. James D. Cummins, *The Potomac River American Shad Restoration Project 2004 Summary Report* (Rockville, MD: Interstate Commission on the Potomac River, 2004), 1–2; Angus Phillips, "Future Remains Bleak for Potomac River Shad Fishing," *WP*, May 13, 1980; David Montgomery, "For Shad, an Amends; Scientists Devise a Better 'Fish Ladder,'" *WP*, October 12, 1999.

80. Cummins, *The Potomac River American Shad Restoration Project*, 1–2.

81. Montgomery, "For Shad, an Amends."

82. Robert W. Adler, *Restoring Colorado River Ecosystems: A Troubled Sense of Immensity* (Washington. D.C.: Island Press, 2007), 26–54.

83. Jacqueline L. Salmon, "Volunteers Wade Right In to Save Plants; Wetlands Vegetation Facing Destruction During Building of New Wilson Bridge," *WP*, March 25, 2001; Griff Witte, "Restoring Damaged Wetlands; Bridge Project Aims to Replace Habitats Throughout Region," *WP*, July 17, 2003.

84. Adler, *Restoring Colorado River Ecosystems*.

85. Potomac Conservancy, *State of the Nation's River 2008: Potomac Water Runoff* (Silver Spring, MD, 2008), http://potomac.org/sonr/ (accessed April 14, 2014); Potomac Riverkeeper, *Protecting the Potomac: Spring 2007 Status Report* (Washington, DC, 2007), http://potomacriverkeeper.org/sites/default/files/attachments/protectingthepotomac07.23.2007_low

_res.pdf. This and other webpages with date of last access are no longer available on the site, but can be found using the Internet Archive's Wayback Machine. Anita Huslin, "Survey Finds Md. Streams in Poor Health; Watershed Damage from Development and Pollution Widespread," *WP*, September 25, 2000; Kim Hosen, "Protecting Our Waterways," op-ed, *WP*, August 11, 2002.

86. Potomac Conservancy, *State of the Nation's River 2008*.

87. Ibid.

88. Potomac Conservancy, *State of the Nation's River 2010: Farms and Forests: Rural Land Use in the Potomac Watershed* (Washington, DC, 2010), http://potomac.org/sonr/ (accessed April 14, 2014); *Poisoned Waters*, online transcript.

89. Eric Lipton, "Poultry Poses Growing Potomac Hazard; Chicken Production Employs Many but May Taint Water for Many More," *WP*, June 1, 1997; John Johnson, "A Diminishing Potomac Hazard," op-ed, *WP*, June 14, 1997; *Poisoned Waters*, online transcript.

90. Eric Lipton, "Potomac Seen as River with Rough Going Ahead," *WP*, April 17, 1997.

91. Gross and Dodge, *Clean Water Act*, 110–129; Andreen, "Water Quality Today," 562–564, 592–593; Hoornbeek, *Water Pollution Policies*; Kelly Barker," Extended Controls Target Chesapeake; Sewage, Runoff Named as Problems," *WP*, August 15, 1999.

92. U.S. Department of Justice, "D.C. Will Overhaul Blue Plains Treatment Plant," press release, April 5, 1996, http://www.justice.gov/opa/pr/1996/April96/157.txt.htm; Susan Levine, "Where Sewage Comes Clean; Plant Outflow Raises Quality of Potomac," *WP*, September 12, 2000; D'Vera Cohn, "EPA Notes Improvements in D.C.'s Water System," *WP*, February 7, 1997.

93. Debbi Wilgoren, "WASA Agrees to Build Tunnels to Stem Sewage Spills," *WP*, December 3, 2004; Ashley Halsey III, "Meet Lady Bird, A Massive Machine Digging Out a Solution to D.C. Wastewater Woes," *WP*, February 15, 2014.

94. Halsey, "Meet Lady Bird."; Ashley Halsey III, "You Asked for More About Lady Bird, We Answered," *WP*, February 18, 2014.

95. Halsey, "You Asked for More About Lady Bird." On shortfalls in federal capital investment for municipal wastewater infrastructure as a problem in improving water quality, see Andreen, "Water Quality Today," 592.

96. O'Leary, *Environmental Change*, 45, 160, 170.

97. Edward P. Weber, *Pluralism by the Rules: Conflict and Cooperation in Environmental Regulation* (Washington. D.C.: Georgetown University Press, 1998).

98. Alice Ferguson Foundation, "History," Alice Ferguson Foundation website, http://fergusonfoundation.org/history/ (accessed January 20, 2015). The foundation's website has a wealth of educational resources for teachers and students.

99. Eugene L. Meyer, "Region Springs into Action for River Cleanup," *WP*, April 5, 2001; Derrill Holly, "Officials Resolve to Tackle Trash in Potomac Watershed," *WP*, March 23, 2006; Alice Ferguson Foundation, "Trash-Free Potomac Watershed Initiative: Cleanup History," http://fergusonfoundation.org/trash-free-potomac-watershed-initiative/potomac-river-watershed-cleanup/cleanup-history/ (accessed January 20, 2015).

100. Holly, "Officials Resolve to Tackle Trash"; Opinion Works Inc., *Why People Litter in the Potomac River Watershed* (Accokeek, MD: Alice Ferguson Foundation, 2008), http://fergusonfoundation.org/pdf/08_OpinionWorksSurvey.pdf (accessed February 24, 2013).

101. Eugene L. Meyer, "For Fifth Graders, a Classroom in the Open Air: Students from Tulip Grove Elementary School in Bowie Investigate Nature," *WP*, May 9, 1996.

102. Fears, "Guardian of the Potomac"; Potomac Riverkeeper, *About Us*, http://potomacriverkeeper.org/mission (accessed August 11, 2017).

103. Potomac Riverkeeper Network, *History*, http://potomacriverkeeper.org/history (accessed April 22, 2014).

104. Leef Smith, "River Patrol to Keep Environmental Watch on Potomac," *WP*, June 7, 2001; Sheila Walsh, "Keeping Tabs on the Watershed; Teams of Volunteers Monitor Streams," *WP*, November 15, 2001.

105. Walsh, "Keeping Tabs on the Watershed."

106. Fears, "Guardian of the Potomac."

107. Ibid.

108. Ibid.; Potomac Riverkeeper, *Potomac Riverkeeper Annual Reports* (Washington, D.C., 2007–2009), http://www.potomacriverkeeper.org/annual-reports (accessed February 24, 2013). Fears, "Guardian of the Potomac."

109. Potomac Riverkeeper, *Annual Reports.*; *Poisoned Waters*, online transcript; H. Hendrick Belin, "The New Polluters of the Potomac," *WP*, April 19, 2009; National Institute of Environmental Health Sciences, "Endocrine Disruptors," http://www.niehs.nih.gov/health/topics /agents/endocrine/ (accessed October 27, 2015).

110. Potomac Riverkeeper Network, "Lawsuit Forces Potomac River Plant to Halt Water Pollution Violations and Pay for Millions in Improvements," press release, October 21, 2015, http://www.potomacriverkeepernetwork.org/s/151020-PRK-WSSC-Consent-Decree.pdf (accessed October 27, 2015).

111. Ibid.; Katherine Shaver, "WSSC Agrees to Reduce Pollution in Potomac River from Treatment Plant," *WP*, October 21, 2015.

112. Potomac Riverkeeper Network, "Lawsuit Forces Potomac River Plant to Halt Water Pollution."

113. Ibid.

114. Shaver, "WSSC Agrees to Reduce Pollution."

Chapter 2. Where Have All the Forests Gone?

1. Adam Rome, *The Genius of Earth Day: How a 1970 Teach-In Unexpectedly Made the First Green Generation* (New York: Hill and Wang, 2013).

2. "200 Back Purchase of Burling Site," *Washington Post* [*WP*], May 29, 1970; "Burling Park Backed with Film, Songs," *Washington Star*, May 29, 1970; Sharon Francis, "The Burling Tract" (unpublished manuscript, 1971), 22–23 (in author's possession, obtained from John Adams, July 16, 2014).

3. Susan Daniel, "Burling Song" [1970], in folder 1389, box 46, Marian K. Agnew Papers, ca. 1967–1993 (MSS1 Ag635 a FA2), Virginia Historical Society, Richmond, VA.

4. Samuel P. Hays, *Beauty, Health, and Permanence: Environmental Politics in the United States, 1955–1985* (New York: Cambridge University Press, 1987), 13–39, 71–98, 137–158; Adam Rome, *The Bulldozer in the Countryside: Suburban Sprawl and the Rise of American Environmentalism* (New York: Cambridge University Press, 2001), 119–152; Karl Boyd Brooks, *Before Earth Day: The Origins of American Environmental Law, 1945–1970* (Lawrence: University Press of Kansas, 2009), 94; Christopher C. Sellers, *Crabgrass Crucible: Suburban Nature and the Rise of Modern Environmentalism in Twentieth-Century America* (Chapel Hill: University of North Carolina Press, 2012), 39–67.

5. Rome, *The Bulldozer in the Countryside*, 87–118, 153–188; Sellers, *Crabgrass Crucible.*

6. On the ties between slow growth and land preservation, see Tom Daniels and Mark Lapping, "Land Preservation: An Essential Ingredient in Smart Growth," *Journal of Planning*

Literature 19 (2005): 316–329; Daniel Press, *Saving Open Space: The Politics of Local Preservation in California* (Berkeley: University of California Press, 2002), 38–42, 59–60.

7. John A. Powell. "Opportunity-Based Housing," *Journal of Affordable Housing and Community Development Law* 12 (2002): 188–228.

8. Robert D. Bullard, Glenn S. Johnson, and Angel O. Torres, "Environmental Costs and Consequences of Sprawl," in *Sprawl City: Race, Politics, and Planning in Atlanta*, ed. Robert D. Bullard, Glenn S. Johnson, and Angel O. Torres (Washington, D.C.: Island Press, 2000), 22; Brooks, *Before Earth Day*, 7, 94; James Longhurst, *Citizen Environmentalists* (Medford, MA: Tufts University Press, published by University Press of New England, 2010).

9. Christopher Bonastia, *Knocking on the Door: The Federal Government's Attempt to Desegregate the Suburbs* (Princeton, NJ: Princeton University Press, 2006).

10. Brian Patrick Larkin, "The Forty-Year 'First Step': The Fair Housing Act as an Incomplete Tool for Suburban Integration," *Columbia Law Review* 107, no. 7 (November 2007): 1631.

11. On charges of elitism among environmentalists, see e.g. Denton E. Morrison and Riley E. Dunlap, "Environmentalism and Elitism: A Conceptual and Empirical Analysis," *Environmental Management* 10, no. 5 (1986): 581–589; Diane M. Samdahl, "Social Determinants of Environmental Concern," *Environment and Behavior* 21, no. 1 (January 1989): 57–81.

12. Board of Supervisors of Fairfax County, Virginia v. G. Wallace Carper et al., 200 Va. 653, 107 S.E. 2d 390 (1959); Russ Banham, *The Fight for Fairfax: A Struggle for a Great American County* (Fairfax, VA: George Mason University Press, 2009), 48–50.

13. Grace Dawson, *No Little Plans: Fairfax County's PLUS Program for Managing Growth* (Washington, D.C.: Urban Institute, 1977), 14–21; Lucille Harrigan and Alexander von Hoffman, *Happy to Grow: Development and Planning in Fairfax County, Virginia* (Cambridge, MA: Joint Center for Housing Studies, Harvard University, 2004), http://www.jchs.harvard.edu/sites /jchs.harvard.edu/files/w04-2_von_hoffman.pdf (accessed August 12, 2017). The close supervision that the state exerted over localities operated under a legal principle known as the Dillon Rule. While this often manifested itself in state oversight of local planning, it also extended to the structure of the judicial system. Judges in the state of Virginia, even at the local level, were appointed by the state legislature rather than elected, which made them more responsive to the interests of the party that appointed them rather than local communities.

14. U.S. Census Bureau, *Census of Population and Housing*, 1940 and 1970, in Minnesota Population Center, *National Historic Geographic Information System: Version 2.0* (Minneapolis: University of Minnesota, 2011), http://www.nhgis.org (accessed November 3, 2012); Dawson, *No Little Plans*, 23–24; Harrigan and von Hoffman, *Happy to Grow*, 9–13.

15. Fairfax County Planning Division, *The Vanishing Land: Proposals for Open Space Preservation* (1962), 28–29. Prince George's County had four parks totaling 3,104 acres while Washington, D.C., had two parks with 1,852 acres.

16. Hays, *Beauty, Health, and Permanence*, 13–39, 71–98, 137–158.

17. Fairfax County Planning Division, *The Vanishing Land*.

18. University of Virginia Student Legal Research Group, "Open Space Law in the State of Virginia," in Fairfax County Planning Division, *The Vanishing Land*, 71–81.

19. Kirk Scharfenberg, "Suburban Park Policy Accents the People," *WP*, May 22, 1969.

20. Land and Water Conservation Fund Coalition, *The Land and Water Conservation Fund in YOUR State*, https://www.lwcfcoalition.com/tools (accessed August 12, 2017).

21. David Berry, "Preservation of Open Space and the Concept of Value," *American Journal of Economics and Sociology* 35, no. 2 (April 1976): 113–124; Hays, *Beauty, Health, and*

Permanence, 13–39, 139–158; Rome, *The Bulldozer in the Countryside*, 87–118, 153–188; Press, *Saving Open Space*, 38–42, 69–74; Jeffrey C. Sanders, "The Battle for Fort Lawton: Competing Environmental Claims in Postwar Seattle," *Pacific Historical Review* 77, no. 2 (May 2008): 203–235; Sellers, *Crabgrass Crucible*.

22. Woolpert, Inc., "Scotts Run Watershed," *Final Middle Potomac Watershed Management Plan*, vol. 1 (2008), 5-1–5-2, http://www.fairfaxcounty.gov/dpwes/watersheds/publications/mp/01_mp_wmp_ada.pdf (accessed August 12, 2017); Citizens for Burling Park, "Why Burling Park," [1970], 2, item #1, MSS box 1-02, Burling Tract Controversy, City of Fairfax Regional Public Library, Fairfax, VA. For more information on the Burling tract's ecology, see Gary P. Fleming, *Summary of Classified Ecological Communities in the Potomac Gorge, Virginia Riverbend Park to Spout Run* (2004), cited in Fairfax County Park Authority, Resource Management Division, *Natural Resource Management Plan for Riverbend Park: A Potomac Gorge Conservation Site*, rev. ed. (Fairfax, VA: Fairfax County Park Authority, 2011), 49–53, http://www.fairfaxcounty.gov/parks/riverbend/pdf/go-ape/Riverbend-NRMP-2011.pdf (accessed November 28, 2011).

23. Colman McCarthy, "The Unsilent Spring out on the Burling Tract," *WP*, March 30, 1970; Kenneth Bredemeier, "A Fight to Keep Homes from a Piece of Nature," *WP*, February 19, 1970.

24. Ibid.

25. Bredemeier, "A Fight to Keep Homes."

26. Francis, "The Burling Tract," 13.

27. Bullard, Johnson, and Torres, "Environmental Costs and Consequences of Sprawl," 22; Press, *Saving Open Space*, 69–74; Morrison and Dunlap, "Environmentalism and Elitism"; Samdahl, "Social Determinants of Environmental Concern"; George Lipsitz, "The Racialization of Space and the Spatialization of Race: Theorizing the Hidden Architecture of Landscape," *Landscape Journal* 26, no. 1 (2007): 10–23.

28. John B. Willmann, "Proposed Ordinance on Slopes Arouses Builders in Fairfax," *WP*, January 17, 1970; "Stronger Policy Seen on Steep Slope Building," *WP*, January 31, 1970; Bredemeier, "A Fight to Keep Homes"; Michael Kernan, "Battling the Bulldozers," *WP*, July 31, 1970; Francis, "The Burling Tract," 16–18.

29. "Hickel Hits Use of Tract for Housing," *WP*, December 17, 1969.

30. James D. Bell to William M. Lightsey, letter, January 14, 1970, item #1, Burling Tract Controversy.

31. On how development pressures inflate land costs, see Eric T. Freyfogle, *The Land We Share: Price Property and the Common Good* (Washington, D.C.: Island Press, 2003), 227.

32. Northern Virginia Regional Park Authority, "Regional Park Authority Acceptance of Conservation Agreement Offered by Burling Tract Developers: Explanation and Related Background Information," February 27, 1970, in Fairfax County Park Authority, Public Hearing, April 29, 1970, item #1, Burling Tract Controversy.

33. Bredemeier, "A Fight to Keep Homes."

34. Ronald B. Kessler, "U.S. Offers $1.2 Million to Save Scenic Tract," *WP*, February 7, 1970.

35. McCarthy, "The Unsilent Spring."

36. Rome, *The Bulldozer in the Countryside*, 222; Hays, *Beauty, Health, and Permanence*, 13–39.

37. Kenneth Bredemeier, "Hickel Asks Fairfax Planners to Preserve Tract on Potomac," *WP*, February 10, 1970; Bredemeier, "A Fight to Keep Homes"; Francis, "The Burling Tract," 18–19, 27.

38. "What's a Nice Air Force Wife Doing on a Picket Line?" *Family*, March 17, 1971.

39. Fairfax County Board of Supervisors, Minutes, vol. 59, March 11, 1970, 155–157, Fairfax Regional Library; Kenneth Bredemeier, "Fairfax Approves Developer's Plan," *WP*, March 12, 1970; McCarthy, "The Unsilent Spring."

40. Fairfax County Board of Supervisors, Minutes, vol. 59, March 11, 1970, 161–163.

41. Bredemeier, "Fairfax Approves Developer's Plan."

42. Press, *Saving Open Space*, 38–42; Sanders, "The Battle for Fort Lawton." In 1970, President Richard Nixon signed the first environmental education act into law. The National Environmental Education Act of 1970 (Public Law 91-516) included a grants program for teachers and curriculum development. For a period account of environmental education, see William B. Stapp et al., "The Concept of Environmental Education," *Journal of Environmental Education* 1, no. 1 (July 1969): 30–31.

43. Bredemeier, "Fairfax Approves Developer's Plan." For a follow-up statement from Bradley, see Harriet Bradley, "Burling Developers Pledge 'Best Possible' Control Techniques," letter to the editor, *Providence Journal* [McLean, VA], March 20, 1970.

44. Press, *Saving Open Space*, 74.

45. Robert O. Self, *American Babylon: Race and the Struggle for Postwar Oakland* (Princeton, NJ: Princeton University Press, 2003).

46. Freyfogle, *The Land We Share*, 179–201; Richard K. Olson and Thomas A. Lyson, eds., *Under the Blade: The Conversion of Agricultural Landscapes* (Boulder, CO: Westview Press, 1999), 147–162; Berry, "Preservation of Open Space"; Craig R. Smith, "Institutional Determinants of Collaboration: An Empirical Study of County Open-Space Protection," *Journal of Public Administration Research and Theory* 19 (2007): 3; Daniels and Lapping, "Land Preservation," 318–319; Press, *Saving Open Space*, 74.

47. McCarthy, "The Unsilent Spring."

48. Garrett Hardin, "The Tragedy of the Commons," *Science* 162 (December 1968): 1243–1248, http://www.sciencemag.org/content/162/3859/1243.full.pdf (accessed October 31, 2015).

49. Freyfogle, *The Land We Share*, 7–8, 158–201.

50. Ibid., 203–280.

51. Roberta Horning, "The Burling Tract Battle: They'd Rather Hike Than Fight, But . . ." *Washington Star*, November 3, 1969, item #5, Burling Tract Controversy; Morrison and Dunlap, "Environmentalism and Elitism"; Samdahl, "Social Determinants of Environmental Concern."

52. Stephen Schmidt and Kurt Paulsen, "Is Open-Space Preservation a Form of Exclusionary Zoning? The Evolution of Municipal Open-Space Policies in New Jersey," *Urban Affairs Review* 45 (2009): 92–118; Press, *Saving Open Space*, 59–60, 64–66; Smith, "Institutional Determinants of Collaboration," 7.

53. Kenneth T. Jackson, *Crabgrass Frontier: The Suburbanization of the United States* (New York: Oxford University Press, 1985), 203–218; Matthew D. Lassiter, *The Silent Majority: Suburban Politics in the Sunbelt South* (Princeton, NJ: Princeton University Press, 2006), 7, 11–14; David M. P. Freund, *Colored Property: State Policy and White Racial Politics in Suburban America* (Chicago: University of Chicago Press, 2007), 18–19, 216–217; Bonastia, *Knocking on the Door*.

54. McCarthy, "The Unsilent Spring."

55. Larkin, "The Forty-Year 'First Step,'" 1631.

56. Kenneth Bredemeier, "Fairfax Defers Tract Action," *WP*, April 9, 1970; Schmidt and Paulsen, "Is Open-Space Preservation a Form of Exclusionary Zoning," 98.

57. Press, *Saving Open Space*, 38–42, 59–60, 64–66.

58. Freyfogle, *The Land We Share*, 179–201, 227; Robert J. Brulle, *Agency, Democracy, and Nature: The U.S. Environmental Movement from a Critical Theory Perspective* (Cambridge, MA: MIT Press, 2000), 191.

59. Beverly Crawford, "Preserve Rather Than Houses: Scott's Run Nature Preserve," *McLean* [Virginia] *Connection*, July 18, 2002; Adam Rome, "William Whyte, Open Space, and Environmental Activism," *Geographical Review* 88, no. 2 (April 1998): 261; Brooks, *Before Earth Day*, 94.

60. Anne D. Shreve, "On 'Shame,' and the Burling Tract," letter to the editor, *Providence Journal*, April 24, 1970, item #5, Burling Tract Controversy.

61. Francis, "The Burling Tract," 20–21.

62. A district park was supposed to be a major recreational area. The park authority's plan for the Burling tract included playing fields, courts, trails, etc., with forty to fifty acres for active recreation. Fairfax County Park Authority, "Public Hearing: Burling Tract," statement, April 29, 1970, item #1, Burling Tract Controversy.

63. "Dranesville Will Vote on Buying Park," *WP*, May 7, 1970; "Fairfax Pledges Park Cash," *WP*, May 15, 1970.

64. Fairfax County Park Authority, "Staff Presentation—Burling Tract," April 29, 1970, in folder 1385, box 46, Marian K. Agnew Papers, ca. 1967–1993 (MSS1 Ag635 a FA2), Virginia Historical Society, Richmond, VA; "3 Ways Told to Finance Burling Park," *WP*, May 2, 1970.

65. Harriet F. Bradley, Statement on the Burling Tract, April 27, 1970, item #1, Burling Tract Controversy.

66. Susan Daniel, Richard DeSanti, and Jeffrey Wieser, "2350 Signatures on Burling Petition," letter to the editor, *Providence Journal*, May 22, 1970.

67. Citizens for Burling Park, "Why Burling Park," 2.

68. Press, *Saving Open Space*, 59–60, 64–66.

69. Arnold Berleant, *The Aesthetics of Environment* (Philadelphia: Temple University Press, 1992), 169, 171; Joan Iverson Nassauer, "Cultural Sustainability: Aligning Aesthetics and Ecology," in *Placing Nature: Culture and Landscape Ecology* (Washington, D.C.: Island Press, 1997), 68; David Orr, *The Nature of Design: Ecology, Culture, and Human Intention* (Oxford: Oxford University Press, 2002), 178–179; Yuriko Saito, "The Role of Aesthetics in Civic Environmentalism," in *The Aesthetics of Human Environments*, ed. Arnold Berleant and Allen Carlson (Ontario: Broadview Press, 2007), 206; Richard Brewer, *Conservancy: The Land Trust Movement in America* (Hanover, NH: University Press of New England, 2003), 57–77.

70. "Dranesville Will Vote on Buying Park," *WP*, May 7, 1970; "Fairfax Pledges Park Cash," *WP*, May 15, 1970; Donald B. Bowman, "On the Burling Tract," letter to the editor, *WP*, July 24, 1970; "Fairfax Opens Way to Land Purchase," *WP*, May 30, 1970.

71. "Fairfax Pledges Park Cash," *WP*, May 15, 1970.

72. "200 Back Purchase of Burling Site," *WP*, May 29, 1970; "Burling Park Backed with Film, Songs," *Washington Star*, May 29, 1970; Francis, "The Burling Tract," 22–23.

73. Susan Daniel, "Burling Song" [1970], in folder 1389, box 46, Agnew Papers.

74. "Fairfax Opens Way to Land Purchase."

75. Marian Agnew, "We Will Wonder Why We Argued," op-ed, *Providence Journal*, July 3, 1970, item #5, Burling Tract Controversy.

76. "McLean Area Deciding on Tax to Buy Burling," *WP*, July 9, 1970; "The Burling Dispute and the System," editorial, *WP*, July 21, 1970. For a newspaper article from a local high school student, see Jeff Wieser, "Burling as a Park," *Providence Journal*, July 3, 1970, in folder 1385, box 46, Agnew Papers.

77. Vote for Burling Park, pamphlet [1970], in folder 1384, box 46, Agnew Papers.

78. Frederick Kunkle, "Activists Were Green Before It Was Trendy: Fairfax Set to Commemorate the Battle for Scott's Run," *WP*, June 11, 2009; John Adams, "Georgetown Pike & Potomac River Association," in *McLean Citizens Association: Anthology of Local Histories*, ed. Jan Auerbach (2009), http://www.mcleancitizens.org/anthology_4.pdf (accessed October 23, 2011).

79. Fairfax County Chamber of Commerce, Burling Tract Committee, advertisement, *Providence Journal*, July 10, 1970, item #4, Burling Tract Controversy.

80. Press, *Saving Open Space*, 74.

81. Ibid., 38–42; Rome, *The Bulldozer in the Countryside*, 222; "Burling," advertisement, *Providence Journal*, July 10, 1970, item #4, Burling Tract Controversy.

82. Kenneth Bredemeier, "Vote in Va. Today Will Decide Dispute over Burling Tract," *WP*, July 14, 1970.

83. "Vote Backs Purchase of Burling Site," *WP*, July 15, 1970.

84. Ibid.

85. "The Burling Dispute and the System," editorial, *WP*, July 21, 1970.

86. Freyfogle, *The Land We Share*, 227.

87. Kenneth Bredemeier, "Builder Blocks Access Trails at Controversial Burling Site," *WP*, July 17, 1970.

88. "Holton Seeks Project Delay at Burling Site," *WP*, July 22, 1970.

89. William N. Curry and Kenneth Bredemeier, "Developers Reject Offer for Burling," *WP*, July 23, 1970.

90. Kenneth Bredemeier, "Fairfax Burling Suit Eyed," *WP*, July 24, 1970.

91. Kenneth Bredemeier, "Fairfax Board Condemns Burling Site," *WP*, July 28, 1970.

92. Kenneth Bredemeier, "Developer Halts Work at Burling," *WP*, July 29, 1970.

93. Richard J. Lazarus, *The Making of Environmental Law* (Chicago: University of Chicago Press, 2004); Brooks, *Before Earth Day*, 7.

94. Freyfogle, *The Land We Share*, 8, 203–253.

95. Bredemeier, "Fairfax Board Condemns Burling Site."

96. Longhurst, *Citizen Environmentalists*, x.

97. Bredemeier, "Developer Halts Work."

98. William N. Curry, "County Loses Delay Bid: Clearing Renewed in Burling's Woods," *WP*, July 30, 1970.

99. Kenneth Bredemeier, "Bulldozers Rumbling in Wilderness; Senators Enter Burling Tract Fight," *WP*, July 31, 1970.

100. "$3.6 Million Price Tag: Developers Agree to Sell Burling Site," *WP*, August 6, 1970.

101. "Va. to Give Funds for Burling," *WP*, August 19, 1970. The state's contribution came courtesy of a near doubling of the federal funds the Virginia Outdoor Commission on Recreation received from the Department of the Interior's Land and Water Conservation Program.

102. "Fairfax Gets Burling Tract," *WP*, September 5, 1970.

103. "Seek to Void Referendum; 31 File Suit on Burling Vote," *WP*, August 16, 1970; "Fairfax Gets Burling Tract," *WP*, September 5, 1970; Hank Burchard, "Burling Tract Sale Is Upheld," *WP*, January 9, 1971. The suit alleged that the purchase of the Burling tract was unlawful because the decision to hold the ballot referendum was arbitrary and obligated residents to pay taxes for a park that would primarily serve residents outside of the local district.

104. Stewart L. Udall, "Youths Save a Public Park," *Bangor* [Maine] *Daily News*, October 2, 1970. In a related story, Fairfax officials received a 640-acre parcel of hilly and wooded land,

nearly twice the size of the Burling, as a gift from the estate of political columnist David Lawrence two days before Christmas, 1970. The property was valued at approximately $5 million
and given to the county for use as a park. Kenneth Bredemeier, "Fairfax Gets Gift of Land; Tract
Valued at $5 Million Will Be Park," *WP*, December 24, 1970.

105. Fairfax County Park Authority, "Great Parks, Great Communities: McLean Planning
District," http://www.fairfaxcounty.gov/parks/plandev/downloads/gpgc_mclean.pdf (accessed
August 11, 2017); Fairfax County Park Authority, "Scotts Run Nature Preserve," Master Plan
Archives, http://www.fairfaxcounty.gov/parks/plandev/mparchives.htm (accessed January
16, 2012); Marty Smith, "How Does Scott's Run?" Fairfax County Park Authority, http://www
.fairfaxcounty.gov/parks/resources/archives/scottsrun.htm (accessed January 16, 2012).

106. Kunkle, "Activists Were Green Before It Was Trendy."

107. Kenneth Bredemeier, "Fairfax Environmentalists Eye Challenge to Supervisors," *WP*,
April 3, 1971.

108. Banham, *The Fight for Fairfax*, 103–105. Montgomery County also stepped up its
efforts to limit growth and was generally more successful. On differences between Fairfax and
Montgomery, see Peter Siskind, "Suburban Growth and Its Discontents: The Logic and Limits of
Reform on the Postwar Northeast Corridor," in *The New Suburban History*, ed. Kevin M. Kruse
and Thomas J. Sugrue (Chicago: University of Chicago Press, 2006), 164–170.

109. The county hired Robert H. Freilich, the attorney who developed the ordinance for
Ramapo, as a consultant for PLUS. Dawson, *No Little Plans*.

110. Banham, *The Fight for Fairfax*, 106–123, 159–163; Siskind, "Suburban Growth and Its
Discontents," 169. The two most important cases in Fairfax were *Board of Supervisors of Fairfax County v. Allman*, 215 Va. 434, 211 S.E.2d 48 (1975), which dealt with public facilities and
Board of Supervisors v. Horne, 216 Va. 113, 215 S.E.2d 453 (1975), which pertained to site and
subdivision planning.

111. Francis, "The Burling Tract," 30.

112. John Adams, "Georgetown Pike," in Auerbach, *McLean Citizens Association*.

113. John B. Willmann, "Area Home Builder Survives by Changing Styling and $$ Range,"
WP, February 28, 1976.

114. Bonastia, *Knocking on the Door*; Larkin, "The Forty-Year 'First Step.'"

115. Katherine Salant, "In Reston, a Touch of 19th-Century Chicago, or Paris," *WP*, March
6, 1999.

116. Brewer, *Conservancy*, 8–9; Sally K. Fairfax et al., *Buying Nature: The Limits of Land
Acquisition as a Conservation Strategy, 1780–2004* (Cambridge, MA: MIT Press, 2005), 151.

Chapter 3. Desperate for Growth

1. Amy Alexander, statement, quoted in National Capital Planning Commission, Pub-
lic Scoping Meeting in re: National Harbor Project, Oxon Hill, Maryland (January 20, 1999),
27–28, box 7, Record Group 328, National Capital Planning Commission [NCPC], Develop-
ment Proposals Project Files, National Archives and Records Administration, Washington, D.C.

2. Brian Patrick Larkin, "The Forty-Year 'First Step': The Fair Housing Act as an Incomplete
Tool for Suburban Integration," *Columbia Law Review* 107, no. 7 (November 2007): 1631.

3. On the property tax revolt in Prince George's, see Karyn R. Lacy, *Blue-Chip Black: Race,
Class, and Status in the New Black Middle Class* (Berkeley: University of California Press, 2007),
194–197.

4. John A. Powell, "Opportunity-Based Housing," *Journal of Affordable Housing and Community Development Law* 12 (2002): 188–228.

5. Denton E. Morrison and Riley E. Dunlap, "Environmentalism and Elitism: A Conceptual and Empirical Analysis," *Environmental Management* 10, no. 5 (1986): 581–589; Diane M. Samdahl, "Social Determinants of Environmental Concern," *Environment and Behavior* 21, no. 1 (January 1989): 57–81.

6. Matthew J. Lindstrom and Zachary A. Smith, *The National Environmental Policy Act: Judicial Misconstruction, Legislative Indifference and Executive Neglect* (College Station: Texas A&M University Press, 2001), 9–12; Michael R. Greenberg, *The Environmental Impact Statement After Two Generations: Managing Environment Power* (New York: Routledge, 2012), 1, 13–16.

7. Kenneth T. Jackson, *Crabgrass Frontier: The Suburbanization of the United States* (New York: Oxford University Press, 1985), 203–218; Matthew D. Lassiter, *The Silent Majority: Suburban Politics in the Sunbelt South* (Princeton, NJ: Princeton University Press, 2006), 7, 11–14; David M. P. Freund, *Colored Property: State Policy and White Racial Politics in Suburban America* (Chicago: University of Chicago Press, 2007), 18–19, 216–217; Kevin Fox Gotham, *Race, Real Estate, and Uneven Development: The Kansas City Experience, 1900–2000* (Albany: State University of New York Press, 2002); Robert O. Self, *American Babylon: Race and the Struggle for Postwar Oakland* (Princeton, NJ: Princeton University Press, 2003); Kevin M. Kruse, *White Flight: Atlanta and the Making of Modern Conservatism* (Princeton, NJ: Princeton University Press, 2005), 6–10; Lizabeth A. Cohen, *A Consumers' Republic: The Politics of Mass Consumption in Postwar America* (New York: Alfred A. Knopf, 2003), 8–9, 11, 289.

8. Andrew Wiese, *Places of Their Own: African American Suburbanization in the Twentieth Century* (Chicago: University of Chicago Press, 2003), 211–213, 243–249; Michael Eastman, "Low-Income Blacks Pushed into P.G.," *Washington Post* [*WP*], October 11, 1979.

9. Wiese, *Places of Their Own*, 219–230; United States Commission on Civil Rights, *A Long Day's Journey Into Light: School Desegregation in Prince George's County*, Clearinghouse Publication 52 (Washington, D.C.: United States Commission on Civil Rights, 1976); Larkin, "The Forty-Year 'First Step,'" 1631.

10. U.S. Census Bureau, *Census of Population and Housing*, 1970, 1980, in Minnesota Population Center, *National Historic Geographic Information System: Version 2.0* (Minneapolis: University of Minnesota, 2011), http://www.nhgis.org (accessed November 3, 2012).

11. Wiese, *Places of Their Own*, 218–219; Powell, "Opportunity-Based Housing," 196–197.

12. Maryland-National Capital Park and Planning Commission (M-NCPPC), *Prince George's County Shopping Center Directory* (Upper Marlboro, MD: M-NCPPC, 2008), 1–2, http://www.mncppcapps.org/planning/Publications/PDFs/227/2008%20Shopping%20Center %20Directory.pdf (accessed August 13, 2017); and "Shopping Center Inventory: Montgomery County, Maryland," in Shopping Centers in Montgomery (Upper Marlboro, MD, 2002), http://www.montgomeryplanning.org/community/plan_areas/other/shopctrs_mc/index.shtm (accessed July 29, 2012); Cohen, *A Consumers' Republic*, 257, 259, 288; Powell, "Opportunity-Based Housing."

13. George Lipsitz, "The Racialization of Space and the Spatialization of Race: Theorizing the Hidden Architecture of Landscape," *Landscape Journal* 26, no. 1 (2007): 14.

14. Lacy, *Blue-Chip Black*, 194–197. On other cases, see Lisa McGirr, *Suburban Warriors: The Origins of the New American Right* (Princeton, NJ: Princeton University Press, 2001), 237–239; Self, *American Babylon*, 317–326.

15. Lacy, *Blue-Chip Black*, 194–197.

16. Paul Schwartzman, "Activist Won't Give Up Fight—or Home," *WP*, May 3, 2004; Ahmar Musitkhan, "Activist Celebrates Fight to Save Home," *WP*, January 17, 2008.

17. Eugene L. Meyer, "The Supersalesman Behind P.G.'s Bay of the Americas," *WP*, July 6, 1983.

18. Eugene L. Meyer, "The Political Voyage of P.G.'s Smoot Bay Project," *WP*, July 4, 1983.

19. James H. Burch, Company, *Above and Beyond It All: Bay of the Americas General Concept Plan, Smoot Bay Waterfront Center* (Fort Washington, MD: Fedco Systems Inc., 1983), box 1, NCPC. box 1, NCPC.

20. Meyer, "The Political Voyage of P.G.'s Smoot Bay Project."

21. Paul Hodge, "Waterfront Project May Make Waves," *WP*, September 15, 1982; John C. Grover to Helen M. Scharf, letter, December 2, 1982, box 1, NCPC; John C. Grover to Helen M. Scharf, letter, December 2, 1982, box 1, NCPC; Leon Wynter, "Smoot Bay Project Stirs Concerns of Congestion," *WP*, January 26, 1983; Paul Hodge, "Smoot Bay Project Stirs Concerns of Congestion," *WP*, January 26, 1983.

22. Meyer, "The Political Voyage of P.G.'s Smoot Bay Project."

23. Rudolph A. Pyatt, "Glendening's Warning," *WP*, November 16, 1984.

24. Ibid.

25. R. H. Melton, "Election Results Delivered Strong Message on Growth: Development Embraced in Md., Opposed in Va.," *WP*, November 9, 1986.

26. Marcia McAllister, "'Bay of Americas' Site Reported Sold," *WP*, October 18, 1984; Eugene L. Meyer, "His Port in a Storm; Tysons Builder Banks on Potomac Project," *WP*, February 27, 1995; Sandra R. Gregg, "P.G. Hopes to Build a Better Georgetown; PortAmerica Plan: Pizzazz AND Parking," *WP*, July 22, 1985.

27. Marcia McAllister, "50-Story Tower Proposed for Potomac Shore," *WP*, August 26, 1985; Eugene L. Meyer, "'Visual Gateway' to Prince George's: 52-Story Tower the Centerpiece of $1 Billion PortAmerica Project" *WP*, January 24, 1986.

28. Gregg, "P.G. Hopes to Build a Better Georgetown."

29. Ibid.

30. A Bill to Authorize the Secretary of the Interior to Convey Certain Land Located in the State of Maryland to the Maryland-National Capital Park and Planning Commission, Public Law 99–215, 99th Cong., 1st sess. (December 26, 1985); National Capital Planning Commission, Statement of NCPC on Conceptual Site Plan Application for PortAmerica Before the Prince George's County Planning Board, July 7, 1986, box 1, NCPC.

31. For earlier statements, see Barbara Vobejda, "P.G. Skyscraper Plans Denounced," *WP*, April 18, 1986; Manus J. Fish Jr. to John Rhoads, letter, May 1, 1986, box 2, NCPC; Eugene L. Meyer, "Park Agency Seeks to Bar PortAmerica; Access over Parkland Would Be Denied," *WP*, July 4, 1986.

32. Public debate had flared up periodically since the early 1960s over the visibility of high-rise office buildings, particularly at Rosslyn, in Arlington. See Sandra G. Boodman, "Federal Agencies Plead in Vain to Restrict Rosslyn Skyline," *WP*, October 29, 1978; Sandra G. Boodman, "High-Rise Va. Buildings Held an 'Act of Urban Vandalism,'" *WP*, January 23, 1979.

33. U.S. Senate, Senate Committee on the Environment and Public Works, PortAmerica Project Oversight, 99th Cong., 2nd sess., October 1, 1986, 30–47, 170–173. On aesthetics in the environment see Arnold Berleant, *The Aesthetics of Environment* (Philadelphia: Temple

University Press, 1992); Allen Carlson, "Nature and Positive Aesthetics," in *Nature, Aesthetics, and Environmentalism: From Beauty to Duty*, ed. Allen Carlson and Sheila Lintott (New York: Columbia University Press, 2007), 211–237.

34. William C. Baker to Don Bozarth, letter, February 24, 1987, box 2, NCPC; Ken Wilson to Ronald Wilson, letter, March 8, 1988, box 5, NCPC. On the rise of grassroots activism to address ecosystem issues, see Douglas Bevington, *The Rebirth of Environmentalism: Grassroots Activism from the Spotted Owl to the Polar Bear* (Washington, D.C.: Island Press, 2009).

35. Senate Committee, PortAmerica Project Oversight, 8–13, 21, 52–54, 68–78.

36. Eugene L. Meyer, "PortAmerica Plan Scaled Down: New Blueprint Puts 22-Story Tower on Pr. George's Riverfront," *WP*, October 28, 1987; J. Randall Evans to Ron Wilson, letter, March 8 1988, box 5, NCPC.

37. James T. Lewis Enterprises, *PortAmerica: Conceptual Site Plan* (Fort Washington, MD: FSI Design Group, 1988); and *PortAmerica: Revised Conceptual Site Plan* (Fort Washington, MD: FSI Design Group, 1989), box 4, NCPC.

38. Kirstin Downey Grimsley, "PortAmerica: From Dream to Wasteland; Project Site on Potomac Now Belongs to RTC," *WP*, January 30, 1993; Rudolph A. Pyatt Jr. "PortAmerica: Lewis Picks Up the Pieces of a Monument to His Persistence," *WP*, March 31, 1994; Eugene L. Meyer, "His Port in a Storm; Tysons Builder Banks on Potomac Project," *WP*, February 27, 1995; James T. Lewis to Reginald Griffith, letter, February 1, 1996, box 5, NCPC.

39. At the time of Peterson's purchase, the Smoot Bay site was under receivership because one of PortAmerica's financiers had gone bankrupt. The Resolution Trust Corporation (RTC) was established to deal with the fallout from many of the savings and loan institutions that failed in the early 1990s, including those that financed PortAmerica. The Federal Deposit Insurance Corporation later took over control of the site from the RTC.

40. David Montgomery, "PortAmerica Site in Private Hands," *WP*, March 11, 1996; Junior Achievement of Greater Washington, "Milton V. Peterson," Washington Business Hall of Fame Past Laureates, 2008, http://www.myja.org/halloffame/history/laureates/biography_Milton_Peterson.html (accessed February 27, 2012); Russ Banham, *The Fight for Fairfax: A Struggle for a Great American County* (Fairfax, VA: George Mason University Press, 2009), 170–172, 208–214, 232–234; John Arundel, "For Milt Peterson, Building a Real Estate Empire Meant Building a Family First," *localKicks*, March, 14, 2012, http://www.localkicks.com/article_print.jsp?ID=5095 (accessed February 21, 2014).

41. Larkin, "The Forty Year 'First Step.'"

42. Cited in Mark Goldstein, "Maryland's Changing Demographics: Leadership Challenge XV" (June 13, 2006), http://slideplayer.com/slide/4692444/ (accessed August 13, 2017).

43. Lacy, *Blue-Chip Black*, 186–187.

44. Maryland National Capital Park and Planning Commission, *Shopping Center Directory*, 1–2.

45. Washington Post, Washington Post Prince George's County Poll, July 1994, computer file, ICPSR version (Radnor, PA: Chilton Research Services [producer], 1994; Ann Arbor, MI: Inter-university Consortium for Political and Social Research [distributor], 2005).

46. Wiese, *Places of Their Own*, 274–281; Lacy, *Blue-Chip Black*, 2–3, 9–17, 48–49.

47. More than a third of African American residents stated in the lead-up to the election that it was important for the next county executive to be African American, compared to less than 10 percent of whites. Washington Post, Washington Post Prince George's County Poll (1994).

48. "Wayne Curry: Biography," The HistoryMakers, September 29, 2004, http://www.thehistorymakers.com/biography/wayne-curry-40 (accessed July 17, 2014); John Rivera, "Curry Already Changing Prince George's History," *Baltimore Sun*, December 27, 1994.

49. Rivera, "Curry Already Changing Prince George's History."

50. Rudolph A. Pyatt Jr., "In Prince George's, Planning a Harbor for Economic Growth," *WP*, March 6, 1997; Eugene L. Meyer, "Curry Offers Up His Dream of a Booming County," *WP*, March 1, 1997.

51. Rudolph A. Pyatt Jr., "Prince George's Policy of Slower Growth," *WP*, February 20, 1989; Retha Hill, "Glendening No Longer Developers' Darling," *WP*, August 27, 1989.

52. Edward J. Malecki, "Jockeying for Position: What It Means and Why It Matters to Regional Development Policy When Places Compete," *Regional Studies* 38, no. 9 (December 2004): 1104–1108; Daphne T. Greenwood and Richard P. F. Holt, *Local Economic Development in the 21st Century* (Armonk, NY: M. E. Sharpe, 2010), 8–9, 14–25.

53. A 1995 study found that nearly twenty million people visited the Washington area annually, spending nearly $5 billion and producing another $3 billion in local economic activity through the spending of those whose jobs benefited from the tourist economy. Fifty-six percent of total tourist spending went to the suburbs. Overall, tourism made up 5 percent of the metropolitan area's gross regional product. Stephen S. Fuller, *The Impact of the Hospitality Industry on the Metropolitan Washington Economy* (Washington, D.C.: Greater Washington Research Center, 1995), 1–2.

54. Maryann Haggerty, "Developer Plans Resort in Prince George's; Curry, Glendening Back Entertainment Complex at PortAmerica Site," *WP*, March 1, 1997.

55. Ibid.; Terry M. Neal and Robert E. Pierre, "Pr. George's Smooths Way for Project on the Potomac; Council Votes to Speed Zoning Approval Process," *WP*, June 18, 1997.

56. The site plan discussed here was only for the waterfront parcel because the Beltway parcel was not contiguous and, according to local zoning, was a separate site requiring its own plans.

57. The Peterson Companies L.C., National Harbor: Conceptual Site Plan (Fairfax, VA, 1998), box 5, NCPC; Jackie Spinner, "Developer Has Grand Plans for Md. River Tract," *WP*, February 19, 1998. The five zones were the Point, with a hotel and conference center; the Central Waterfront, the hub of tourist activity; North Cove, a mix of hotel, retail, and entertainment; the Pier, a nightlife spot; and Uplands Resort, a mountain-style resort.

58. Rudolph A. Pyatt Jr., "Fill in the Fine Print Before Putting River Resort Proposal on a Fast Tract," *WP*, April 9, 1998.

59. NCPC, *Extending the Legacy: Planning America's Capital for the Twenty-First Century* (Washington, D.C., 1997), 34, 51–52.

60. Stewart Schwartz to NCPC, letter, May 29, 1998, box 6, NCPC; George L. Maurer to NCPC, letter, May 26, 1998, box 6, NCPC; Richard C. Zurowski to Maurice Foushee, letter, May 23, 1998, box 6, NCPC; Helen H. O'Leary to Maurice Foushee, letter, May 28 1998, box 6, NCPC; Jeb Byrne to NCPC, statement, May 25, 1998, box 6, NCPC.

61. SWCA, Inc., Biological Assessment for Impacts to Bald Eagle From the National Harbor Project, Prince George's County, Maryland (August 25, 1998), box 6, NCPC. Even with the study's findings, Peterson shifted some of the development at Smoot Bay to better accommodate the eagles. Institute for Public Representation, *Annual Report 2000–01* (Washington, D.C.: Georgetown University Law Center, 2001), 19–21, https://www.law.georgetown.edu/academics/academic-programs/clinical-programs/our-clinics/IPR/upload/ar00_01.pdf (accessed August 13, 2017).

62. Rick Tyler to Maurice Foushee, letter, May 26, 1998, box 6, NCPC.

63. Jackie Spinner, "Tourists, Not Residents, to Be Resort's Market; Developer Hopes for 12 Million a Year," *WP*, April 7, 1998.

64. NCPC, Draft Proposed National Harbor Project Environmental Impact Statement (Washington, D.C.: NCPC, December 1998), v, box 8, NCPC; Jackie Spinner, "Final Public Showdown over Md. Resort Plan; Foes, Backers of National Harbor Pack Hearing in Pr. George's School to Press Views," *WP*, January 21, 1999.

65. Andrew MacDonald, statement for Public Scoping Meeting, 61–66. For an earlier statement, see Andrew H. MacDonald to Maurice K. Foushee, letter, May 28, 1998, box 6, NCPC. Other organizations that recommended avoiding intensive development of the waterfront parcel included the Chesapeake Bay Foundation and the Coalition for Smarter Growth.

66. Jackie Spinner, "National Harbor Foes Take New Tack," *WP*, January 27, 1999.

67. Ibid.; Jackie Spinner, "Pr. George's Plan Compares Favorably in Environmental Study," *WP*, December 23, 1998.

68. Wayne K. Curry to Eugene Keller, letter, February 5, 1999, quoted in National Capital Planning Commission, Public Scoping Meeting in re: National Harbor Project, Oxon Hill, Maryland (January 20, 1999), box 7, NCPC.

69. NCPC, Public Scoping Meeting, 28–31.

70. Amy Alexander, statement for Public Scoping Meeting, 27–28.

71. Spinner, "Final Public Showdown."

72. Ibid.

73. Morrison and Dunlap, "Environmentalism and Elitism"; Samdahl, "Social Determinants of Environmental Concern."

74. "Norris McDonald, President of the African American Environmentalist Association, Answers Questions," *Grist*, April 5, 2005, http://grist.org/article/norris/ (accessed March 27, 2013).

75. For this familiar critique, see Morrison and Dunlap, "Environmentalism and Elitism"; Samdahl, "Social Determinants of Environmental Concern."

76. "Norris McDonald . . . Answers Questions"; Ronald Sandler and Phaedra C. Pezzullo, eds., *Environmental Justice and Environmentalism: The Social Justice Challenge to the Environmental Movement* (Cambridge, MA: MIT Press, 2007).

77. "Norris McDonald . . . Answers Questions."

78. African American Environmentalist Association, http://www.aaenvironment.com (accessed March 25, 2012); African American Environmentalist Association, "AAEA Criteria for Supporting/Opposing Development Projects," http://aaenvironment.com/Development.htm (accessed August 8, 2012).

79. Norris MacDonald, statement for Public Scoping Meeting, 144.

80. Judson Berger, "Peers: Activist in the Way," *Gazette*, February 10, 2015, http://www.gazette.net/gazette_archive/2005/200506/fort_washington/news/259712-1.html (accessed September 4, 2015).

81. Ibid.

82. Courtland Milloy, "Opryland Isn't Music to All Ears," *WP*, January 12, 2000; Rudolph A. Pyatt Jr., "Down at National Harbor, an Environment of Divisiveness," *WP*, September 2, 1999.

83. Nathaniel Tuff, statement for Public Scoping Meeting, 30. Karyn Lacy downplays the role of race in public attitudes about the project. She argues that proximity to the site was more important. Lacy, *Blue-Chip Black*, 193.

84. Jackie Spinner, "National Harbor Plans Get Boost; Proposed Resort in Pr. George's Passes Environmental Review," *WP*, April 18, 1999.

85. "Unhorse the Riders," editorial, *WP*, October 24, 1999; Jeb Byrne, "National Harbor: And the Environment?" op-ed, *WP*, January 23, 2000. The bill was H.R. 3423, Section 356, part of the Consolidated Appropriations Act, Public Law 106-113. On this, see Natural Resources Defense Council, "Chapter 4: FY 2000 Budget Riders Report," *At the Crossroads: Environmental Threats and Opportunities in the 106th Congress* (Washington, D.C.: Natural Resources Defense Council, March 2000), http://www.nrdc.org/legislation/crossroads/chap4.asp (accessed March 25, 2012). Fifteen years earlier, Hoyer secured passage of a bill that transferred federal parkland to the bi-county planning commission as a right-of-way for Smoot Bay in exchange for the NCPC receiving veto power and conducting the federal environmental review process for development at Smoot Bay.

86. Jackie Spinner, "Lavish Harbor Complex Planned; Opryland Firm Makes Md. Deal," *WP*, January 11, 2000; Jackie Spinner, "Harbor Project Ready to Set Sail; Latest Proposal Includes Shops, Eateries, Hotel Rooms and Conference Center," *WP*, January 12, 2000.

87. Deborah Brevard, "Major League Project," letter to the editor, *WP*, February 2, 2000. A column in the *Washington Post* a week earlier featured several other letters in support of the Gaylord complex and National Harbor. Janice McCullagh, "Time to Sell Quality of Life," letter to the editor, *WP*, January 26, 2000; William R. Murray, "Need Upscale Project," letter to the editor, *WP*, January 26, 2000; Fred B. Houson, "Tremendous Opportunity," letter to the editor, *WP*, January 26, 2000.

88. Eugene L. Meyer, "Curry Offers Up His Dream of a Booming County."

89. Spinner, "Lavish Harbor Complex Planned."

90. The state paid for nearby interchanges at I-295 and I-495, constructed 1,750 parking spots, defrayed the costs of a visitors' center, and earmarked $33 million for preparing the waterfront for a boardwalk. Paul Schwartzman, "Curry Pledges $122 Million for National Harbor," *WP*, March 22, 2000.

91. Heywood Sanders, statement for hearing on *Build It and They Will Come: Do Taxpayer-Financed Sports Stadiums, Convention Centers and Hotels Deliver As Promised for America's Cities*, Hearing Before the Subcommittee on Domestic Policy of the Committee on Oversight and Government Reform, 110th Congress, 1st session, March 29, 2007, 144–145; Alan Peters and Peter Fisher, "The Failure of Economic Development Incentives," *Journal of the American Planning Association* 70, no. 1 (Winter 2004): 33–35.

92. Lacy, *Blue-Chip Black*, 203–205; Wiese, *Places of Their Own*, 279–281; Paul Schwartzman, "National Harbor Aid Hits Resistance; Public Money to Help Build Private Project," *WP*, March 26, 2000; Rudolph A. Pyatt Jr., "Prince George's Complex Raises Questions About Government's Role in Luring Business," *WP*, March 30, 2000.

93. Pyatt, "Prince George's Complex Raises Questions."

94. Stan Fetter, "Harbor Spending Matters," letter to the editor, *WP*, May 18, 2000.

95. Schwartzman, "National Harbor Aid Hits Resistance."

96. Spinner, "Lavish Harbor Complex Planned."

97. Vladimir Parma, "No to National Harbor," letter to the editor, *WP*, August 11, 1999; On the economics of tourism, see Carolyn Adams, David Bartelt, David Elsh, and Ira Goldstein, *Restructuring the Philadelphia Region: Metropolitan Divisions and Inequality* (Philadelphia: Temple University Press, 2008), 42.

98. On this question, see Edward J. Blakely and Ted K. Bradshaw, *Planning Local Economic Development: Theory and Practice*, 3rd ed. (Thousand Oaks, CA: Sage, 2002), 54–56, 67; Daphne T. Greenwood and Richard P. F. Holt, *Local Economic Development in the 21st Century* (Armonk, NY: M. E. Sharpe, 2010), 8–45; Audrey G. McFarlane, "Race, Space, and Place: The Geography of Economic Development," *San Diego Law Review* 36 (1999): 304–309.

99. Paul Schwartzman, "Standing Guard: Profiles of Nine Civic Watchdogs," *WP*, August 12, 2004.

100. "Friends of the Forest," *WP*, February 4, 1999.

101. Spinner, "National Harbor Foes."

102. Schwartzman, "Activist Won't Give Up Fight"; Schwartzman, "Standing Guard."

103. Rosalind S. Helderman, "Candidate Armed with Self-Assurance on Campaign Trail; Donna Edwards on Stump Ahead of Tuesday Vote," *WP*, June 12, 2008.

104. Musitkhan, "Activist Celebrates Fight."

105. Ovetta Wiggins, "National Harbor Neighbors Drop Lawsuit; Developer Agrees to Financing Improvements in Oxon Hill, Including Trails, Support for Metro," *WP*, August 12, 2004; Steven Pearlstein, "Developer's Tenacity Saves National Harbor," *WP*, August 18, 2004.

106. Schwartzman, "Activist Won't Give Up Fight."

107. Musitkhan, "Activist Celebrates Fight."

108. "Jack Johnson: Biography," The HistoryMakers, April 26, 2007, http://www.thehistorymakers.com/biography/jack-johnson-41 (accessed July 17, 2014).

109. Ovetta Wiggins, "Vote Clears the Way for National Harbor; Prince George's Council Approves Bonds for Roads," *WP*, July 7, 2004.

110. Ovetta Wiggins, "Ground Broken for $2 Billion National Harbor Project in Md.," *WP*, December 3, 2004.

111. Olga Khazan, "Facing National Harbor's Retail Challenges," *WP*, March 5, 2012.

112. Blakely and Bradshaw, *Planning Local Economic Development*, 191, 231.

113. Arundel, "For Milt Peterson."

114. Ovetta Wiggins, "National Harbor's Housing Boon; High-End Homes May Bolster County," *WP*, October 10, 2005; Rosalind S. Helderman, "Compromise Reached on Harbor Hotel," *WP*, July 19, 2006; Anita Huslin, "Gaylord's Potential Has D.C. Squirming," *WP*, June 11, 2007; Dana Hedgepeth, "National Harbor to Get More Hotels; Additions Challenge District Business," *WP*, April 17, 2006; Jackie Spinner, "The Deal That Sealed National Harbor; Partnership Between Developer, Pr. George's Leader Brought Project to Life," *WP*, April 25, 2008.

115. Ovetta Wiggins, "Direct Access Planned for National Harbor; Road Changes Designed to Ease Traffic, Steer Cars away from Neighborhoods," *WP*, June 9, 2007; Jonathan O'Connell, "For National Harbor, Seven Years of Change," *WP*, December 12, 2011; Alia E. Dsatagir, "Hot Chocolate 15K/5K Race Called 'Epic Fail,'" *DCIST*, http://dcist.com/2011/12/hot_chocolate_15k_5k_race_called_ep.php (accessed March 25, 2012); Thomas Heath, "Disney Scraps Plan to Build Resort Hotel at National Harbor," *WP*, November 27, 2011.

116. Matt Zapotosky, "Residents Blame National Harbor for Sewage Spills; Utility Says Rain, Power Outages Caused Unusually Large Overflows into Creek," *WP*, June 23, 2008.

117. Jonathan O'Connell, "Why Developer Milt Peterson Is Now Ready to Roll the Dice on a Casino at National Harbor," *WP*, September 23, 2012.

118. O'Connell, "For National Harbor, Seven Years of Change"; Dsatagir, "Hot Chocolate 15K/5K Race"; Heath, "Disney Scraps Plan to Build Resort."

119. Pamela Prah, "Does the Country Have Too Many Casinos," *Pew Charitable Trusts* (June 26, 2013), http://www.pewtrusts.org/en/research-and-analysis/blogs/stateline/2013/06/26 /does-the-country-have-too-many-casinos (accessed November 9, 2015).

120. Paul Schwartzman, "Gambling Is Project's Wild Card; National Harbor Neighbors, County Officials Are Vocal, but Developer Is Mum," *WP*, December 27, 2003.

121. Ibid.

122. O'Connell, "Why Developer Milt Peterson Is Now Ready"; Luz Lazo, "MGM Casino Gets Prince George's Council Backing for Casino Construction at National Harbor," *WP*, July 21, 2014.

123. John Wagner and Miranda S. Spivack, "$1 Billion Casino at National Harbor Proposed by Prince George's Executive Baker," *WP*, February 16, 2012; Rosalind S. Helderman, "Candidate Armed with Self-Assurance on Campaign Trail; Donna Edwards on Stump Ahead of Tuesday Vote," *WP*, June 12, 2008.

124. O'Connell, "Why Developer Milt Peterson Is Now Ready"; Lazo, "MGM Casino Gets Prince George's Council Backing."

125. Lazo, "MGM Casino Gets Prince George's Council Backing."

126. Peterson Companies, National Harbor website, http://www.nationalharbor.com/ (accessed July 23, 2014). MGM National Harbor, MGM National Harbor Fact Sheets, http://newsroom.mgmnationalharbor.com/mgm-national-harbor/fact-sheets/fact-sheets/ (accessed August 13, 2017).

Chapter 4. The Road to Sprawl

1. Zachary M. Schrag, *The Great Society Subway: A History of the Washington Metro* (Baltimore: Johns Hopkins University Press, 2006).

2. Mike Tidwell, "A LOOK AT . . . Sprawl; Escaping L.A. on the Potomac," *Washington Post* [*WP*], May 3, 1998.

3. Edward Weiner, *Urban Transportation Planning in the United States: An Historical Overview*, 5th ed. (Washington, D.C.: U.S. Department of Transportation, 1997), 46–66.

4. On highway planning and public participation after 1970, see the thematic issue of the *Journal of Planning History* 11, no. 1 (February 2012).

5. Michael R. Greenberg, *The Environmental Impact Statement After Two Generations: Managing Environmental Power* (New York: Routledge, 2012), 11–16; Matthew J. Lindstrom and Zachary A. Smith, *The National Environmental Policy Act: Judicial Misconstruction, Legislative Indifference and Executive Neglect* (College Station: Texas A&M University Press, 2001), 9–12, 101.

6. Richard Hogan, *The Failure of Planning: Permitting Sprawl in San Diego Suburbs, 1970–1999* (Columbus: Ohio State University Press, 2003), 89.

7. Mark H. Rose, *Interstate: Express Highway Politics*, rev. ed. (Knoxville: University of Tennessee Press, 1990), 40, 59–60, 93–97; Tom Lewis, *Divided Highways: Building the Interstate Highways, Transforming American Life* (New York: Viking, 1997), 86, 134; John F. Bauman, "The Expressway 'Motorists Loved to Hate': Philadelphia and the First Era of Postwar Highway Planning, 1943–1956," *Pennsylvania Magazine of History and Biography* 115, no. 4 (October 1991): 503–533.

8. National Capital Transportation Act of 1960, Public Law 86-669, July 14, 1960.

9. M-NCPPC, *On Wedges and Corridors; General Plan for the Physical Development of the Maryland-Washington Regional District in Montgomery and Prince George's Counties* (Silver Spring, MD: M-NCPPC, 1964).

10. For a discussion of U.S. freeway revolts, see Raymond A. Mohl, "Stop the Road: Freeway Revolts in American Cities," *Journal of Urban History* 30 (July 2004): 674–706. On the Washington area, see Zachary M. Schrag, "The Freeway Fight in Washington, D.C.: The Three Sisters Bridge in Three Administrations," *Journal of Urban History* 30 (2004): 648–673; Bob Levey and Jane Freundel Levey, "End of the Roads," *WP*, November 26, 2000.

11. For primary source documentation on Washington's freeway battles, see Emergency Committee on the Transportation Crisis (ECTC), Collection No. 36, D.C. Public Library, Washington, D.C.

12. Levey and Levey, "End of the Roads."

13. Weiner, *Urban Transportation Planning*, 61–62; Lewis, *Divided Highways*, 223–233.

14. Levey and Levey, "End of the Roads."

15. Federal Highway Administration (FHWA), Maryland Transportation Authority (MTA), and Maryland State Highway Administration (MD SHA), *Intercounty Connector from I-270 to US 1, Final Environmental Impact Statement/Final Section 4(f) Evaluation*, Project No. AT376B11, vol. 1 (Baltimore, 2006), S-4, I-3.

16. Elsa L. Walsh, "$16 Million Road to Nowhere; The Inter-County Connector: Its Time Has Come and Gone," *WP*, December 10, 1981; Jack Eisen, "Md. Vetoes I-95 Extension into District," *WP*, July 13, 1973; Ron Shaffer, "Freeway Money Eyed for Subway," *WP*, January 25, 1975; Douglas B. Feaver, "No New Freeways Slated for District," *WP*, October 30, 1978; Schrag, *The Great Society Subway*, 223–242.

17. "The Montgomery County Executive," editorial, *WP*, September 9, 1978.

18. Paul Hodge, "Opposition Again Marks Intercounty Connector Workshop," *WP*, August 8, 1980; Walsh, "$16 Million Road to Nowhere"; FHWA, MTA, and MD SHA, *Final Environmental Impact Statement*, S4-4; Weiner, *Urban Transportation Planning*, 46–66; Sidney M. Milkis, "Remaking Government Institutions in the 1970s: Participatory Democracy and the Triumph of Administrative Politics," *Journal of Policy History* 10, no. 1 (1998): 51–74; Thomas J. Sugrue, "All Politics Is Local: The Persistence of Localism in Twentieth-Century America," in *The Democratic Experiment: New Directions in American Political History*, ed. Meg Jacobs, William J. Novak, and Julian E. Zelizer (Princeton, NJ: Princeton University Press, 2003), 301–326.

19. Paul Hodge, "Public Debates Plans for Roads Connecting Montgomery and P.G.," *WP*, October 11, 1979.

20. Maryland State Highway Administration (MD SHA), "Project Status Report: Intercounty Connector / Rockville Facilities (ICC/RF) and Interstate Route 370 (I-370)," Project Planning Studies (Baltimore, 1980), box 17, Collection No. 2007-92, Carol S. Petzold Papers, 1987–2006, unprocessed, University of Maryland.

21. Maryland State Highway Administration, "Interim Alternates Brochure," Intercounty Connector / Rockville Facility Project Planning Study (August 1980); and Project Status Report: Intercounty Connector / Rockville Facility (ICC/RF) Project Planning Study (March 1981).

22. Walsh, "$16 Million Road to Nowhere."

23. R. H. Melton, "Montgomery Citizens Assail Road Plan," *WP*, September 14, 1983.

24. R. H. Melton, "Foes of Inter-County Road Claim Md. Supports It Before Hearings," *WP*, November 22, 1983.

25. Hodge, "Opposition Again Marks Intercounty Connector Workshop"; Walsh, "$16 Million Road to Nowhere"; Melton, "Montgomery Citizens Assail Road Plan"; R. H. Melton, "Debate Surrounds Connector Highway Proposal," *WP*, September 29, 1983.

26. R. H. Melton, "Montgomery Council Votes for Highway to Link Up with P.G.," *WP*, December 3, 1983; R. H. Melton, "Montgomery House Delegation Backs Road from Gaithersburg to Laurel," *WP*, December 20, 1983; R. H. Melton, "Intercounty Highway Designated," *WP*, June 28, 1984.

27. "The Beltway; In 2005: 'A Minute a Mile Slower,'" *WP*, July 27, 1986.

28. Montgomery County Planning Board to Montgomery County Elected Officials, Intercounty Connector - Rockville Facility Study: Answers to Questions Posed by Montgomery County Council's Transportation and Environment Committee, memorandum series, October 27, 1983, 1–2, folder: Transp: 1980–1990, box 15, Coll. No. 2007-92, Petzold Papers.

29. Edward Walsh, "Rockville Freeway Plans Stir Opposition," *WP*, January 28, 1972; John Burgess, "Suburb-to-Suburb Commuting Is Traffic Pattern of the Future," *WP*, April 24, 1983; Melton, "Foes of Inter-County Road"; Stephen J. Lynton, "Panel Says Area Roads, Bridges Being Ignored; Taking 'Back Seat' to Metro," *WP*, November 20, 1984; Carol S. Petzold, "Connector Necessary to County," *Rockville* [Maryland] *Gazette*, March 18, 1987, folder: Transp: 1980–1990, box 15, Coll. No. 2007-92, Petzold Papers.

30. On Garrott, see Josh Kurtz, "Idamae Garrott Remembered for Intensity," *Gazette.Net*, June 16, 1999; Karen Lee, "Friends, Colleagues Remember Garrott as Woman of Conviction," *Montgomery Journal* [1999].

31. Idamae Garrott, "Connector: A Faulty Solution," *Montgomery County Sentinel*, September 23, 1983.

32. Neil Pedersen, statement for hearing, Intercounty Connector, I 370 to MD 28, May 31, 1988, Rockville, Maryland (Rockville: MD DOT, MD SHA, and Montgomery County Department of Transportation, 1988), 17–18, in folder: Public Hearing Transcript, box 15, Coll. No. 2007-92, Petzold Papers.

33. Melton, "Foes of Inter-County Road"; Frank Vrataric, statement for hearing, Intercounty Connector, I 370 to MD 28, 43–46.

34. Allen Bender, statement for hearing, Intercounty Connector, I 370 to MD 28, 51–52.

35. Walter A. Rosenbaum, *Environmental Politics and Policy*, 4th ed. (Washington, D.C.: CQ Press, 1998), 29, 39; Keith Bartholomew, "Land Use-Transportation Scenario Planning: Promise and Reality," *Transportation* (2006): n.p.

36. Thomas Williams, statement for hearing, Intercounty Connector, I 370 to MD 28, 134.

37. Christopher Bosso, *Environment, Inc.* (Lawrence: University Press of Kansas, 2005).

38. Robert J. Duffy, *The Green Agenda in American Politics: New Strategies for the Twenty-First Century* (Lawrence: University Press of Kansas, 2003), 7, 118; Mary Graham, *The Morning After Earth Day: Practical Environmental Politics* (Washington, D.C.: Brookings Institution Press, 1999).

39. Susan DeFord, "Environmentalists Organize to Exert Pressure on County," *WP*, October 4, 1990.

40. Weiner, *Urban Transportation Planning*, 140–152; Richard F. Weingroff, "Creating a Landmark: The Intermodal Surface Transportation Act of 1991," *Public Roads* 65, no. 3 (November/December 2001).

41. Myron Orfield, *Metropolitics: A Regional Agenda for Community and Stability* (Washington, D.C.: Brookings Institution Press, 1997); Carlton Wade Basmajian, *Atlanta Unbound: Enabling Sprawl through Policy and Planning* (Philadelphia: Temple University Press, 2015).

42. Robert Jay Dilger, *American Transportation Policy* (Westport, CT: Praeger, 2003), 53–61; Weiner, *Urban Transportation Planning*, 157; Weingroff, "Creating a Landmark"; Genevieve

Giuliano, "Where Is the 'Region' in Regional Transportation Planning?" in *Up Against the Sprawl: Public Policy and the Making of Southern California*, ed. Jennifer Wolch, Manuel Pastor Jr., and Peter Dreier (Minneapolis: University of Minnesota Press, 2004), 151–170.

43. Schrag, *The Great Society Subway*, 222.

44. Letter to Hon. Ida Ruben and Hon. Gene Counihan, June 23, 1993, box 15, Coll. No. 2007-92, Petzold Papers; Joe Anderson to Carol S. Petzold, letter, August 11, 1993, box 15, Coll. No. 2007-92, Petzold Papers; FHWA, MTA and MD SHA, *Intercounty Connector from I-270 to US 1, Final Environmental Impact Statement/Final Section 4(f) Evaluation*, S-5.

45. Charles Babington and Michael Abramowitz, "A Road Paved with Bias," *WP*, September 2, 1993; Audrey Osborne, "County Gives OK to ICC Citizens Group," *Olney* [Maryland] *Gazette*, October 23, 1993, folder: Transp: ICC 1993-1994, box 15, Coll. No. 2007-92, Petzold Papers.

46. Phyllis Brush, "ICC Would Divert Regional Traffic: Bauman Defends ICC," *Wheaton News*, October 18, 1990, box 15, Coll. No. 2007-92, Petzold Papers; "Intercounty Connector Planning Study: Interview Summary [for Carol S. Petzold]," June 6, 1993, box 15, Coll. No. 2007-92, Petzold Papers; Stephen C. Fehr, "Traffic Snarl Up Ahead, Report Says; Md. Study Makes Case For an East-West Link," *WP*, June 13, 1995; Jennie M. Forehand to Estelle W. Meador, letter, March 18, 1997, box 23, Coll. No. 2008-54, Forehand Papers, University of Maryland, College Park.

47. For a batch of letters from residents of Silver Spring to Montgomery County Council president William Hanna, see folder: Transp: 1993-1994, box 15, Coll. No. 2007-92, Petzold Papers.

48. The report noted the ICC would improve only seven out of forty-four saturated traffic intersections during peak morning rush hour and only eight of forty-nine intersections during afternoon rush hour. Frank Vrataric, "Official ICC Study Proves ICC Will Not Relieve Traffic Congestion," press release [1996], box 15, Coll. No. 2007-92, Petzold Papers.

49. A case from the Bay Area found that planners had not adequately addressed the impact of a highway project on air quality. Mark Evan Garrett and Martin Wachs, *Transportation Planning on Trial: The Clean Air Act and Travel Forecasting* (Thousand Oaks, CA: Sage, 1996).

50. Frank Vrataric, editorial, *WP*, June 5, 1994; Baird Straughan, letter to the editor, *WP*, September 22, 1997; Julie Carlston, "Testimony Presented to the Montgomery County Delegation to the Maryland General Assembly, Transportation Issues," October 30, 1997, box 16, Collection No. 2007-93, Adrienne A. Mandel Papers, unprocessed, University of Maryland, College Park.

51. ICC-SCAR, "No ICC in MC," flyer [n.d., pre-1995], folder: Transp: ICC 1993–1994, box 15, Coll. No. 2007-92, Petzold Papers; Carl Henn [of Stop That Infernal Road!], "Official ICC Study Proves ICC Will Not Relieve Traffic Congestion," memo, folder: Transp: ICC 1996, box 15, Coll. No. 2007-92, Petzold Papers; Montgomery Intercounty Connector Coalition to Kumar P. Barve [Chairman, MC House Delegation], letter, March 10, 1998, folder: Transp: ICC 1997, box 15, Coll. No. 2007-92, Petzold Papers; Montgomery County Council Transportation and Environment Committee, "An Independent Analysis of the Intercounty Connector Study," January 1997, folder: Transp: ICC [1996–2006?], box 8, Collection No. 2008-55, Carol S. Petzold Papers, 1989–2006, unprocessed, Special Collections and University Archives, University of Maryland, College Park, MD.

52. Gregg Zoroya, "Md. Blasts EPA Rejection of Highway Route; Ruling on Proposed Montgomery-P.G. Connector Called Premature," *WP*, October 25, 1994.

53. Ibid.

54. Greenberg, *The Environmental Impact Statement*, 11–16, 20–21.

55. Aaron Handler to Adrienne Mandel, letter, October 21, 1994, box 16, Coll. No. 2007-93, Mandel Papers. For early scholarship on NIMBY, see Denis J. Brion, "An Essay on LULU, NIMBY, and the Problem of Distributive Justice," *B.C. Environmental Affairs Law Review* 15 (1987–1988): 437–503. For a local critique, see e.g. Joseph H. FitzGerald, "Menace to Society," op-ed, *WP*, November 12, 1995.

56. Greater Washington Consumer Survey, Inc., Survey of Voter Attitudes by Legislative District Regarding the Intercounty Connector (Washington, D.C.: Greater Washington Board of Trade, November 22, 1996), folder: Transp: ICC Polls, box 17, Coll. No. 2007-92, Petzold Papers. Charles Babington and Peter Behr, "Businesses Push to Get Area Moving; Board of Trade Launches Own Transportation Study," *WP*, June 9, 1996.

57. Aaron Handler, "Presentation before the Transportation and Environmental Committee of the Montgomery County Council," March 5, 1997, 17, in "An Independent Analysis of the Intercounty Connector Study," January 1997, box 8, Coll. No. 2008-55, Petzold Papers.

58. Maryland State Highway Administration, *Draft Environmental Impact Statement and Major Investment Study, Section 4(f) Evaluation: Intercounty Connector, I-270 to US 1, Montgomery and Prince George's Counties, Maryland*, vol. 1 (Baltimore: Maryland Department of Transportation, 1997), S-3–4, I-4–6, I-18–20.

59. Gus Bauman, Testimony Before Maryland State Highway Administration and U.S. Army Corps of Engineers on the Intercounty Connector Study, May 29, 1997, 2, folder 30, box 2, Coll. No. 2010-101, Carol S. Petzold Papers, 1979–2006, University of Maryland.

60. Charles A. Dukes Jr., "A Failure to Make the Connection in Montgomery," editorial, *WP*, November 9, 1997.

61. David L. Winstead to Adrienne A. Mandel, letter, October 10, 1997, folder: ICC 1998, box 16, Coll. No. 2007-93, Mandel Papers.

62. Karl Vick, "For Md. Connector, EPA Prefers Alternate Route; Agency Rejects Leading Option for Highway," *WP*, August 2, 1997; EPA to Susan J. Binder, letter, August 1, 1997, box 16, Coll. No. 2007-93, Mandel Papers; Willie R. Taylor to Susan Binder, letter, August 19, 1997, box 16, Coll. No. 2007-93, Mandel Papers.

63. The EPA's preferred routing was estimated to claim 40 acres of parkland, 10 acres of wetland, and 236 acres of forest, while displacing the tenants of forty-five homes and seven businesses.

64. Ray C. Dintaman Jr. to Neil J. Pedersen, letter, July 23, 1997, box 16, Coll. No. 2007-93, Mandel Papers; Elder A. Ghigiarelli Jr. to Neil J. Pedersen, letter, August 26, 1997, box 16, Coll. No. 2007-93, Mandel Papers.

65. Alice Reid, "Opponents Dominate First Hearing in Montgomery on Intercounty Connector," *WP*, May 30, 1997.

66. Karl Vick, "Vote to Protect Land May Scuttle Freeway Plan; Montgomery's Action on Paint Branch Watershed Deals Blow to Long-Planned East-West Link," *WP*, July 12, 1995; Sandra Otto, "Environmentally Sensitive Design of Transportation Facilities," *Journal of Transportation Engineering* 126, no. 5 (2000): 364–365.

67. Steve Vogel, "New Route Touted for Connector; Montgomery Board Suggests Hybrid Plan," *WP*, August 8, 1997; Manuel Perez-Rivas, "Md. Rejects Stretch of Connector; But East-West Road Is Needed, State Says," *WP*, September 10, 1997.

68. Lois Sherman, testimony, October 30, 1997, box 16, Coll. No. 2007-93, Mandel Papers.

69. Carl Henn, testimony, October 30, 1997, box 16, Coll. No. 2007-93, Mandel Papers; Julie Carlston, testimony, October 30, 1997, box 16, Coll. No. 2007-93, Mandel Papers; David Dunmire, testimony, October 30, 1997, box 16, Coll. No. 2007-93, Mandel Papers.

70. Nancy Dacek, "Why WE Bypassed the Connector," *WP*, November 23, 1997.

71. For a study that supports efforts to better plan transportation and land use as a way to enhance regional mobility, see Environmental Protection Agency, *Our Built and Natural Environments: A Technical Review of the Interactions Between Land Use, Transportation, and Environmental Quality* (Washington, D.C.: EPA, 2000).

72. Cited in ibid., 20.

73. James J. MacKenzie, "Driving the Road to Sustainable Ground Transportation," in *Frontiers of Sustainability: Environmentally Sound Agriculture, Forestry, Transportation, and Power Production*, ed. Roger C. Dower, Daryl Ditz, Paul Faeth, Nels Johnson, Keith Kozloff, and James J. Mackenzie (Washington, D.C.: Island Press, 1997), 121–190; Transportation Research Board of the National Academies, *Surface Transportation Environmental Research: A Long-Term Strategy*, Special Report 268 (Washington: Transportation Research Board, 2002), 1–2, 20.

74. Jerry Walters and Reid Ewing, "Measuring the Benefits of Compact Development on Vehicle Miles and Climate Change," *Environmental Practice* 11 (2009): 196–208.

75. EPA, *Our Built and Natural Environments*, 68.

76. Tidwell, "Escaping L.A. on the Potomac." Tidwell later founded the Chesapeake Climate Action Network, a grassroots nonprofit focused on global warming in the Washington area and broader region. Mike Tidwell, "A Climate Change Activist Prepares for the Worst," *WP*, February 25, 2011.

77. Elizabeth Gearin, "Smart Growth or Smart Growth Machine? The Smart Growth Movement and Its Implications," in *Up Against the Sprawl: Public Policy and the Making of Southern California*, ed. Jennifer Wolch, Manuel Pastor Jr., and Peter Dreier (Minneapolis: University of Minnesota Press, 2004).

78. Weingroff, "Creating a Landmark"; Giuliano, "Where Is the 'Region,'" 151–154; Liam A. McCann, "TEA-21: Paving Over Efforts to Stem Urban Sprawl and Reduce America's Dependence on the Automobile," *William and Mary Environmental Law and Policy Review* 23 (1998–1999): 857–892.

79. Tidwell, "Escaping L.A. on the Potomac."

80. Edward Abramic, "An Intercounty Greenway?" letter to the editor, *WP*, November 9, 1997.

81. Dunmire, statement (1997), folder: ICC 1998, box 16, Coll. No. 2007-93, Mandel Papers.

82. Rosenbaum, *Environmental Politics and Policy*, 29, 39.

83. Michael E. Ruane, "For the Intercounty Connector, Another Setback; In 5 to 3 Vote, Montgomery Council Takes a Stand in Favor of Alternatives to New Highway," *WP*, October 29, 1997; Jackie Spinner, "Curry Prefers Six-Lane Connector; Executive, Duncan at Odds on Road," *WP*, March 27, 1999.

84. Daniel LeDuc, "Governor Abandons Road Plan; Reversal May Kill Montgomery-Pr. George's Project," *WP*, March 7, 1998; Alan Sipress, "Panel Urges Downsized Connector; Toll Road Would Join Maryland Suburbs," *WP*, June 27, 1999; State of Maryland, Office of the Governor, "Governor Glendening Announces That He Will Not Build Intercounty Connector," press release, September 22, 1999, box 23, Coll. No. 2008-54, Forehand Papers.

85. Bannon Research, Public Opinion Survey of Registered Voters in Montgomery County, Maryland, June 30, 1998, folder: ICC 1998, box 16, Coll. No. 2007-93, Mandel Papers.

86. Alan Sipress, "Glendening Kills Intercounty Connector," *WP*, September 23, 1999.

87. Scott Wilson, "Duncan Endorses 'Parkway-Like' Link of I-270, I-95; Md. Panel Nearing Decision on Connector," *WP*, February 18, 1999.

88. Michael E. Ruane, "Legislator Is a Redevelopment Engine," *WP*, April 18, 1998.

89. Candus Thomson, "Legislative Leaders Eager to Revive Road," *Baltimore Sun*, November 17, 1999.

90. Amy Argetsinger, "Montgomery Won't Sell Its Connector Property," *WP*, February 5, 2000; Michael H. Cottman, "Council Leaves Connector Out of Plan; Transportation Vote Infuriates Duncan," *WP*, July 31, 2002; Michael H. Cottman, "Study Fuels Debate over Intercounty Connector; Duncan, Council Members Dispute Effects on Traffic," *WP*, August 22, 2002.

91. Security also became an important issue after September 11, 2001, and Hurricanes Katrina and Rita in 2005. This was built into one of the justifications for the ICC. Federal Highway Administration and Federal Transit Administration, *The Transportation Planning Process: Key Issues* (Washington, D.C.: U.S. DOT, 2007), 44-45.

92. Michael H. Cottman, "Montgomery Caught Up in Traffic; In Nearly Every Political Race, Gridlock Is the Key Issue," *WP*, September 4, 2002.

93. Anthony B. Mauger, "We Are Paying the Price of Not Building Roads," *The* [Rockville] *Gazette*, November 15, 2002.

94. Michael H. Cottman, "Montgomery Caught Up in Traffic; In Nearly Every Political Race, Gridlock Is the Key Issue," *WP*, September 4, 2002.

95. Jo Becker, "Election Enhances Duncan's Power; Supporters Already Looking to 2006 Governor's Race," *WP*, November 24, 2002.

96. Michael H. Cottman, "Duncan Aims to Oust Dacek from Montgomery Council; County Executive on Campaign for a Pro-Connector Panel," *WP*, September 12, 2002.

97. Bill Turque, "Friends and Colleagues Remember an 'Unfailingly Graceful' Nancy Dacek," *WP*, January 19, 2015.

98. Becker, "Election Enhances Duncan's Power."

99. Cottman, "Montgomery Caught Up in Traffic"; Dana Hedgpeth and Krissah Williams, "Business Calls It a Win in Maryland; Intercounty Connector Supporters Had Pinned Hopes on Ehrlich," *WP*, November 7, 2002; Lyndsey Layton and Katherine Shaver, "Transportation Plans Turn on Budgets, Ballots; Intercounty Connector Reborn; Uphill Fight for Inner Purple Line," *WP*, November 19, 2002. A 2002 poll for the Maryland gubernatorial election found that 80 percent of voters felt that Robert Ehrlich would do a good job promoting business and economic growth in the state. Washington Post, Washington Post Maryland Governor's Race Poll, October 2002 [computer file], ICPSR version (Horsham, PA: Taylor Nelson Sofres Intersearch [producer], 2002; Ann Arbor, MI: Inter-university Consortium for Political and Social Research [distributor], 2003).

100. George W. Bush, Environmental Stewardship and Transportation Infrastructure Project Reviews, Executive Order 13274, September 18, 2002, in *Federal Register*, 67, no. 184, September 23, 2002, 59449–59450.

101. Katherine Shaver, "Intercounty Connector Study Placed on Federal Fast Track; Road Project to Get Expedited Review," *WP*, February 28, 2003 and "Md. Highway Officials Taking New Look at Connector Options; In Expedited Review, State Aims to Have Plan Approved by 2005," *WP*, June 28, 2003; FHWA, MTA, and MD SHA, *Final Environmental Impact Statement*, S-8, I-3; Federal Highway Administration, Maryland Division, Record of Decision: Intercounty Connector Project, Montgomery and Prince George's Counties, Maryland (Baltimore, 2006), 4–6.

102. Maryland Department of Transportation, "Governor Ehrlich Appoints Neil J. Pedersen to Head Maryland State Highway Administration," press release, May 7, 2003, http://

msa.maryland.gov/megafile/msa/speccol/sc5300/sc5339/000113/002000/002409/unrestricted
/20063624e.pdf (accessed February 22, 2014).

103. Audubon Naturalist Society of the Central Atlantic States, Inc., et al. v. United States Department of Transportation, et al.; and Environmental Defense, et al. v. United States Department of Transportation, et al., United States District Court for the District of Maryland, Southern Division, 524 F. Supp. 2d 642, November 8, 2007.

104. Ibid.; FHWA, MTA, and MD SHA, *Final Environmental Impact Statement*, III-29-32; Metropolitan Washington Council of Governments, "Transportation Planning Board Gives Green Light to Intercounty Connector (ICC)," press release, November 17, 2004, http://www .mwcog.org (accessed December 29, 2011); Katherine Shaver, "Fortunes Shift for East-West Rail Plan; Purple Line Stalls, Connector Thrives," *WP*, January 16, 2005.

105. The three Maryland agencies were the Department of Transportation, State Highway Administration, and the Maryland Transportation Authority. The last was responsible for mass transit in the state and was involved in the EIS process because the ICC was to include express bus service along its route.

106. FHWA, MTA, and MD SHA, *Final Environmental Impact Statement*, I-1. The reference to "homeland security" reflected concerns about responding to emergencies after September 11 and Hurricane Katrina. It also harkened back to the Cold War era, a time when highway building and decentralization were responses to reducing the impact of nuclear attack.

107. U.S. Department of Transportation, Federal Highway Administration, "NEPA and Transportation Decisionmaking: Environmental Impacts," http://environment.fhwa.dot.gov /projdev/tdmimpacts.asp (accessed April 11, 2014).

108. U.S. Department of Transportation, Federal Highway Administration, "NEPA and Transportation Decisionmaking: Mitigation of Environment Impacts," http://environment.fhwa .dot.gov/projdev/tdmmitig2.asp (accessed April 11, 2014).

109. FHWA and FTA, *Transportation Planning Process: Key Issues*, 44–45.

110. Rosenbaum, *Environmental Politics and Policy*, 29, 39.

111. U.S DOT FHWA Maryland Division, Intercounty Connector, I-270 to US 1: Record of Responses to Public Comments (Baltimore, 2006), http://cdm16064.contentdm.oclc.org/cdm /ref/collection/p266901coll7/id/791 (accessed August 13, 2017).

112. Katherine Shaver, "ICC Funding Plans Debt Irks Some Lawmakers," *WP*, March 3, 2005; Katherine Shaver, "ICC Puts Strain on Maryland's Transportation Funds," *WP*, November 22, 2011; Katherine Shaver, "Maryland's Intercounty Connector Toll Revenue Falls Short of Early Forecasts," *WP*, November 30, 2013. For a breakdown of project costs, see Federal Highway Administration, Office of Innovative Program Delivery, Project Profiles: Intercounty Connector, http://www.fhwa .dot.gov/ipd/project_profiles/md_icc.aspx (accessed April 11, 2014). The estimated cost of the project was $2.425 billion. Approximately $770 million came from federal funds, nearly all from the sale of bonds backed by future federal aid receipts. The rest came from state funds including $695 million in toll revenue bonds and cash and a $516 million loan backed by future toll revenue as well as a $180 million grant from the Maryland Transportation Trust Fund and $265 million from the state's general fund and general bonds not tied to future toll revenue.

113. FHWA, Record of Decision, 7–9.

114. For a listing of the mitigation and environmental stewardship measures and their location, see ibid., 21.

115. Audubon Naturalist Society and Environmental Defense v. United States Department of Transportation 24 F. Supp. 2d 642 (2007); Margie Hyslop and C. Benjamin Ford, "Council

Activists Mull Next Step After ICC Ruling," *Gazette Regional News* [unknown locality], November 15, 2007. The litigants alleged violations of NEPA, the Federal Highway Act, the Clean Water Act, and the Clean Air Act.

116. Matthew Mosk and Eric M. Weiss, "For Ehrlich, Connector Highway Issue Is Promising but Low-Risk," *WP*, October 13, 2006.

117. Lindsey Robbins, "ICC Pieces Fall into Place for Konterra; Land Swap Paves Way for 2,200-Acre Laurel Development," *Gazette.Net*, April 21, 2011, http://ww2.gazette.net/stories /04212011/busiplo163111_32533.php (accessed September 16, 2011).

118. Shaver, "ICC Puts Strain on Maryland's Transportation Funds"; Eugene L. Meyer, "The Road Less Traveled," *Bethesda Magazine* (September–October 2013), http://www .bethesdamagazine.com/Bethesda-Magazine/September-October-2013/The-Intercounty -Connector/ (accessed July 31, 2014); Shaver, "Maryland's Intercounty Connector Toll Revenue Falls Short."

119. Shaver, "ICC Puts Strain on Maryland's Transportation Funds"; Shaver, "Maryland's Intercounty Connector Toll Revenue Falls Short."

Chapter 5. A Master Plan for Agriculture

1. Nathan Carrick, "More County Farmland Preserved; Easement Placed on 75-Acre Etchison Property," *Gazette.Net*, February 4, 2009.

2. Sarah Krouse, "Montgomery County Farmers Looking for New Agriculture Policy," *Washington Business Journal*, August 31, 2009. Of the 93,000-acre total, approximately 71,000 acres was protected through conservation easements. Agricultural Preservation Advisory Board (APAB), *Montgomery County Farmland Preservation Annual Report FY1980–FY2009* (Rockville, MD: Montgomery County Department of Economic Development, 2009), https://www .montgomerycountymd.gov/agservices/Resources/Files/agpreservation/2013AGannualreport .pdf (accessed August 15, 2017).

3. Tom Daniels and Mark Lapping, "Land Preservation: An Essential Ingredient in Smart Growth," *Journal of Planning Literature* 19 (2005): 316–329; Daniel Press, *Saving Open Space: The Politics of Local Preservation in California* (Berkeley: University of California Press, 2002), 23–28; Daniel Hellerstein et al., *Farmland Protection: The Role of Public Preferences for Rural Amenities*, Agricultural Economic Report No. 815 (Washington, D.C.: Economic Research Service, U.S. Department of Agriculture [USDA], 2002), https://www.ers.usda.gov/webdocs /publications/41479/17291_aer815b_1_.pdf?v=41061 (accessed August 15, 2017), 21–22.

4. Press, *Saving Open Space*, 48, 59–60, 64–66; Stephan Schmidt and Kurt Paulsen, "Is Open-Space Preservation a Form of Exclusionary Zoning? The Evolution of Municipal Open-Space Policies in New Jersey," *Urban Affairs Review* 45 (2009): 92–118; Mark Friedberger, "The Rural-Urban Fringe in the Late Twentieth Century," *Agricultural History* 74, no. 2 (Spring 2000): 502; Richard K. Olson and Thomas A. Lyson, eds., *Under the Blade: The Conversion of Agricultural Landscapes* (Boulder, CO: Westview Press, 1999), 88–90; Craig R. Smith, "Institutional Determinants of Collaboration: An Empirical Study of County Open-Space Protection," *Journal of Public Administration Research and Theory* 19 (2007): 1–21; Olson and Lyson, *Under the Blade*, 133.

5. Hellerstein et al., *Farmland Protection*; Schmidt and Paulsen, "Is Open-Space Preservation," 104–105; Smith, "Institutional Determinants of Collaboration"; Olson and Lyson, *Under the Blade*, 133.

6. While scholarship has brought the suburbs into urban history, rural communities have often been left out. For a model of thinking about interconnections between regional

communities and role of hinterlands in shaping metropolitan growth, see Andrew Needham and Allen Dieterich-Ward, "Beyond the Metropolis: Metropolitan Growth and Regional Transformation in Postwar America," *Journal of Urban History* 35, no. 7 (November 2009): 943–969.

7. Hellerstein et al., *Farmland Protection*; Brian Roe, Elena G. Irwin, and Hazel A. Morrow-Jones, "The Effects of Farmland, Farmland Preservation, and Other Neighborhood Amenities on Housing Values and Residential Growth," *Land Economics* 80, no. 1 (February 2004): 55–75.

8. Deborah Carter Park and Philip M. Coppack, "The Role of Rural Sentiment and Vernacular Landscapes in Contriving Sense of Place in the City's Countryside," *Geografiska Annaler: Series B, Human Geography* 76, no. 3 (1994): 161–172; Randal S. Beeman and James A. Pritchard, *A Green and Permanent Land: Ecology and Agriculture in the Twentieth Century* (Lawrence: University Press of Kansas, 2001), 2–3.

9. Christopher S. Elmendorf, "Ideas, Incentives, Gifts, and Governance: Toward Conservation Stewardship of Private Land, in Cultural and Psychological Perspective," *University of Illinois Law Review* (2003): 423–506.

10. Ibid.

11. U.S. Bureau of the Census, *Census of Population and Housing*, 1950 and 1970, Maryland, in *National Historic Geographic Information System NHGIS* (Minneapolis: Minnesota Population Center, University of Minnesota), http://nhgis.org (accessed November 3, 2012).

12. John Fraser Hart, "Half a Century of Cropland Change," *Geographical Review* 91, no. 3 (July 2001): 525–543.

13. Bruce L. Gardner, *American Agriculture in the Twentieth Century: How It Flourished and What It Cost* (Cambridge, MA: Harvard University Press, 2002); Tim Lehman, *Public Values, Private Lands: Farmland Preservation Policy, 1933–1985* (Chapel Hill: University of North Carolina Press, 1995); David B. Danbom, *Born in the Country: A History of Rural America*, 2nd ed. (Baltimore: Johns Hopkins University Press, 2006), 206–250.

14. The number of farms dropped from 1,555 to 654, while the value of agricultural products per farm increased from $6,868 to $15,615. USDA, National Agricultural Statistics Service, *Farm Characteristics—Montgomery County [Maryland], 1949–2007*, 1, http://www.montgomerycountymd.gov/agservices/resources/files/agdata1949-2007.pdf (accessed August 15, 2017).

15. Cited in Maryland-National Capital Park and Planning Commission (M-NCPPC), *Functional Master Plan for the Preservation of Agriculture and Rural Open Space in Montgomery County* (Silver Spring, MD: M-NCPPC, 1980), 14. On the postwar suburbanization of Montgomery, see Peter Siskind, "Growth and Its Discontents: Localism, Protest and the Politics of Development on the Postwar Northeast Corridor" (PhD diss., University of Pennsylvania, 2002), 125–128.

16. Alice Bonner, "Hanson Focus on Montgomery Fuss: Planning Chief's 'Strong Leadership' Hit as 'Grand Scheme,'" *Washington Post* [*WP*], July 14, 1975.

17. Maryland Department of Agriculture, Department of Mental Hygiene, and Department of State Planning, *The Effects of Large-Lot Zoning on the Depletion of Agricultural Land* (Annapolis, MD, 1977), cited in Cynthia Giordano and Frank Schnidman, "Agricultural Preservation in Montgomery County, Maryland," *Journal of Soil and Water Conservation* (September–October 1979): 209; M-NCPPC, *Preservation of Agriculture and Rural Open Space*, 6, 12, 32. Some officials maintained the public facilities ordinance was an issue of public health rather than growth management. Royce Hanson, "Montgomery County—Steady, Moderate Growth and

Change," *Realtor*, July 1978, 18. On growth management in Montgomery in the 1970s, see Siskind, "Growth and Its Discontents," 94–97, 152–161.

18. In 1975, the Department of Economic and Agricultural Development became the Department of Economic Development as local agriculture was moved to another office and treated as a land use issue rather than an industry. Jeremy Criss and John Zawitoski, interview by author, Derwood, MD, June 23, 2011.

19. Elsa L. Walsh, "Saving Montgomery's Farmland; They Gave a Hearing, but Nobody Came," *WP*, June 12, 1980.

20. Sugarloaf Regional Trails, *Environmental, Social, and Cultural Aspects of Farmland Retention* (Montgomery County, MD, 1977), 41. On definitions of an ecological understanding of private property, Eric T. Freyfogle, *The Land We Share: Private Property and the Common Good* (Washington, D.C.: Island Press, 2003), 203–227. Park and Coppack, "The Role of Rural Sentiment"; Beeman and Pritchard, *A Green and Permanent Land*, 2–3.

21. Olson and Lyson, *Under the Blade*, 201; Ralph E. Heimlich and William D. Anderson, *Development at the Urban Fringe and Beyond: Impacts on Agriculture and Rural Land*, Agricultural Economic Report No. 803 (Washington, D.C.: Economic Research Service, USDA, 2001), vi, h https://www.ers.usda.gov/webdocs/publications/41350/19084_aer803_1_.pdf?v=41061 (accessed August 15, 2017); Hellerstein et al., *Farmland Protection*, iv, 1.

22. M-NCPPC, *Preservation of Agriculture and Rural Open Space*, 14. Farmland dropped from 150,284 acres in 1971 to 131,516 acres by 1979. USDA, *Farm Characteristics—Montgomery County*, 1.

23. USDA, *Farm Characteristics—Montgomery County*, 1.

24. Gardner, *American Agriculture in the Twentieth Century*, 78; Rene Johnson, *Changes in Montgomery County Agriculture, 1969 to 1978* (January 1980), 5, cited in M-NCPPC, *Preservation of Agriculture and Rural Open Space*, 24.

25. Lehman, *Public Values, Private Lands*, 43–44, 70–81, 93–95, 133.

26. Giordano and Schnidman, "Agricultural Preservation in Montgomery County," 208.

27. Lehman, *Public Values, Private Lands*, 101.

28. Ed Bruske, "Olney's Growing Pains; Plan Will Save Farms, Shift Growth to Town Center," *WP*, June 12, 1980; Timothy W. Warman, *Preservation of Agricultural Land in Montgomery County: Issues in 1987* (n.p., 1987), 2–3, box 7, SC2007-13, Neal Potter Papers, Montgomery County Historical Society, Rockville, MD; American Farmland Trust, "Montgomery County, Maryland TDR Program," in APAB, *Montgomery County Farmland Preservation Annual Report*; Robert A. Johnston and Mary E. Madison, "From Landmarks to Landscapes: A Review of Current Practices in the Transfer of Development Rights," *Journal of the American Planning Association* 63, no. 3 (1997): 369.

29. For thinking about the relationship between growth management and rural land preservation in the early 1980s, see e.g. National Agricultural Lands Study, *Final Report 1981* (Washington, D.C., 1981), 16; Wendell Fletcher and Charles E. Little, *The American Cropland Crisis: Why US Farmland Is Being Lost and How Citizens and Governments Are Trying to Save What's Left* (Bethesda, MD: American Land Forum, 1982), 46–48.

30. Walsh, "Saving Montgomery's Farmland"; Olson and Lyson, *Under the Blade*, 70.

31. M-NCPPC, *Preservation of Agriculture and Rural Open Space*, 1; Walsh, "Saving Montgomery's Farmland."

32. M-NCPPC, *Preservation of Agriculture and Rural Open Space*, iv, 27–30. On preservation in 1970s Montgomery, see Giordano and Schnidman, "Agricultural Preservation

in Montgomery County." For an overview of the issue in the 1970s, see David Berry and Thomas Plaut, "Retaining Agricultural Activities Under Urban Pressures: A Review of Land Use Conflicts and Policies," *Policy Science* 9 (1978): 153–178; Owen J. Furuseth, "The Oregon Agricultural Program: A Review and Assessment," *Natural Resources Journal* 20 (1980): 603–614. On the influence of growth pressures on agricultural land in metropolitan areas, see Charles Barnard, Keith Wiebe, and Vince Breneman, "Urban Influence: Effects on US Farmland Markets and Value," in *Government Policy and Farmland Markets: The Maintenance of Farmer Wealth*, ed. Charles B. Moss and Andrew Schmitz (Ames: Iowa State Press, 2003), 319–341.

33. M-NCPPC, *Preservation of Agriculture and Rural Open Space*, i. Emphasis in original.

34. Landowners had to retain at least one development right for each parcel of land they owned, so they could not sell all of the TDRs, which would have rendered the property undevelopable.

35. M-NCPPC, *Preservation of Agriculture and Rural Open Space*, 38–47, 59, 62, 65–71; James R. Cohen and Ilana Preuss, "An Analysis of Social Equity Issues in the Montgomery County (MD) Transfer of Development Rights Program," working paper, September 3, 2002 (College Park, MD: National Center for Smart Growth Research and Education, 2002), 5, http://smartgrowth.umd.edu/assets/cohenpreuss_2002.pdf (accessed July 21, 2010); Johnston and Madison, "From Landmarks to Landscapes," 369–370.

36. M-NCPPC, *Preservation of Agriculture and Rural Open Space*, i.

37. USDA, *Farm Characteristics—Montgomery County*, 3.

38. Beef cattle operations declined from 348 to 136, and poultry from 40 to 3. USDA, *Farm Characteristics—Montgomery County*, 3.

39. Criss and Zawitoski, interview.

40. Hellerstein et al., *Farmland Protection*, iv, 1, 12, 15; Bruce R. Beattie, "The Disappearance of Agricultural Land: Fact or Fiction?" in *Agriculture and the Environment: Searching for Greener Pastures*, ed. Terry L. Anderson and Bruce Yandle (Stanford, CA: Stanford University, Hoover Institution Press, 2001), 19, 21–22; Park and Coppack, "The Role of Rural Sentiment"; Julia D. Mahoney, "Perpetual Restrictions on Land and the Problems of the Future," *Virginia Law Review* 88, no. 4 (June 2002): 739–787; Beeman and Pritchard, *A Green and Permanent Land*, 2–3; Arnold Berleant, *The Aesthetics of Environment* (Philadelphia: Temple University Press, 1992), 38, 57–58.

41. Janis Johnson, "Cheered and Jeered, but Remembered," *WP*, September 1, 1978; "Royce Hanson," *WP*, June 22, 2006.

42. Janis Johnson, "Montgomery Panel Kills Farm Preservation Plan," *WP*, March 23, 1979.

43. Park and Coppack, "The Role of Rural Sentiment"; Beeman and Pritchard, *A Green and Permanent Land*, 2–3.

44. Elsa L. Walsh, "Farmland's Uncertain Future," *WP*, September 11, 1980.

45. Press, *Saving Open Space*, 59–60, 64–66.

46. A local judge upheld that the 1980 plan's reduction of the developable density of land in the Agricultural Reserve was not an unconstitutional taking because it was reasonably related to advancing the public welfare, part of detailed public study, and did not result in the complete loss of value. Moreover, he noted that the TDR program helped to offset the impact of downzoning. Raymond A. Dufour [Law No. 56964], Frederick L. Horman et al. [Law No. 56968], Ray Gustin III et al. [Law No. 56969], Elizabeth S. Dietz et al. [Law No. 56970] and Leonard Abel et al. [56983], Circuit Court for Montgomery County, MD, January 20, 1983, folder 18, box 19,

American Farmland Trust Records [AFT], 1979–1999, Collection Number CMSS CONS148, Denver Public Library, Denver, CO.

47. Paul Hodge, "Montgomery Readies Plan to Protect Farms," *WP*, August 13, 1981.

48. Paul Hodge, "First Use of TDRs Saves Farm Land," *WP*, June 30, 1982; Maryland-National Capital Park and Planning Commission, "First Transfer of Development Rights Approved by Planning Board," news release, June 25, 1982, folder 18, box 19, AFT.

49. Eugene L. Meyer, "Saving Farmland; Citizens Oppose County Plan to Preserve Its Open Spaces," *WP*, July 7, 1982.

50. Ibid.

51. Meyer, "Saving Farmland."

52. "The Montgomery County Executive," editorial, *WP*, September 9, 1978. On tax-revolt movements elsewhere, see Chapter 3 on Prince George's as well as Lisa McGirr, *Suburban Warriors: The Origins of the New American Right* (Princeton, NJ: Princeton University Press, 2001), 237–239; and Robert O. Self, *American Babylon: Race and the Struggle for Postwar Oakland* (Princeton, NJ: Princeton University Press, 2003), 317–326.

53. *West Montgomery County Citizens Association v. Maryland-National Capital Park and Planning Commission*, 309 Md. 183, 522 A.2d 1328 (1987); Jo-Ann Armao, "Kramer Urges Transfer Rights; Zoning Technique Criticized by Some," *WP*, May 19, 1987.

54. Dinah Wisenberg, "A Farewell to Farms? Urbanization, Low Prices, High Costs Are Forcing Farmers to Quit," *Sentinel* [Montgomery County], June 26, 1986; Warman, *Preservation of Agricultural Land*, "Table 5: Farmland in Montgomery County; Change 1986 to 1987 with Reference to 1979," 6. At the time, one-third of the county's farmland was outside of the reserve and under greater development pressures because of its proximity to urban areas.

55. in Warman, *Preservation of Agricultural Land*, "Table 9: Preservation of Montgomery County Agricultural Land; August 1987," 7. The MALPF preserved 1,679 acres while the MET preserved 1,865 acres.

56. Warman, *Preservation of Agricultural Land*, 13.

57. Neal Potter to council members, memorandum, December 3, 1987, box 7, Potter Papers.

58. Warman left his position with the county in 1993 to become the director of federal policy for the American Farmland Trust; he is one of several Montgomery-based figures with ties to the AFT.

59. Claudia Levy, "Keeping Montgomery Evergreen," *WP*, October 22, 1989.

60. Ibid.

61. Office of Economic Development and the Agricultural Preservation Advisory Board (Montgomery County, MD), *Agricultural Preservation Easement Purchase Program* (1991), 12; Richard Brewer, *Conservancy: The Land Trust Movement in America* (Hanover, NH: University Press of New England, 2003), 247. On open space preservation, see Stephanie Pincetl, "The Preservation of Nature at the Urban Fringe," in *Up Against the Sprawl: Public Policy and the Making of Southern California*, ed. Jennifer Wolch, Manuel Pastor Jr., and Peter Dreier (Minneapolis: University of Minnesota Press, 2004), 225–251. On the balance between open space preservation and preserving farming, see Hellerstein et al., *Farmland Protection*, iv, ix, 1; Beattie, "The Disappearance of Agricultural Land," 19, 21–22; Samuel R. Staley, "The Political Economy of Land Conversion on the Urban Fringe," in Anderson and Yandle, *Agriculture and the Environment*, 65–80.

62. Warman, *Preservation of Agricultural Land*, 7–9, 12–14.

63. Edward Thompson Jr., "Testimony in Support of Bill No. 56–87," 3, box 7, Potter Papers.

64. Office of the County Executive (Montgomery County), *Executive Regulation: Agricultural Land Preservation Districts and Easement Purchases, No. 66–91*, in Office of Economic Development and the Agricultural Preservation Advisory Board (APAB), *Agricultural Preservation Easement Purchase Program: FY 1991 Annual Report* (July 1991).

65. Chapter 2B Agricultural Land Preservation (1988), 395–407, in Office of Economic Development and APAB, *Agricultural Preservation Easement Purchase Program*; Internal Audit Section, Department of Finance, Montgomery County, *Office of Economic Development and Review of Agricultural Transfer Tax Program for the Year Ended June 30, 1990, Agreed-Upon Procedures*, July 11, 1991, folder 4, box 3, Potter Papers; APAB, *Montgomery County Farmland Preservation Annual Report*, 6.

66. Office of Economic Development and APAB, *Agricultural Preservation Easement Purchase Program*, 10.

67. Ibid., 16; APAB, *Montgomery County Farmland Preservation Annual Report*, 7.

68. Warman, *Preservation of Agricultural Land*, 7; Office of Economic Development and the Agricultural Preservation Advisory Board, *Agricultural Preservation Easement Purchase Program* (1991).

69. Christopher Bosso, *Environment, Inc.* (Lawrence: University Press of Kansas, 2005); Robert J. Duffy, *The Green Agenda in American Politics: New Strategies for the Twenty-First Century* (Lawrence: University Press of Kansas, 2003), 7, 118; Mary Graham, *The Morning After Earth Day: Practical Environmental Politics* (Washington, D.C.: Brookings Institution Press, 1999).

70. American Farmland Trust, "Preliminary Report of the Farmland Protection Working Group," March 1995, folder 10, box 9, AFT.

71. Liz Spayd, "Poolesville Fears Effect on Services of Saudi Plan for Mosque, Schools," *WP*, September 20, 1993.

72. Dolores Milmoe, interview by author, Poolesville, MD, June 23, 2011; Caroline Taylor, interview by author, Poolesville, MD, June 23, 2011; Louis Aguilar, "Potter Joins Opposition to Saudi Project in Poolesville," *WP*, September 1, 1994.

73. Charles Babington, "Saudis Propose a Pipeline from the Potomac: Offer Could Clinch Deal for Mosque, School," *WP*, May 12, 1994; Aguilar, "Potter Joins Opposition"; Montgomery County Agricultural Preservation Advisory Board, "Statement of Position," August 2, 1994, folder 5, box 29, AFT.

74. Louis Aguilar, "Plans for Saudi School, Mosque Stirs Controversy in Poolesville," *WP*, October 26, 1994.

75. Louis Aguilar, "Battle Lines in Poolesville over Site for Saudi School; Annexation Bid Triggers Rumors and Rancor," *WP*, January 22, 1995.

76. Louis Aguilar, "Poolesville Voters Reject Annexation Plan; Saudi Proposal Defeated in Controversy Tinged with Charges of Racism," *WP*, February 12, 1995; Peter Pae, "Saudi School Effort Turns to Loudoun; Divisive Bid to Build in Montgomery Ends," *WP*, November 9, 1997; Rosalind S. Helderman, "Islamic Saudi School Drops Plan for Campus in Loudoun," *WP*, July 8, 2004.

77. Taylor, interview.

78. Richard A. Harris and Sidney M. Milkis, *The Politics of Regulatory Change: A Tale of Two Agencies* (New York: Oxford University Press, 1989); Bosso, *Environment, Inc.*; Duffy, *The Green Agenda*.

79. Stuart Leavenworth, "Saving a Rural Legacy," *News and Observer* [Raleigh, NC], November 10, 1998.

80. Stephen C. Fehr, "Montgomery's Line of Defense Against the Suburban Invasion," *WP*, March 25, 1997.

81. Cohen and Preuss, "An Analysis of Social Equity Issues," 21–25.

82. Cited in M-NCPPC, Montgomery County Department of Park and Planning, *Rustic Roads Functional Master Plan, Clarksburg Master Plan and Hyattstown Special Study Area, Boyds Master Plan and Gaithersburg Vicinity Master Plan Amendment; Planning Board Draft* (Silver Spring, MD, December 2002), 1.

83. Montgomery County Department of Park and Planning, M-NCPPC, *Rustic Roads Functional Master Plan* (Silver Spring, MD, 1996); and Rustic Roads Functional Master Plan, http://www.montgomeryplanning.org/community/plan_areas/rural_area/master_plans/rustic _roads/rustic_toc.shtm (accessed October 9, 2010); Nancy Trejos, "Where the 'Rustic' Clogs the Road; Montgomery Rules Make It Tough for Farmers to Maneuver," *WP*, April 24, 2006.

84. Trejos, "Where the 'Rustic' Clogs the Road."

85. Park and Coppack, "The Role of Rural Sentiment."

86. Trejos, "Where the 'Rustic' Clogs the Road."

87. Susan DeFord, "Saving the County's Rural Byways; Future of Rustic Road Program Pits Preservationists Against Farmers," *WP*, December 3, 1998; Criss and John Zawitoski, interview.

88. Maryland Department of Natural Resources, "Maryland's Rural Legacy Program," http://dnr.maryland.gov/land/Pages/RuralLegacy/home.aspx (accessed August 15, 2017).

89. The difference between the RLP and the two local programs was that the state and county jointly held easements acquired through the RLP APAB, *Montgomery County Farmland Preservation Annual Report*, 8–9.

90. Ibid., 10–11.

91. National Center for Smart Growth Research and Education, *Indicators of Smart Growth in Maryland* (College Park: University of Maryland, 2011), 16, 26–27, http://smartgrowth .umd.edu/assets/documents/indicators/2011_smart_growth_indicators_report.pdf (accessed November 23, 2011); Elizabeth Gearin, "Smart Growth or Smart Growth Machine? The Smart Growth Movement and Its Implications," in *Up Against the Sprawl: Public Policy and the Making of Southern California*, ed. Jennifer Wolch, Manuel Pastor Jr., and Peter Dreier (Minneapolis: University of Minnesota Press, 2004), 279–307.

92. Daniels and Lapping, "Land Preservation."

93. Ibid., 320.

94. Ibid., 317. Between 1980 and 2002, the number of land trusts in the United States rose from 400 to over 1,200. For a history of the land trust movement, see Brewer, *Conservancy*.

95. Maryland Department of Natural Resources, "Directory of Maryland Land Trusts / Land Conservation Organizations" (2009), http://dnr.maryland.gov/met/landtrustslists.pdf (accessed April 24, 2012). Most of the land trusts were located in New England, although mid-Atlantic states such as Maryland also saw a rise in their number.

96. Anita Huslin, "Land Deal Places Montgomery Tract into Preservation," *WP*, December 14, 2001.

97. Julie Ann Gustanski, "Protecting the Land: Conservation Easements, Voluntary Actions, and Private Lands," in *Protecting the Land: Conservation Easements Past, Present, and Future*, ed. Julie Ann Gustanski and Robert H. Squires (Washington, D.C.: Island Press, 2000), 9–25. For a brief overview of the work of the Trust for Public Land, see Brewer, *Conservancy*, 216–226.

98. The Trust for Public Land, "800 Acres Protected for Maryland Park," press release, March 3, 2002, The Trust for Public Land, http://www.tpl.org/news/press-releases/800-acres

-protected-for-maryland.html (accessed April 7, 2012). For more information about Mike Rubin, see "Mike Rubin," *Conservation Montgomery*, http://www.conservationmontgomery.org /rubin.html (accessed April 7, 2012). On the Montgomery Countryside Alliance, see Montgomery Countryside Alliance, "Montgomery Countryside Alliance: A Brief History," http://www .mocoalliance.org/a-brief-history.html (accessed August 15, 2017).

99. Sara Stefanini, "'Megachurch' Plans Decried; Water and Traffic Problems Envisioned in Rural Zone," *Gazette* [Damascus, MD], May 11, 2005.

100. Ibid.

101. Nancy Trejos, "Size Curbs Sought for Churches on Md. Reserve; With Plans in Limbo, Congregations Vow Fight," *WP*, April 25, 2005.

102. Jacqueline Mah, "Two Churches Press to Build in Agricultural Reserve," *Gazette* [Damascus, MD], December 8, 2004.

103. Tim Craig, "Churches' Development Plans Cause Flap in Md.," *WP*, June 30, 2005.

104. Trejos, "Size Curbs Sought for Churches on Md. Reserve."

105. Nancy Trejos, "Montgomery Megachurches Curb Advances; Planning Board Backs Utility Limits and Size Constraints in Agricultural Reserve," *WP*, November 5, 2005.

106. Nancy Trejos, "County Curtails Megachurches' Rush on Reserve; Montgomery Ends New Access to Utilities in Agrarian Area," *WP*, November 30, 2005.

107. Ibid.

108. Ann E. Marimow, "Veteran Tapped to Chair Planners," *WP*, July 26, 2006.

109. Montgomery County, Maryland, press release, January 29, 2009, http://www2 .montgomerycountymd.gov/mcgportalapps/Press_Detail.aspx?Item_ID=4255 (accessed August 15, 2017); APAB, *Montgomery County Farmland Preservation Annual Report*, 13; "County Reaches Milestone in Agricultural Preservation," *WP*, January 29. 2009; "Reserve Hits 70,000 Acres," *Potomac Almanac* [Montgomery County, MD], February 4–10, 2009.

110. APAB, *Montgomery County Farmland Preservation Annual Report*, 5. By 2009, the MALPF had preserved 4,280 acres, while the MET and private land trusts had preserved 2,086 acres.

111. APAB, *Montgomery Farmland Preservation Annual Report*, 13.

112. Press, *Saving Open Space*, 47–48; Daniels and Lapping, "Land Preservation," 320.

113. USDA, *Farm Characteristics—Montgomery County*, 1.

114. Ibid., 3. Data from 1982 to 2007 showed drops in dairy farms (from 52 to 8); beef cattle operations (from 136 to 63); other livestock (from 257 to 53), and cash grain operations (from 119 to 34).

115. Ibid.; Montgomery County Department of Economic Development, *Agricultural Fact Sheet for Montgomery County*, https://www.montgomerycountymd.gov/agservices/Resources /Files/Ag%20Census/agfactsheetmay2016.pdf (accessed August 15, 2017). For a discussion of agricultural adaptation in metropolitan America, see Ralph E. Heimlich and Charles H. Barnard, "Agricultural Adaptation to Urbanization: Farm Types and Agricultural Sustainability in US Metropolitan Areas," in *Rural Sustainable Development in America*, ed. Ivonne Audirac (New York: John Wiley and Sons, 1997), 283–303.

116. Peter Whoriskey, "Farmland Acreage Dips in Montgomery; 'Reserve' Program Not Halting Decline," *WP*, June 4, 2004.

117. Department of Economic Development. Agricultural Services Division, *2008 Farm Directory: Montgomery County* (2009), http://www.montgomerycountymd.gov/agservices /resources/files/farmdirectory_120108.pdf (accessed August 17, 2017).

118. Agricultural Services Division, *2011 Farm Tour and Harvest Sale*, brochure, http://www6 .montgomerycountymd.gov/content/ded/agservices/pdffiles/farmtourifront.pdf (accessed August 3, 2012); and *Fall 2009 Festival of Farms*, brochure, http://www6.montgomerycountymd .gov/content/ded/agservices/pdffiles/festivaloffarms.pdf (accessed August 3, 2012).

119. University of Maryland Extension, "Entries Serving Montgomery County (for the Community Supported Agriculture (CSA) Category," *MarylandAgriculture.inf*, http://www .marylandagriculture.info/county_info.cfm?countyid=6&categoryid=46 (accessed April 24, 2012). On the history of community supported agriculture in the United States, see, e.g., Trauger M. Groh and Steven McFadden, *Farms of Tomorrow Revisited: Community Supported Farms, Farm Supported Communities* (Biodynamic Farming and Gardening Association, 1998); Elizabeth Henderson and Robyn Van En, *Sharing the Harvest: A Citizen's Guide to Community Supported Agriculture*, rev. and expanded ed. (White River Junction, VT: Chelsea Green, 2007).

120. Between 1975 and 1995, public officials treated agriculture primarily as a land use, with little support for economic development.

121. Criss and Zawitoski, interview.

122. Agricultural Services Division, *The Dilemma of Montgomery County's Agricultural Reserve: Competing Interests of Agricultural and Open Space Preservation*, information sheet, December 4, 2009, author's possession.

123. Brewer, *Conservancy*, 247.

124. Taylor, interview.

125. Edward Thompson Jr., "Hybrid Farmland Protection Programs: A New Paradigm for Growth Management," *William and Mary Environmental Law and Policy Review* 23, no. 3 (1999): 831–839; Ralph E. Grossi, "A Green Evolution: Retooling Agricultural Policy to Greater Sustainability," *Journal of Soil and Water Conservation* 48, no. 4 (July–August 1993): 285–288.

Chapter 6. Saving Farms from Development

1. Glenn Frankel and Peter Pae, "In Loudoun, Two Worlds Collide; County's Explosive Growth Clashes with Traditions of Its Rural Past," *Washington Post* [*WP*], March 24, 1997; Michael Laris and Peter Whoriskey, "Loudoun's Ambitious Plan to Create a Perfect Suburb," *WP*, July 22, 2001.

2. Tom Daniels and Mark Lapping, "Land Preservation: An Essential Ingredient in Smart Growth," *Journal of Planning Literature* 19 (2005): 316–329; Daniel Press, *Saving Open Space: The Politics of Local Preservation in California* (Berkeley: University of California Press, 2002), 23–28; Daniel Hellerstein et al., *Farmland Protection: The Role of Public Preferences for Rural Amenities*, Agricultural Economic Report No. 815 (Washington, D.C.: Economic Research Service, U.S. Department of Agriculture [USDA], 2002), http://www.ers.usda.gov/publications /aer815/ (accessed August 5, 2010), 21–22.

3. Deborah Carter Park and Philip M. Coppack, "The Role of Rural Sentiment and Vernacular Landscapes in Contriving Sense of Place in the City's Countryside," *Geografiska Annaler: Series B, Human Geography* 76, no. 3 (1994): 161–172; Susan Carr and Joyce Tait, "Farmers' Attitudes to Conservation," *Built Environment* 16, no. 3 (1990): 218–231.

4. Hellerstein et al., *Farmland Protection*; Brian Roe, Elena G. Irwin, and Hazel A. Morrow-Jones, "The Effects of Farmland, Farmland Preservation, and Other Neighborhood Amenities on Housing Values and Residential Growth," *Land Economics* 80, no. 1 (February 2004): 55–75; John C. Bergstrom, "Postproductivism and Changing Rural Land Use Values and Preferences," in *Land Use Problems and Conflicts: Causes, Consequences and Solutions*, ed. Stephan J. Goetz,

James S. Shortle, and John C. Bergstrom (New York: Routledge, 2005), 64–76; Christopher S. Elmendorf, "Ideas, Incentives, Gifts, and Governance: Toward Conservation Stewardship of Private Land, in Cultural and Psychological Perspective," *University of Illinois Law Review* (2003): 423–506.

5. Ralph E. Heimlich and Charles H. Barnard, "Agricultural Adaptation to Urbanization: Farm Types and Agricultural Sustainability in US Metropolitan Areas," in *Rural Sustainable Development in America*, ed. Ivonne Audirac (New York: John Wiley and Sons, 1997), 283–303.

6. While scholarship has brought the suburbs into urban history, rural communities have often been left out. For a model of thinking about the connections between regional communities and role of hinterlands in shaping metropolitan growth, see Andrew Needham and Allen Dieterich-Ward, "Beyond the Metropolis: Metropolitan Growth and Regional Transformation in Postwar America," *Journal of Urban History* 35, no. 7 (November 2009): 943–969.

7. Northern Virginia Regional Commission, "Table 1.1: Population Growth 1930–2000," *Northern Virginia Databook* (2003), http://www.novaregion.org/index.aspx?NID=227 (accessed May 8, 2012).

8. National Trust for Historic Preservation, "The Development of Rural Conservation Programs: A Case Study of Loudoun County, Va.," *Information* 29 (1981), 2.

9. Charles Preston Poland Jr., *From Frontier to Suburbia* (Marceline, MO: Walsworth, 1976), 359, 362; Eugene M. Scheel, "1000 Years of Loudoun; Making Room in a Rural Enclave," *WP*, December 30, 1999.

10. Margaret Morton, "Frank Raflo: In Memoriam, 1919–2009," obituary, *Leesburg* [Virginia] *Today*, March 18, 2009; Donnel Nunes, "Supervisor Races in Loudoun—An Issue of Growth," *WP*, September 25, 1975; Lee Hockstader, "Loudoun Leader Makes a Splash; Raflo Seeks to Control Growth," *WP*, April 10, 1985; John F. Harris, "Loudoun's Favorite 'Troublemaker' Retires; Announcement by Supervisor Frank Raflo Marks End of an Era," *WP*, November 18, 1986.

11. "Summary of Denis Brion's 12/31/94 'Loudoun County Transferrable Development Rights' Proposal," [1985], folder 21, box 33, American Farmland Trust [AFT] Records, 1979–1999, Coll. No. C MSS CONS148, Denver Public Library, Denver, Colorado.

12. On this idea historically, see Eric T. Freyfogle, *The Land We Share: Private Property and the Common Good* (Washington, D.C.: Island Press, 2003), 108–124.

13. National Trust for Historic Preservation, "A Case Study of Loudoun County," 2.

14. Kenneth Bredemeier, "New Land-Use Classification: Loudoun Tax Favoring Farmers Passes," *WP*, September 30, 1972. On the limits of "differential assessment," see Robert A. Blewett and Julia I. Lane, "Development Rights and the Differential Assessment of Agricultural Land: Fractional Valuation of Farmland Is Ineffective for Preserving Open Space and Subsidizes Speculation," *American Journal of Economics and Sociology* 47, no. 2 (April 1988): 195–205.

15. National Trust for Historic Preservation, "A Case Study of Loudoun County," 21.

16. Bredemeier, "New Land-Use Classification"; National Trust for Historic Preservation, "A Case Study of Loudoun County," 20–23.

17. Freyfogle, *The Land We Share*, 179–201.

18. National Trust for Historic Preservation, "A Case Study of Loudoun County," 1.

19. Ibid., 8–20.

20. Ibid., 4.

21. Dallas D. Miner, *Farmland Retention in the Washington Metropolitan Area: An Examination of the Status of the Agricultural Industry, Rationale for the Retention of Farmland, and*

Alternative Preservation Techniques (Washington, D.C.: Metropolitan Washington Council of Governments, 1976), xi; Tim Lehman, *Public Values, Private Lands: Farmland Preservation Policy, 1933–1985* (Chapel Hill: University of North Carolina Press, 1995); Daniels and Lapping, "Land Preservation."

22. Loudoun County Department of Planning, Zoning and Community Development, *Rural Land Management Plan: An Element of the Loudoun County Comprehensive Plan* (Leesburg, VA, 1984), 1; Elsa L. Walsh, "Coming Home to the Country; Population Boom in the 'New' Suburbs," *WP*, August 20, 1981.

23. Anne Cocroft, "Loudoun Becomes a New Battleground in Land-Use Wars," *WP*, November 17, 1983.

24. Ibid.

25. Loudoun County Department of Planning, Zoning and Community Development, *Rural Land Management Plan*, 1; Walsh, "Coming Home to the Country."

26. Anne Cocroft, "Land Wars Spread to Loudoun County," *WP*, November 17, 1983.

27. Wendy Swallow, "Rural Plan Approved: Loudoun Group Agrees on Proposed Changes," *WP*, July 9, 1983; Wendy Swallow, "Transferable Development Rights: Loudoun to Ask Assembly for Land-Use Control," *WP*, October 1, 1983.

28. John F. Harris, "Loudoun Proposal Hotly Debated; Open Spaces Protection Plan Is Praised, Blasted at Hearing," *WP*, December 10, 1985; John F. Harris, "Loudoun Moves to Limit Rural Development," *WP*, January 3, 1986.

29. Virginia exerted unusual control over its localities under the Dillon Rule. As a result, Loudoun had to work with the state more closely than localities in Maryland. Loudoun County Department of Planning, Zoning and Community Development, *Rural Land Management Plan*, 7.

30. National Trust for Historic Preservation, "A Case Study of Loudoun County," 7.

31. Swallow, "Transferable Development Rights."

32. Ibid.; Swallow, "Rural Plan Approved"; Harris, "Loudoun Moves to Limit Rural Development"; John F. Harris, "Fate of Open-Space Bill Miffs Loudoun Official: Raflo Says Lobbies Took 'Country Boys,'" *WP*, February 12, 1986. The state finally approved use of a TDR program in 2006.

33. John F. Harris, "Loudoun's Farmers to Get Official Voice," *WP*, December 5, 1985.

34. Stephen Turnham, "Farms Growth with County; Land Use More Specialized," *WP*, January 24, 1991; John F. Harris, "New Wave on the Old Farm; Neotraditionalists Go to Loudoun County," *WP*, July 7, 1985.

35. John F. Harris, "Loudoun Taxpayers Are Feeling the Bite; Some Property Assessments Go Up 30 Percent," *WP*, March 26, 1986.

36. Stephen J. Lynton and Jane Fruendel, "Saudi Prince, Company Buy Godfrey Farm," *WP*, June 29, 1979; United Press International, "Former Arthur Godfrey Estate Being Converted to Private Resort," *WP*, June 27, 1981; Stella Dawson, "Partnership Plans Resort on Former Arthur Godfrey Farm," *WP*, November 16, 1985; Cornelius F. Foote Jr., "Estate Sale Offer Worries Loudoun; Preservation Groups Keep Close Eye on Beacon Hill Site," *WP*, December 26, 1987; John Kelly, "Answer Man: Herd of Arthur Godfrey," *WP*, May 3, 2004.

37. Timothy J. Krawczel to E. William Chapman, letter, May 15, 1986, folder 1, box 1, MS 031, Catoctin Mountain Alliance [CMA], 1985–1995, Thomas Balch Library, Leesburg, VA; Joseph C. Davis Jr. to James M. Wordsworth, letter, May 21, 1986, folder 1, box 1, CMA.

38. John F. Harris, "Luxury Development, Resort Set for Loudoun," *WP*, September 27, 1985; Timothy J. Krawczel to Thomas Walls, letter, November 6, 1985, folder 2, box 1, CMA;

Dawson, "Partnership Plans Resort on Former Arthur Godfrey Farm"; Donna Acquaviva, "Beacon Hill Opposition Forms," *WP*, June 11, 1987; Hellerstein et al., *Farmland Protection*.

39. "Powell Harrison Dies; Loudoun Citizen of the 20th Century and Conservation Leader," *Fairfax Times*, November 7, 2000.

40. B. Powell Harrison to Bruce M. Brownell, letter, November 11, 1985, folder 2, box 1, CMA.

41. Ibid.; Joseph C. Davis Jr. to Loudoun County Planning Commission, letter, March 12, 1986, folder 4, box 1, CMA; Joseph C. Davis to John A. Stowers, letter, April 9, 1986, folder 4, box 1, CMA; Acquaviva, "Beacon Hill Opposition Forms"; B. Powell Harrison, Joseph Davis Jr., and Hanes to Loudoun County Planning Commission, letter, June 15, 1987, folder 9, box 1, CMA; B. Powell Harrison to "Friend of the Catoctin," letter, July 30, 1991, 1, folder 4, box 2, CMA.

42. Clive Carnie, "Planners Reject Proposal for Beacon Hill Farm Development," *WP*, December 17, 1987.

43. On twentieth-century attitudes toward private property rights, see Freyfogle, *The Land We Share*, 2, 229–253; Edward Thompson Jr., "Takings and Givings: Toward Common Ground on the Property Rights Issue," *Journal of Soil and Water Conservation* 47, no. 5 (September–October 1992): 376–377.

44. Carnie, "Planners Reject Proposal."

45. Loudoun County, *Mountainside Development Overlay District (745)* cited in Beacon Hill Farm Associates II Limited Partnership v. Loudoun County Board of Supervisors, 875 F2d 1081 (U.S. Court of Appeals, Fourth Circuit), May 26, 1989.

46. Clive Carnie, "Loudoun Restricts Development in Mountain Areas," *WP*, December 24, 1987.

47. John F. Harris, "Loudoun Board Elects Betty Tatum Chairman; She Is First Woman to Head Governing Body," *WP*, January 6, 1987.

48. On Common Ground . . . A Loudon Consortium, letter, January 25, 1988, folder 12, box 1, CMA; B. Powell Harrison to Betty W. Tatum, letter, June 3, 1988, folder 1, box 2, CMA; Burr Powell Harrison, interview by Eugene M. Scheel, January 17, 1992, Thomas Balch Library, Leesburg, VA; Walter A. Rosenbaum, *Environmental Politics and Policy*, 4th ed. (Washington, D.C.: CQ Press, 1998), 29.

49. Betty W. Tatum to B. Powell Harrison, letter, June 14, 1988, folder 1, box 2, CMA.

50. For an overview of the "growth imperative" in the social science literature, see Phil Hubbard et al., "Geographies of Governance," *Thinking Geographically: Space, Theory and Contemporary Human Geography* (New York: Continuum, 2002), 175–203; Jonathan S. Davies and David L. Imbroscio, eds., *Theories of Urban Politics*, 2nd ed. (Thousand Oaks, CA: Sage, 2009).

51. Roger K. Lewis, "Loudoun Acts to Shape Plans for Its Future; County Aims to Avert Uncontrolled Growth," *WP*, September 10, 1988; Cornelius F. Foote Jr., "Loudoun Envisions Urban-Rural Balance," *WP*, November 13, 1988; Cornelius F. Foote Jr., "Developer Revises Plan for Beacon Hill Project; Group Drops Lawsuit Against Loudoun," *WP*, December 10, 1988.

52. Village of Euclid, Ohio v. Ambler Realty Co., 272 US 365 (1926); Freyfogle, *The Land We Share*, 86–91.

53. Beacon Hill Farm Associates v. Loudoun County; Cornelius F. Foote Jr., "Court Told to Hear Loudoun Developer's Lawsuit: Company Is Challenging County's Mountainside Restrictions," *WP*, May 31, 1989.

54. Loudoun County Board of Supervisors, *The Vision for Rural Loudoun County*, white paper, April 3, 1989, vertical file, "1981–1990," Thomas Balch Library, Leesburg, VA.

55. Beacon Hill Farm Associates II Limited Partnership, *Adjustment of the Boundary of the Rural Fringe Area of the "Rural Land Management Plan" and the "Leesburg Area Management Plan,"* Land Development Application CPAM 89–16, October 13, 1989, folder 1, box 4, CMA.

56. Tekla H. Cox to Loudoun County Planning Commission, memo, March 21, 1990, folder 1, box 4, CMA.

57. Harrison to CMA, letter, April 6, 1990, folder 5, box 4, CMA; Harrison, "Statement at Planning Commission Hearing," April 11, 1990, folder 5, box 4, CMA; B. Powell Harrison to Board Members [Together for Loudoun County, Presidents of Piedmont Environmental Council, Loudoun Restoration & Preservation Society, the Preservation Society of Loudoun County], letter, April 10, 1991, folder 4, box 2, CMA; Harrison to Friend of the Catoctins, letter, July 30, 1991, folder 4, box 2, CMA; Harrison to Committee for Loudoun's Future, letter, August 7, 1991, folder 4, box 2, CMA.

58. Harrison, letter, June 12, 1992, folder 7, box 2, CMA.

59. Even with the approval of the Beacon Hill proposal, development of the site stalled for a decade as a national recession in the early 1990s led the Beacon Hill Farm Associates to sell the property and ownership changed hands several more times. Finally, in the early 2000s, a new developer opened the Beacon Hill Golf and Equestrian Community. Rajiv Chandrasekaran, "Development Approved at Beacon Hill, Ex-Godfrey Estate," *WP*, April 27, 1995; Justin Blum, "Beacon Hill Development to Be Sold; Critics of Project Fear Loss of Rural Landscape," *WP*, April 25, 1999; "Welcome to Beacon Hill Community," Beacon Hill Homeowners Association website, http://www.beacon-hill.us/Beacon-Hill-homeowners-association-Web-site~2183~176.htm (accessed May 6, 2012).

60. Cornelius F. Foote, Jr., "Official Feels Pressure of Loudoun Growth; Bolen's Laid-Back Style Questioned As Debate Over Development Intensifies," *WP*, February 6, 1989; Steve Bates, "Loudoun's Bolen Resigns amid Rumors of Dismissal," *WP*, May 2, 1991.

61. Robert O'Harrow Jr., "Loudoun's Christian Right on March from Pulpit to Public Policy," *WP*, September 27, 1992; Stephen Turnham, "Board Sets New Planning Commission," *WP*, January 9, 1992.

62. On exurbanization, see David Marcouiller, Mark Lapping, and Owen Furuseth, eds., *Rural Housing, Exurbanization, and Amenity-Driven Development: Contrasting the "Haves" and the "Have Nots"* (Burlington, VT: Ashgate, 2011); Arthur C. Nelson, "The Exurban Battleground," in *Contested Countryside: The Rural Urban Fringe in North America*, ed. Owen J. Furuseth and Mark B. Lapping (Surrey, United Kingdom: Ashgate, 1999): 137–149; Mark Friedberger, "The Rural-Urban Fringe in the Late Twentieth Century," *Agricultural History* 74, no. 2 (Spring 2000): 502–514.

63. Northern Virginia Regional Commission, "Table 1.1: Population Growth 1930–2000"; Frankel and Pae, "In Loudoun, Two Worlds Collide"; "Table A–1. Comparative Demographic Overview, 1990 and 2000. Loudoun County, Northern Virginia, Metropolitan Washington DC and United States," in Loudoun County, *Revised General Plan* (Leesburg, VA, 2001).

64. William F. Powers, "Loudoun's Road to Opportunity; As Highway Takes Shape, Landowners Hope for Economic Bonanza," *WP*, October 23, 1993; Stephen C. Fehr, "Highway Links Loudoun to Region's Growing Pains," *WP*, September 24, 1995; Peter Finn and Peter Pae, "The Road to a New Loudoun? Residents Fear Greenway's Toll Will Be Farmland Lost to Development," *WP*, September 24, 1995.

65. Justin Blum, "Dulles Greenway a 'Double-Edged Sword'; Road Brings Business Loudoun Wants and the Housing Development It Doesn't," *WP*, July 26, 1999.

66. Steve Bates, "Silence of the Farmers' Tax Activism Is Limited, but Concerns Are Great," *WP*, May 2, 1991.

67. Steve Bates, "Loudoun's Well-Kept Secret," *WP*, September 8, 1990; Robert O'Harrow Jr., "Development Knocks on Round Hill's Door," *WP*, January 12, 1991; Peter Pae, "Towns in Loudoun Look to Annex Land; Strategy Expands Growth Debate," *WP*, June 17, 1996.

68. Louie Estrada, "Historic Leesburg Confronts Reality of Today's Urban Sprawl," *WP*, May 14, 1994.

69. Frankel and Pae, "In Loudoun, Two Worlds Collide."

70. Leef Smith, "An Agricultural Way of Life Withers; County's Farming Heritage Is Dying as Debt, Drought and Development Squeeze Industry," *WP*, October 7, 1993; Louie Estrada, "Fewer Hands for the Farmers; Labor Crunch a Growing Concern," *WP*, November 21, 1996; American Farmland Trust, "Farming on the Edge Press Conference," Washington, D.C., National Press Club, 1993?, folder 10, box 27, AFT.

71. Stephen Turnham, "Farms Grow with County; Land Use More Specialized," *WP*, January 24, 1991; Stephen Turnham, "Nurseries Blossom in Va. Countryside; As Land Prices Rise, Farm Sizes Shrink," *WP*, September 5, 1991; Peter Pae, "Loudoun County Farms Show A New Taste for the Exotic," *WP*, April 10, 1994. On farming on the urban fringe, see Ralph E. Heimlich, "Metropolitan Agriculture: Farming in the City's Shadow," *APA Journal* (Autumn 1989): 457–465; Ralph E. Heimlich and Charles H. Barnard, "Agricultural Adaptation to Urbanization: Farm Types and Agricultural Sustainability in US Metropolitan Areas," in *Rural Sustainable Development in America*, ed. Ivonne Audirac (New York: John Wiley and Sons, 1997), 283–303.

72. United States Department of Agriculture (USDA), *Census of Agriculture: Historical Census Publications*, http://www.agcensus.usda.gov/Publications (accessed December 1, 2013).

73. USDA, *Census of Agriculture*, 1992, 1997, 2002; Peter Pae, "In Loudoun, Growing Steady; New Farmers and Methods Help Acreage Remain Constant Despite Development," *WP*, June 30, 1997.

74. Laura B. DeLind, "Considerably More Than Vegetables, a Lot Less Than Community: The Dilemma of Community Supported Agriculture," in *Fighting for the Farm: Rural America Transformed*, ed. Jane Adams (Philadelphia: University of Pennsylvania Press, 2002), 192–206; Heimlich, "Metropolitan Agriculture."

75. Leef Smith, "Organic Success; Lovettsville Farm Lures Lovers of Natural Food," *WP*, December 2, 1993.

76. DeLind, "Considerably More Than Vegetables."

77. Pae, "In Loudoun, Growing Steady."

78. Peter Pae, "County Prepares for a Burgeoning Future; Planned Communities Seen as a Way to Handle Growth," *WP*, January 20, 1994; Peter Pae, "Development Booms Again in Loudoun; Latest Building Plan Is Largest Since '80s," *WP*, March 21, 1996; Frankel and Pae, "In Loudoun, Two Worlds Collide."

79. Jennifer Lenhart and Peter Pae, "Drawing a Line In Loudoun Co; Some Residents Eager to Slow Rising Tide of Development," *WP*, September 11, 1997.

80. Dan Eggen and Peter Pae, "Anti-Development Forces Massing Along Home Front; Traffic, Taxes, Crowded Schools Rouse Suburbs," *WP*, December 14, 1997.

81. Dan Eggen, "Suburban Developers Find Public Anger Building," *WP*, July 19, 1998

82. Peter Pae, "Supervisors Reject Broad Run Village; Board's Decision Called 'Historic,'" *WP*, November 20, 1997; Peter Pae, "Rejected Developer Sues Loudoun's Supervisors; Revisions

to County Land-use Policy Disputed," *WP*, December 23, 1997; Friedberger, "The Rural-Urban Fringe," 502.

83. Justin Blum, "In Busy Loudoun, Building a Revolt; Volunteers Learned to Tap Anti-Sprawl Fervor, Funds," *WP*, November 14, 1999; Lisa Rein, "Threats to Growth Plan Energize Anti-Sprawlers; Group to Fund Like-Minded Candidates," *WP*, February 20, 2000; Deborah Lynn Guber, *The Grassroots of a Green Revolution: Polling America on the Environment* (Cambridge, MA: MIT Press, 2003), 70.

84. Justin Blum, "Slow-Growth Vote Reshapes Board; 8 of 9 Victors Vow to Push for Curbs," *WP*, November 4, 1999; Maria Glod, "It's Official: Slow-Growth Proponent York Sworn In as Board Chairman," *WP*, December 23, 1999.

85. Ralph E. Heimlich and William D. Anderson, *Development at the Urban Fringe and Beyond: Impacts on Agriculture and Rural Land*, Agricultural Economic Report No. 803 (Washington, D.C.: Economic Research Service, USDA, 2001), vi, https://www.ers.usda.gov/webdocs /publications/41350/19084_aer803_1_.pdf?v=41061 (accessed August 16, 2017); American Farmland Trust, "Preliminary Report of the Farmland Protection Working Group," March 1995, folder 10, box 9, AFT.

86. American Farmland Trust, "American Farmland Trust Encourages Private Land Conservation Initiatives," news release, April 27, 1999; Ralph Grossi, Testimony on the Conservation and Reinvestment Act of 1999 (S. 25) the Resources 2000 Act (S. 446) and the Clinton Administration's Lands Legacy Proposal, U.S. Senate Committee on Environment and Natural Resources, April 27, 1999, folder 27, box 11, AFT.

87. Peter Pae, "Farm Survey Taps Deep Commitment; As Profits Dip, County Growers Resist Selling Out; Survey Kindles Tax Debate," *WP*, July 10, 1997.

88. Maria Glod, "County Urged to Speed Up Preservation; $4 Million Proposed for Buying Land Rights," *WP*, January 20, 2000. Localities did not need approval from the state legislature to set up a PDR program.

89. Frankel and Pae, "In Loudoun, Two Worlds Collide."

90. Michael Laris, "Supervisors Pass Plans for Spending; PDRs, Teachers, Schools Get Funding," *WP*, April 6, 2000; Martin P. Bromser-Kloeden, "PDRs Should Be Supported," letter to the editor, *WP*, February 6, 2000.

91. Daniels and Lapping, "Land Preservation"; Press, *Saving Open Space*, 59–60, 64–66.

92. Dan Eggen and Justin Blum, "Faceoff on Growth in Va.; Developers, Localities Vie for Assembly Backing," *WP*, December 27, 1998.

93. Justin Blum, "Lawmakers Hear Debate on Growth; Both Sides Press Their Points in Loudoun," *WP*, March 26, 1999; Justin Blum, "Va. Kills Plans to Let Localities Slow Growth," *WP*, February 9, 2000.

94. Department of Economic Development (Leesburg, VA), *2001 Survey of Loudoun Residents*. October 2001, http://www.loudoun.gov/documentcenter/view/9359 (accessed August 27, 2014).

95. Piedmont Environmental Council, "Mike Kane," *PEC Staff*, http://www.pecva.org/index .php/about/staff-board-listing/423-kane-mike (accessed September 18, 2014). Kane directed the PDR program in Loudoun.

96. "Sage Hill Farms Added to PDR Program," *Fairfax Times*, December 10, 2003.

97. For an overview, see John D. Echeverria and Raymond Booth Eby, eds., *Let the People Judge: Wise Use and the Private Property Rights Movement* (Washington, D.C.: Island Press, 1995); Philip D. Brick and R. McGreggor Cawley, eds., *A Wolf in the Garden: The Land Rights*

Movement and the New Environmental Debate (Lanham, MD: Rowman and Littlefield, 1996). For more general conservative opposition to environmental regulation at the national level, see Judith A. Layzer, *Open for Business: Conservatives' Opposition to Environmental Regulation* (Cambridge, MA: MIT Press, 2012).

98. Michael Laris, "Growth Limits Anger Loudoun Landowners; Farmers Claim Right to Develop Property," *WP*, April 18, 2000; Peter Whoriskey and Michael Laris, "In Loudoun, Farming Serves as a Potent Symbol; Development Debate Obscures Decline of Agriculture," *WP*, July 23, 2001.

99. Maria Glod, "Fears of Withering Land Values; In Loudoun County, Development Curbs Worry Farmers Hoping to Cash In," *WP*, February 20, 2000.

100. Michael Laris, "Loudoun Eyes Cost of Slower Growth; Study Predicts Cuts in Property Values," *WP*, August 12, 2000.

101. Samuel Hays, *Beauty, Health, and Permanence: Environmental Politics in the United States, 1955–1985* (New York: Cambridge University Press, 1987), 288–297; Park and Coppack, "The Role of Rural Sentiment."

102. Hellerstein et al., *Farmland Protection*, iv, 1; Bruce R. Beattie, "The Disappearance of Agricultural Land," in *Agriculture and the Environment: Searching for Greener Pastures*, ed. Terry L. Anderson and Bruce Yandle (Stanford, CA: Hoover Institution Press, 2001), 19, 21–22; Samuel R. Staley, "The Political Economy of Land Conversion on the Urban Fringe," in Anderson and Yandle, *Agriculture and the Environment*, 65–80; Freyfogle, *The Land We Share*, 2, 7–8.

103. Michael Laris, "Planning Board Endorses Downzoning in Rural Areas; Land-Use Proposal Marks Major Departure in Policy," *WP*, June 25, 2000.

104. Michael Laris, "Landowners Cry Foul over Zoning Proposal; Hearing on Consent Issue Heated," *WP*, June 8, 2000.

105. Ibid.

106. Michael Laris, "'Snob' Zoning Assailed in Loudoun," *WP*, June 28, 2000.

107. Ibid.; Martin P. Bromser-Kloeden, "It's All Profit, and Politics," letter to the editor, *WP*, December 7, 2000. On this point more generally see e.g. Heimlich and Anderson, *Development at the Urban Fringe and Beyond*, vi; Friedberger, "The Rural-Urban Fringe," 502.

108. Whoriskey and Laris, "In Loudoun, Farming Serves as a Potent Symbol."

109. Michael Laris, "Board Votes to Take Back Zoning Power; Rhetoric at a Fever Pitch as Growth Curb Passes," *WP*, July 13, 2000.

110. Laris, "'Snob' Zoning Assailed in Loudoun"

111. Ibid.

112. Roe, Irwin, and Morrow-Jones, "The Effects of Farmland, Farmland Preservation, and Other Neighborhood Amenities"; Mary Jane Windle, "A One-Sided Agenda," letter to the editor, *WP*, December 10, 2000. For scholars who dispute the tendency to portray environmentalists as elitists, see Denton E. Morrison and Riley E. Dunlap, "Environmentalism and Elitism: A Conceptual and Empirical Analysis," *Environmental Management* 10, no. 5 (1986): 581–589; Diane M. Samdahl, "Social Determinants of Environmental Concern," *Environment and Behavior* 21, no. 1 (January 1989): 57–81.

113. Department of Economic Development (Leesburg, VA), *2001 Survey of Loudoun Residents*, 10–15.

114. Michael Laris, "Slow-Growth Battle Rages on Among Residents; Hearings Air Public Debate Before Planned Vote in July," *WP*, June 14, 2001; Laris and Whoriskey, "Loudoun's Ambitious Plan to Create a Perfect Suburb."

115. Michael Laris, "Loudoun Adopts Strict Controls on Development; Deputies Rein in Crowd Gathered for 7–2 Vote," *WP*, July 24, 2001.

116. Loudoun County (Va.), *General Plan*, rev. ed. (Leesburg, VA, 2001), Loudoun County, VA official website, Revised General Plan & Amendments, http://www.loudoun.gov/index.aspx ?NID=1066 (accessed May 7, 2012).

117. Loudoun County, *General Plan* (2001), 7–5; Richard Brewer, *Conservancy: The Land Trust Movement in America* (Hanover, NH: University Press of New England, 2003), 247.

118. "Scott K. York," *WP*, December 30, 2001.

119. Laris, "Loudoun Adopts Strict Controls."

120. Michael Laris, "Loudoun Board Adopts Slow-Growth Zoning Blueprint," *WP*, January 7, 2003.

121. Michael Laris, "Nearly 200 Lawsuits Challenge Loudoun Slow-Growth Plan," *WP*, February 6, 2003; Michael Laris, "Loudoun Environmental Rules Contested; Companies Join Flurry of Suits Filed Against Slow-Growth Regulations," *WP*, February 13, 2003; Roger K. Lewis, "In Loudoun County, 'Smart-Growth' Legislation Hits a Snag," *WP*, March 8, 2003.

122. Michael Laris, "Boundaries Start to Blur in Va. Talk on Growth; Loudoun Board Candidates Jockey for Stances," *WP*, October 7, 2003; Michael Laris, "Showdown Over Loudoun; With Growth at Issue, Builders' Cash Fuels Races," *WP*, October 29, 2003; Barbara E. Martinez, "At Forum, Candidates Offer Plans to Support Agriculture," *WP*, November 2, 2003. Deborah Lynn Guber argues that partisan differences rather than socioeconomic status have become the primary determinant of environmental attitudes in the United States. Guber, *The Grassroots of a Green Revolution*, 87.

123. Michael Laris, "Loudoun's Slow-Growth Façade Splits; Election Exposes East-West Schism," *WP*, November 6, 2003; Amy Joyce, "Rural Economy Braces for Pro-Growth Push; New Policies Could Hurt, Area Entrepreneurs Say," *WP*, January 15, 2004; Michael Laris, "Loudoun Building Proposals Pour In; 21 Plans Will Test Rules on Growth," *WP*, September 2, 2004.

124. *Gas Mart Corporation, et al. v. Board of Supervisors of Loudoun County, et al.*, 269 Va. 334; 611 S.E.2d 340 (2005). The public hearing announcement failed to satisfy the "descriptive summary" requirement of Va. Code 15.2–2204(A). This required notices to contain a description of the proposed amendments, a reference to where the public could examine the amendments, and a notice of governing body's intent to adopt the amendments.

125. Michael Laris, "Loudoun Housing Limits Reserved; Va. Court Opens Door to Western Growth," *WP*, March 4, 2005.

126. Michael Laris, "Loudoun Faction Was Set for Fight; Preparation, Money Helped Developers," *WP*, March 13, 2005.

127. "A Shock for Loudoun," editorial, *WP*, March 6, 2005; Campaign for Loudoun's Future, "Supreme Court Rules Loudoun Must Re-Adopt Rural Zoning Due to Question of Lucketts Being a Part of Western Loudoun," press release, March 3, 2005, http://www.loudounsfuture.org /news/releases/2005.03.03.html (accessed April 8, 2012).

128. Michael Laris, "Loudoun Regrets Rejecting '04 Deal; Court Ruling Dims Slow-Growth Hopes," *WP*, March 6, 2005.

129. Campaign for Loudoun's Future, "Residents Urge Passage of the New Rural Zoning Proposal; And Ask Supervisors to Reject Grandfathering Subdivision Proposals Citing Taxes, Traffic, and the Benefits of Loudoun's Rural Economy," press release, June 7, 2006, http://www .loudounsfuture.org/news/releases/2006.06.07.html (accessed April 8, 2012).

130. Loudoun County, "Rural Policy Area Amendments; Public Hearing June 7, 2006; Recorded Comments—Lovettsville Room," 29, *Rural Policy Area Zoning Amendments*, http://inter4.loudoun.gov/Default.aspx?tabid=1113 (accessed April 12, 2012).

131. Ibid., 8.

132. U.S. Census Bureau, *State and Metropolitan Area Data Book: 2010*, 143–148.

133. USDA, "County Profile: Loudoun County, Virginia, *2007 Census of Agriculture*, http://www.agcensus.usda.gov/Publications/2007/Online_Highlights/County_Profiles/Virginia/cp51107.pdf (accessed May 10, 2012); Loudoun Convention & Visitors Association (Visit Loudoun), "Washington DC Wine Country," *Experience Loudoun*, https://www.visitloudoun.org/things-to-do/wine-country/ (accessed August 16, 2017).

134. Campaign for Loudoun's Future, "Residents Urge Passage of the New Rural Zoning Proposal."

135. Daniels and Lapping, "Land Preservation"; Brewer, *Conservancy*, 247.

136. Loudoun County, CPAM 2005-005, Amendments to the Rural Policies of the *Loudoun County Comprehensive Plan* (2006), 2, https://lfportal.loudoun.gov/LFPortalinternet/0/doc/124146/Electronic.aspx (accessed August 16, 2017).

137. Loudoun County, *Attachment 4: Summary of Comprehensive Plan Provisions for the Rural Policy Area, Including Proposed Amendments* (November 2006), http://inter4.loudoun.gov (accessed May 11, 2012).

138. Campaign for Loudoun's Future, "Smart Growth Wins Big In Loudoun Board of Supervisors Races; Loudoun Residents Vote Overwhelmingly for Better Growth and Transportation Management," November 6, 2007, http://www.loudounsfuture.org/news/releases/2007.11.06.html (accessed April 8, 2012). For a slow-growth platform from the Campaign for Loudoun's Future, see Campaign for Loudoun's Future, "A Platform for Loudoun's Future" (August 27, 2007), http://www.loudounsfuture.org/issues/platform.pdf (accessed April 8, 2012).

139. USDA, "County Profile: Loudoun County, Virginia," *2007 Census of Agriculture*. Federal subsidies dropped from $668,000 to $277,000.

140. Loudoun County Office of Rural Economic Development, Loudoun County Agricultural and Forestal District (AFD) Program Frequently Asked Questions, https://www.loudoun.gov/DocumentCenter/View/5534 (accessed August 16, 2017); and Agricultural and Forestal District Ordinances of Loudoun County, https://www.loudoun.gov/index.aspx?NID=2705 (accessed August 16, 2017). The agricultural district program enrolls land for periods ranging from four to ten years.

141. Loudoun County Office of Mapping and Geographic Information, "Loudoun County Conservation Easement Stewardship Program," http://www.loudoun.gov/index.aspx?NID=2816 (accessed September 18, 2014).

Conclusion

1. David Firestone, "90's Suburbs of West and South: Denser in One, Sprawling in Other," *New York Times [NYT]*, April 17, 2001. The nation's population became 15 percent more suburban in the 1990s compared with a growth of 21 percent in the 1980s. In the West, there was a 13 percent decline in rural land that became suburban, with only a slight drop in the South.

2. For a survey of this discussion with a number of source citations, see Shaila Dewan, "Is Suburban Sprawl on Its Way Back?" *NYT*, September 14, 2013. See also Laura Mansnerus, "Suburban Sprawl? Study Says Trend Became History in 90's," *NYT*, May 19, 2004.

3. Joel Kotkin, "So Much for the Death of Sprawl: America's Exurbs Are Booming," *New Geography*, November 4, 2015, available from http://www.newgeography.com/content/005088 -so-much-for-the-death-of-sprawl-americas-exurbs-are-booming (accessed November 4, 2015).

4. For an overview of the "Silver Line," see Dulles Corridor Metrorail Project, http://www .dullesmetro.com/ (accessed November 6, 2016). The unprocessed records of the Dulles Corridor Rail Association, a nonprofit that formed to advocate for the Silver Line, offer a potential wealth of resources to study the long history of the project. Dulles Corridor Rail Association Records, Collection #CO204, Special Collections and Archives, George Mason University Libraries, Fairfax, VA.

SELECTED SOURCES

Archival and Primary Sources

Agnew, Marian K., Papers, ca. 1967–1993. MSS1 Ag635 a FA2. Virginia Historical Society. Richmond, VA.

American Farmland Trust Records, 1979–1999. Coll. No. C MSS CONS148. Denver Public Library. Denver, CO.

Burling Tract Controversy. MSS box 1-02. City of Fairfax Regional Public Library. Fairfax, VA.

Catoctin Mountain Alliance, 1985–1995. MS 031. Thomas Balch Library. Leesburg, VA.

Fairfax County Board of Supervisors. *Minutes* (1970). City of Fairfax Regional Public Library. Fairfax, VA.

Forehand, Jennie M., Papers, 1972–2008. Collection No. 2009-70. University of Maryland Special Collections and University Archives. College Park, MD.

Forehand, Jennie M., Papers, 1976–2006. Collection No. 2008-54, unprocessed. University of Maryland Special Collections and University Archives. College Park, MD.

Mandel, Adrienne A., Papers. Collection No. 2007-93, unprocessed. University of Maryland Special Collections and University Archives. College Park, MD.

National Capital Planning Commission. Development Proposals Project Files. Record Group 328. National Archives and Records Administration. Washington, D.C.

Petzold, Carol S., Papers, 1979–2006. Collection No. 2010-101. University of Maryland Special Collections and University Archives. College Park, MD.

Petzold Carol S., Papers, 1987–2006. Collection No. 2007-92, unprocessed. University of Maryland Special Collections and University Archives. College Park, MD.

Petzold, Carol S., Papers, 1989–2006. Collection No. 2008-55, unprocessed. University of Maryland Special Collections and University Archives. College, Park, MD.

U.S. President. Executive Order No. 13274. "Environmental Stewardship and Transportation Infrastructure Project Reviews." *Federal Register* 67, no. 2 (September 23, 2002): 59449–59450.

Virginia State Water Control Board. Administrative Hearing and Legal Files, 1978–1983. Accession 38493. State Government Records Collection. State Records Center, Library of Virginia. Richmond, VA.

Virginia State Water Control Board. Subject Files of the Virginia State Water Control Board. Office of the Executive Director, 1946–1986. State Records Center, Library of Virginia. Richmond, VA.

Washington Post Maryland Governor's Race Poll, October 2002 [computer file], ICPSR version. Horsham, PA: Taylor Nelson Sofres Intersearch [producer], 2002; Ann Arbor, MI: Interuniversity Consortium for Political and Social Research [distributor], 2003.

Washington Post Prince George's County Poll, July 1994, computer file, ICPSR version. Radnor, PA: Chilton Research Services [producer], 1994; Ann Arbor, MI: Inter-university Consortium for Political and Social Research [distributor], 2005.

Newspapers and Periodicals

Baltimore Sun
Gazette (Rockville, MD)
News-Post (Frederick, MD)
Providence Journal (McLean, VA)
Washington Post
Washington Star

Government Documents

Agricultural Services Division (Montgomery County, MD). *The Dilemma of Montgomery County's Agricultural Reserve: Competing Interests of Agricultural and Open Space Preservation.* In author's possession.

Environmental Protection Agency. *Our Built and National Environments: A Technical Review of the Interactions Between Land Use, Transportation, and Environmental Quality.* Washington, D.C.: EPA, 2000.

Environmental Protection Agency, Office of Sustainable Communities. *Using Smart Growth Strategies to Create More Resilient Communities in the Washington, D.C., Region.* Washington, DC: EPA, 2013. https://www.epa.gov/sites/production/files/2014-06/documents/mwcog-guidebook-final-508-111313.pdf.

Federal Highway Administration. *Flexibility in Highway Design.* Washington, D.C.: FHWA, 1997. https://www.fhwa.dot.gov/environment/publications/flexibility/flexibility.pdf

Federal Highway Administration and Federal Transit Administration. *The Transportation Planning Process: Key Issues.* Washington, D.C.: U.S. Department of Transportation, 2007.

Federal Highway Administration, Maryland Transportation Authority, and Maryland State Highway Administration. *Intercounty Connector from I-279 to US 1, Final Environmental Impact Statement/Final Section 4(f) Evaluation*, Project No. AT376B11. Vol. 1. Baltimore, MD, 2006.

Loudoun County (VA). *General Plan*, rev. ed. Loudoun County, VA, official website. Revised General Plan & Amendments. Leesburg, VA, 2001. http://www.loudoun.gov/index.aspx?NID=1066.

Loudoun County (VA) Department of Planning, Zoning and Community Development. *Rural Land Management Plan: An Element of the Loudoun County Comprehensive Plan.* Leesburg, VA, 1984.

Maryland Department of Transportation, Maryland State Highway Administration. *Project Status Report: Intercounty Connector / Rockville Facilities (ICC/RF) and Interstate Route 370 (I-370).* Project Planning Studies. Baltimore, MD, 1980.

Maryland Department of Transportation and--- and Montgomery County Department of Transportation. *Intercounty Connector, I 370 to MD 28, May 31, 1988, Rockville, Maryland.* In Carol S. Petzold Papers, 1987-2006, Collection No. 2007-92.

Maryland-National Capital Park and Planning Commission. *Functional Master Plan for the Preservation of Agriculture and Rural Open Space in Montgomery County.* Silver Spring, MD, 1980.

———. *On Wedges and Corridors; General Plan for the Physical Development of the Maryland-Washington Regional District in Montgomery and Prince George's Counties.* Silver Spring, MD, 1964.

Maryland State Roads Commission and Maryland-National Capital Park and Planning Commission. *Corridor Feasibility Study for the Outer Circumferential Freeway in Montgomery County, Maryland.* Baltimore, MD, 1969.

Metropolitan Washington Council of Governments. *Economic Trends in Metropolitan Washington: 2004-2008.* Economic Trends (2009). http://www.mwcog.org/uploads/pub-documents /8FZcXA20090710121047.pdf.

———. *Regional Activity Centers and Clusters.* http://www.mwcog.org/uploads/pub-documents /yihZVw20070828145020.pdf.

Montgomery County Department of Park and Planning and Maryland-National Capital Park and Planning Commission. *Rustic Roads Functional Master Plan.* Silver Spring, MD, 1996. http://www.montgomeryplanning.org/community/plan_areas/rural_area/master_plans /rustic_roads/rustic_toc.shtm.

Northern Virginia Regional Commission. "Table 1.1: Population Growth 1930-2000." *Northern Virginia Databook.* Fairfax, VA: Northern Virginia Regional Commission, 2003. http:// www.novaregion.org/index.aspx?NID=227.

Office of Economic Development and the Agricultural Preservation Advisory Board (Montgomery County, MD). *Agricultural Preservation Easement Purchase Program: FY 1991 Annual Report.* Derwood, MD, 1991.

State Water Control Board v. Washington Suburban Sanitary Commission, No. 1813-73, U.S. District Court for the District of Columbia (1974).

United States Census Bureau. *Census of Housing and Population* [1940-2000]. In Minnesota Population Center, *National Historic Geographic Information System: Version 2.0.* Minneapolis: University of Minnesota, 2011. http://www.nhgis.org.

United States Commission on Civil Rights. *A Long Day's Journey into Light: School Desegregation in Prince George's County.* Clearinghouse Publication 52. Washington, D.C.: U.S. Commission on Civil Rights, 1976.

United States Congress. *A Bill to Authorize the Secretary of the Interior to Convey Certain Land Located in the State of Maryland to the Maryland-National Capital Park and Planning Commission.* Public Law 99-215. 99th Cong., 1st sess. December 26, 1985.

United States Department of Agriculture, National Agricultural Statistics Service. *Census of Agriculture Historical Archive.* http://agcensus.mannlib.cornell.edu/AgCensus/homepage .do;jsessionid=6719E209FBA4D487A7FBFB3408253011

———. *Farm Characteristics–Montgomery County [Maryland], 1949–2007.* http://www.mont gomerycountymd.gov/agservices/resources/files/agdata1949-2007.pdf

United States Department of Transportation, Federal Highway Administration, Maryland Division. *Record of Decision: Intercounty Connector Project, Maryland and Prince George's Counties, Maryland.* Baltimore, MD, 2006.

———. *Intercounty Connector, I-270 to US 1: Record of Responses to Public Comments.* Baltimore, MD, 2006. http://dlslibrary.state.md.us/publications/EXEC/MDOT/SHA/ICCRRPC _2006.pdf

United States Senate. Senate Committee on the Environment and Public Works. *Port America Project Oversight.* 99th Cong., 2nd sess. October 1, 1986.

Websites

African American Environmentalists Association: http://aaenvironment.com
Alice Ferguson Foundation: http://fergusonfoundation.org
Anacostia Watershed Society: http://www.anacostiaws.org
Campaign for Loudoun's Future: http://www.loudounsfuture.org/
Chesapeake Bay Foundation: http://www.cbf.org
Intercounty Connector: http://www.iccproject.com
MGM National Harbor: https://www.mgmnationalharbor.com/
Montgomery Countryside Alliance: http://www.mocoalliance.org
National Harbor: https://www.nationalharbor.com/
NEPA and Transportation Decisionmaking: https://www.environment.fhwa.dot.gov/projdev
    /pd3tdm.asp
Potomac Conservancy: http://potomac.org
Potomac Riverkeeper: http://www.potomacriverkeepernetwork.org/
Potomac Watershed Partnership: http://potomacpartnership.org
USDA, *Census of Agriculture:* http://www.agcensus.usda.gov/

INDEX

ACKNOWLEDGMENTS

This book may have a single author but it was made possible only through the support of many people along the way. Marilynn Johnson never wavered in her support of my work or her commitment to my broader professional development. From courses and comprehensive exams to reviewing my drafts, Lynn helped me become a real historian. While I served as a visiting faculty member at Boston College, she continued to offer support by reviewing my book proposal as well as commenting on a newly added chapter that would become crucial to the project. Like a growing number of early-career academics, I wound up making a transition from the professoriat to another sector—in my case, hospital administration. Lynn helped others see how the strengths I cultivated as a historian could be valuable in another setting. For these reasons, among others, I am truly grateful to the guidance and encouragement she has offered over the years.

I also want to thank the broader community of colleagues I found during my time at BC. Mark Gelfand at BC and Sarah Phillips at Boston University offered valuable support during this time in my professional life. I met Sarah at a 2011 workshop where I presented an early version of Chapter 5; her insights fostered my creativity as a scholar and her enthusiasm for my work was inspiring. Ted Miller, Jingge Li, Gráinne McEvoy, Ian Delahanty, Pete Cajka, Seth Meehan, and Clayton Trutor provided insightful feedback as emerging scholars and became good friends.

My work has also benefited from institutional support inside and outside of my local affiliation. The history department at BC provided funding in support of my endeavors, while the Clough Center for the Study of Constitutional Democracy at BC and the Mary Kay Harper Center for Suburban Studies at the Montgomery County Historical Society provided valuable funding for my research. I worked with many librarians and archivists at institutions across Metropolitan Washington, including the University of Maryland, the George Washington University, George Mason University, local libraries in